# Fernando Bujones

## An Autobiography

*With memories by family and friends*

~

**With Zeida Cecilia-Mendez**

Published & distributed by:
Higher Education & Technology Consultants, Inc.
5243 NW 94 Doral Place, Doral, FL 33178



For more information about Fernando Bujones, visit:
**www.fernandobujones.com**

Note: This book is an autobiography written by Fernando Bujones until his death, and completed by Zeida Cecilia-Mendez. It is believed to be a true and accurate account of events which actually took place. It is possible others would report the events differently.

ISBN 10: 0-6152-8496-5
ISBN 13: 978-0-6152-8496-5

First Edition, April 2009
Printed in the United States of America

Book Jacket Cover Design by
Mari "Pasita" Andino
www.pasitadesign.com

*All quotes and reviews used in this book are cited and credited properly with the name of the author and the publication.

# Fernando Bujones

More than an autobiography, this is the diary of a dancer, his will to excel, the incredible years as Principal Dancer with American Ballet Theater and his travels around the world.

~

Z.Cecilia-Méndez

# Dedication

I dedicate this book to my Mother,
to Zeida and Marcia,
to my wife Maria and
my daughter Alejandra.

***Fernando Bujones***

Z.Cecilia-Méndez

# Foreword

*"In all things, success depends upon preparation, and without such preparation, there is sure to be failure. Everything has its beauty, but not everyone sees it..."*
*Confucius*

I write this book with the profound hope I can motivate and inspire others. I've always believed the degree of success in a person is determined by the person's character and inner strength, flexibility, integrity and honesty; that personal achievement comes with the courage of believing in yourself, by having the will to excel and by the power of persistence.

Talent is God-given, and knowing that, talent is humbling. From an early age, I learned talent is a precious gift and a privilege to have, but it means nothing without the work, without the desire to convert it into something lasting, to make it count. Consistent work and unflinching desire is the formula that has worked for me and has allowed me to succeed. In my case, however, I can't take all the credit for my success. If not for the tenacity, the caring, and the trust my family and I have always shared, I wouldn't be who I am today.

I believe one's success is not only determined by his or her own personal talents and efforts, but also by circumstances of life, by the people we surround ourselves with, and by the people who love us, support us, and influence us in our lives.

I consider myself a very fortunate man. I've gained personal happiness and fulfillment in my professional career as a dancer and as a man. Through the love and support of my family, my friends and the public to which I will be forever indebted, dance has given me the opportunity to travel the world, meet extraordinary people and make my life richer.

***Fernando Bujones***

# Acknowledgements

This has been the hardest book to co-author. When Fernando passed away unexpectedly, he and I had been working on his autobiography, but by no means was it close to being finished. He had always kept track of dates, performances, reviews, special occasions and relevant events of his life and his career, and was organizing all that information with the hope of turning it into a book, but now came the time to chronicle those events into proper sequences and add the narration that would tell the complete story.

In writing his memoirs, Fernando described his life and career as he remembered and lived it; he would send me his drafts and I would revise and add whatever additional details and narration was needed. We were over halfway through the process when he died. The shock sent all of us, his family, reeling. I collected the photos, the manuscripts, reviews, everything, locked them up and put them away. For well over a year, I could not bear to even think of it.

One of the last things Fernando said to me and to his wife Maria was *"...please finish the book."* I told him not to worry; we would do it together as soon as he got better. But he didn't. Exactly fifty days after the catastrophic diagnosis, he was gone. There was so much unfinished business to deal with, all so extremely painful. The book became a difficult reminder of such a beautiful life cut short, without notice, and every time I tried to work on it, I would be overcome with grief and end up putting it away, again.

With time, though, even the strongest pain dulls, and I was able to start gradually working on the book. And thanks to the encouragement and support of the many special people whose lives Fernando touched, I finally found a way to finish his story.

First, my thanks to Mary, Fernando's mother, whose absolute faith and belief in this book is without bounds and has helped me through my darkest and most painful hours. My thanks to Howard Sherman, Fernando's public relations agent, the very first person who read a most tentative manuscript, took the time to make most important comments and recommendations, and whose encouraging words convinced me that we indeed had a good story to tell. Thanks to Maria Bujones, whose absolute love and dedication to Fernando, her devotion to detail and organizational skills kept all of Fernando's notes, albums, and photos in immaculate condition. Her endless hours of reading and reviewing the manuscript, most of the times through her tears, has helped the story tremendously. Thanks to Alejandra Bujones, Fernando's loving daughter, who kept up her encouragement and determination to see this book completed.

Many thanks to Richard Adams, our thorough editor and friend for his great and careful review of our manuscript and his wonderful suggestions. To Trish Barnes, Cynthia Gregory, Eleanor D'Antuono, Armando Zetina and Jane Herman, who took the time to sit with me and share their memories and special times with Fernando, my eternal gratitude. Their voices add a most vibrant quality to Fernando's story.

To Tricia and Robert Earl, whose support for Fernando during his five years with the Orlando Ballet helped him achieve his dream of choreographing, teaching and directing a young and most exciting ballet company, thanks! To Olivia Gale, Peter Stark, Elizabeth Gillaspy, Natalia Makarova, Veronica Tennant, Kathie Slattery, and Heather Lescaille, thanks for their touching words remembering Fernando. To my friends, Maria de Varona and Lydia Diaz Cruz, both ex-dancers, whose ballet knowledge, admiration and love for Fernando were of great value but never biased, on the feedback I got from them as they too read the manuscript, encouraging me to go on.

Thanks to Anna Kisselgoff, whose beautiful words grace the Preface of this book, for her eloquent and descriptive reviews of Fernando's performances. Thanks to all the other dance critics from over the world whose contributions and reviews are glowing testimonies of an incredible career.

And to my loving partner, Dr. Kathie Sigler, for the time she has given this project from the start, her unwavering support, dedication, guidance and encouragement, without which I would have never found the strength and resolve to bring this book to completion. Her admiration and love for Fernando, her incredible knowledge and ability with computers were instrumental in the concept, design and layout of this book in more ways than I can ever describe. Thank you, Kathie, from the bottom of my heart.

**Zeida Cecilia-Mendez**

# Preface
## by
## Anna Kisselgoff

I knew Fernando Bujones for more than three decades, beginning with his days as a teenage prodigy. But I knew him essentially – and deeply – through his dancing rather than through close personal contact.

As Chief Dance Critic of the New York Times and in my earlier dance reviewing at the same paper, I had occasion to interview him; with the exception of his unexpected and warm phone call upon my departure from the Times, our other sporadic conversations were in the line of professional duty.

Yet, I felt I knew Fernando well because his dancing so overtly revealed his true nature. I saw his drive for perfection, his unending love of dance and of life and above all, his generosity as both an artist and a person. These qualities in his performances are those that resonate throughout this remarkable memoir, written with typical honesty before his untimely death in 2005.

As someone who does not believe in national stereotypes, I have had trouble with even Fernando's own assessment of the role his "Latin temperament" played in his career. In my view, Fernando had a human warmth that affected the audiences, because he was, as I said, a generous person. This outpouring could translate into passionate dancing.

Those of us who were privileged to see Fernando Bujones at his peak – and even when he was still a very young student – were able to see one of 20th century ballet's greatest classical dancers. When I asked him in an interview whether he was influenced by his two idols, Erik Bruhn and Rudolph Nureyev, he said he hoped to combine Bruhn's purity with Nureyev's power. In the end, this combination came out as specifically and totally Bujones. The Borzoi elegance of his long-legged line, tapering to sleekly pointed feet, did not rein in the explosive fire of his virtuosity.

His two favorite roles were very different. One was James in the Danish version of "La Sylphide," a romantic ballet long identified with Bruhn, Denmark's finest danseur noble. The other role, in "La Bayadere" was Solor, identified with the astounding bravura of the Russian-trained Nureyev. That Fernando triumphed in both ballets is testimony to his gifts and versatility, extended to the very different esthetics he encountered not only at American Ballet Theater but in guest appearances worldwide with more than 30 companies.

The revelation of this book is its detailed account of the sheer amount of labor and training that allowed Fernando to acquire his sensational technique and the dramatic interpretations that were so important to him. From the start, he knew he needed an outside eye and he found it in Zeida Cecilia-Mendez. To have a member of your family as a coach since childhood can be a mixed blessing: read the reminiscences of the Soviet ballerina Galina Ulanova on the less than happy relationship with her prime teacher – her mother. But Fernando's appreciation of Zeida's coaching is a picture of a fruitful, even essential, collaboration. Repeatedly, the image that emerges is of every major role dissected and worked upon. Few dancers start so early to train so assiduously with a personal teacher.

Perhaps that is why Fernando always appeared so confident – so much so that he was once called "unacquainted with self-doubt." Yet, a dancer who knows his own faults and ceaselessly works to correct them is not arrogant. He is striving for the best and understands the consistent effort that leads to such achievement.

Still, all is not work and no play in this memoir. Fernando's life was dance but his life integrated love for others. His devotion for his mother, Mary Calleiro, and to his family, spans a story from his birth in Miami, a brief childhood in Cuba, a difficult move back to the United States, to his training and professional career as dancer and ballet director. Equally touching are Fernando's descriptions of life with his first wife, the late Marcia Kubitschek and their daughter Alejandra, and of his happy marriage to his second wife, Maria Arnillas.

Zeida, as she writes in the epilogue, helped edit this book. But Fernando's voice is clear. It is possible not to agree with him about everything. He gives his side of his break with American Ballet Theater in 1985 – but also includes the company's position. His departure, ironically, gave him a highly amplified worldwide career as ever more companies invited him to perform as a guest artist.

Similarly, Fernando's reasons for joining Ballet Theater right after he trained at New York City Ballet's school are given here with persuasive simplicity. To say he desired a more eclectic repertory than at New York City Ballet would be reason enough, although certainly George Balanchine's choreography at City Ballet would stretch every dancer in a special way with its concealed virtuosity.

Fernando relished the overt virtuosity of the 19th century classics at Ballet Theater where his bravura was anything but concealed. Yet, as he writes, virtuosity alone was not enough and he sought out roles for nuances of dramatic characterization. This memoir is a study in the maturing of an artist. It is a given Fernando would execute double air-turns on both the left and right sides when others did not. What is surprising is how soon he moved from textbook characterizations (according to someone else's book) to illuminating interpretations of his own. Acting became integrated into his entire performances.

The distance he traveled was evident in 1980 with the depth of his portrayal of Jean, the deceptively servile butler in Brigit Culberg's version of Strindberg's "Miss Julie." The astonishing height and power of his jumps could have detracted from his characterization but these physical qualities enhanced his brutal image of a rough, drunken servant bent on class revenge.

Essentially, Fernando remained an American dancer. His relationship with the Boston Ballet (1987-1993), his return to American Ballet Theater in 1990 as well as his teaching and his position as artistic director of the Orlando Ballet in Florida –all chronicled here- took him back home.

The roaring receptions that greeted Fernando upon his return to Ballet Theater and later, at his company farewell performance, showed he had never been absent from the hearts of his American audiences. From prodigy to prodigal, his odyssey was complete.

**Anna Kisselgoff** was named Chief Dance Critic of the New York Times in 1977 and she continued as a staff writer until leaving The Times in 2006. She remains a contributor to The Times. Over the years, she has reviewed ballet, modern dance, folk dance, ethnic dance, tap dance, Michael Jackson and -at the 1988 Olympics- ice dancing and the rodeo. Prior to joining the New York Times, she wrote dance reviews and a range of features for the New York Times International Edition and worked on the English desk of Agence-France Presse in Paris.

Ms. Kisselgoff began studying ballet in New York at the age of four with Valentina Belova, later head of the dance department at Sullins College. She studied ballet for nine years in New York with Jean Yazvinsky, a former dancer in Diaghilev's Ballets Russes. After graduating from Bryn Mawr College, Ms. Kisselgoff studied French History at the Sorbonne and Russian at the School of Oriental Languages in Paris.

She received an M.A. degree from Columbia University in European History and an M.S. from the Columbia Graduate School of Journalism. Ms. Kisselgoff was named a Knight of the Order of the Dannebrog by Queen Margrethe II of Denmark and a Chevalier of the Order of Arts and Letters by the French Government. The President of Iceland personally awarded her the Order of the Falcon. Other awards for her writing include the Distinguished Alumni Award from the Columbia Graduate School of Journalism, an Honorary Doctorate from Adelphi University and the Dean's Award for Distinguished Achievement from the Columbia University Graduate School of Arts and Sciences. Ms. Kisselgoff has taught at Yale University and Barnard College.

# TABLE OF CONTENTS

Z.Cecilia-Méndez

CHAPTER 1

# *A Leap to Freedom*

***GOLD!*** This was the one word I sent back in a telegram to Lucia Chase, the founding artistic director of American Ballet Theater, the ballet company I had already been performing with for over two years. This one word would put it all into perspective. It described the culmination of the dream, of many hours of hard work, in the constant pursuit for perfection and the final achievement perhaps, of the most important event in my career.

**"...Fernando Bujones, candidate number 78, United States of America, Gold Medal and a Special Diploma for Highest Technical Achievement..."** These were the astonishing words I heard from the announcer in an open-air theater filled with ballet dancers representing their countries from all over the world.

It was the early evening of July 24, 1974, and I had just officially become at age nineteen, the first American dancer to win a Gold Medal in the history of the competition. I had won this honor at the "1974 Seventh International Ballet Competitions" in Varna, Bulgaria, more known to the rest of the world as "the Olympics of Dance." Looking back, I now see how young my mind was compared to my physical abilities.

My life begins on March 9, 1955. By coincidence or luck I was born in Miami, Florida, USA, even though I could have been born in Cuba. Both my parents were Cubans from a middle-class family. Married at a very young age they were separated by the time I was a year old. My father, Fernando Bujones senior, is the brother of the famed Cuban actress Minin Bujones, whom the Cuban people adored and to this day, is considered to be one of the greatest dramatic actresses Cuba has produced.

My mother, Mary Aixa Calleiro, a poet, writer, and actress, was also very involved in the theater and the arts. She was the last of twelve brothers and sisters and because of that, she grew up learning to demand her space and her rights from the other eleven. My mother was a fighter, never afraid of anything, always an optimist. Her father, my grandfather, was a Baptist minister and when my grandmother started labor with her last child, it happened so fast my mother was actually born in the church pew. She also was a strict disciplinarian who taught me to believe in myself.

During my early childhood, I was raised by mom and by a friend of the family, Zeida Cecilia-Mendez, who came to live with us when I was four years old. Zeida and I went on to develop a brother-and-sister relationship and without either one of us expecting it, she became one of the most significant persons in my career. My mother set about to bring me up as best she could, doing double duty as mother and as the father I never had at a young age. I was born in Miami, at the insistence of Aunt Laura, her closest sister, and her husband, Doctor Rudolph Ayala. Uncle Rudi was an obstetrician. During the early months of 1955, Uncle Rudi and Aunt Laura urged my mother, already eight months pregnant, to come to Miami so her baby could be born in the United States, under Uncle Rudi's care, which she did. My mother's decision to do so turned out to be a blessing in disguise, since my American citizenship became the only way out for the two of us when the time came to leave Cuba and the political turmoil was making life in that country unbearable.

I am convinced there were two things in life I was destined to do. One was to travel in airplanes; the other was to be around a ballet studio or on stage. Several of my aunts on my father's side were involved in the theater since childhood. My oldest first cousin, Charito Sirgo, became a famous child star and popular TV actress and comedienne since she was fifteen. Her father, Otto Sirgo, was a famous Cuban stage, radio and TV star. My mother was actively writing, acting in plays and teaching ballet to four-and-seven year old children. So the theater was no stranger to me. And my first airplane flight took place when I was less than a month old. I was traveling back to Havana in the arms of my young mother, still recovering from having lived through the traumatic experience of giving birth to me.

Three weeks earlier, at my uncle's private clinic, as my mother recovered from the final push that brought me into this world, there had been a chilling silence in the delivery room. "What's wrong?" she asked. There was no answer - not a sound they tell me - especially no cry from the baby.

Something was definitely wrong. My Uncle Rudi held the baby upside down in disbelief shaking him hard. This baby had come out very fast with the umbilical cord wrapped around his neck, strangling him to death. The baby was blue, as in dead blue.

Dr. Ayala had a reputation. He had never ever lost a baby. Could this be the first baby in his medical career to die in his hands? My mother kept asking, "Why is the baby not crying?" My Aunt Laura, who was the assisting nurse, left the room crying. The tension grew as my uncle continued to work frantically, massaging the baby -- still no reaction. Finally Uncle Rudi smacked the baby strongly on the back with a scream, "Cry damn it!" Almost immediately I responded, with the first scream of my life. I was alive! I had met my first challenge and it had come down to the very last seconds. A miracle had indeed transpired, a miracle of life, one every day I'm grateful for. Four weeks after my birth, my mother and I took a plane back to Havana, Cuba, where we remained for several more years.

By the time I was three years old, family members called me "little Charlie" after Charlie Chaplin because of the way I walked with my feet turned out in my miniature orthopedic boots. Around this time my mother started taking me to the ballet studio while she taught ballet to kindergartners. According to her, I used to sit quietly through the beginning exercises at the barre, but by the time the dancers moved on to the center, I was on my feet trying to reach the gigantic wooden barre above me, mimicking some of the movements I had seen.

One day, some time after my fourth birthday, mom came home with an attractive young lady. Her name was Zeida and she had come to Havana from the Oriente province to pursue her own studies in acting and ballet. She had just arrived in the city and was staying with her aunt at a boarding house. My mom offered to rent her the empty room in our apartment, and Zeida moved in with us. That fortuitous event changed our lives. I not only gained the sister I didn't have, but a private dance coach who turned out to be one of the most influential and important persons in my life. She loved symphonic music and mom had a large classical collection. We would lie in bed as the music played and Zeida would invent stories to go with the music. This little routine made me love classical music, and Beethoven, Brahms, Vivaldi, Bach, Tchaikovsky, Chopin and others soon became familiar friends.

Life continued...and mom hired a piano teacher to give me lessons. I started making some progress, but quickly realized this was not for me. The teacher had a hard time keeping my concentration on the keyboard. I kept getting up and prancing about. I had just turned six, and if at that age jumping around and body movements were exciting to me, food was not. My appetite and eating habits were growing from bad to worse and my mother's patience was running out. In fact, she'd had it! Everything I ate, I threw up! In those days, milk seemed to be the only key to my survival. Mother began to get worried and decided to take me to various doctors. None of them gave her any definite reasons for my lack of appetite. So mom decided to take me to a psychiatrist. We waited in the psychiatrist's office for about ten minutes, then my mother was called in and I was told to wait outside. The doctor explained to her I was physically and mentally healthy, and I was just acting up, craving for attention. The doctor went on, "Don't worry Ms. Calleiro, no child has ever died from hunger when there was food around and your son will not be the first." He suggested I should be placed in some kind of a rigorous exercise program and explained to her this would be the solution to my appetite problem.

Dance! My mother immediately thought... why not? She was teaching and taking ballet lessons and it seemed like the perfect way to begin. Up to that time in Cuba there had been only one professional school of ballet, run and directed by Alicia and Fernando Alonso. Then word got around the new Castro government was going to create and support a full-fledged Cuban school of ballet, with academies in each of the six provinces of Cuba. They would accept only preselected students, all on scholarships, and they would study not only dance, but all the academic disciplines as well. Students would sleep, eat and live at the school during the week, and go home for the weekend. They would be using the Russian system as a model. Mme. Anna Leontieva, an ex Ballet Russe de Montecarlo ballerina who had settled in Havana and had her own small private ballet studio, was appointed director of the new school in Havana. My mother had been

**PLEASE SEND MY BOOK BY RETURN MAIL TO:**

**NAME:** ____________________

**ADDRESS:** ____________________

**CITY/STATE/ZIP:** ____________________

**e-mail:** ____________________ **Telph:** ____________

**Send Check or Money Order to:**

**BUJONES BOOK**
**5243 NW 94$^{TH}$ DORAL PL**
**DORAL, FL. 33178**
**Ph: 305-471-0511**

**Price $35.00 + Shipping & Handling USA: ($7.00 U.S. ea.) International: ($15.00 U.S. ea.)**

**Qty.** ________

**Order Sub-Total $**____________
**Shipping & Handling $** ____________

**Total Order $**____________

**Special Promotional Offer!** 3 Books for only $90.00 **+ Shipping & Handling**

**TO ORDER ON LINE GO TO :** www.fernandobujones.com

**MAKES A GREAT GIFT!**

her student and knew her well, and she was determined to get me enrolled in those classes. The ballet school was called Professional School of Dance Alejo Carpentier, but everyone knew it by "the Ballet School at L y 19."

I had no clue as to what to expect, except I was going to try out for a ballet school. Entering the building I was enthusiastic, but upon seeing hundreds of children all around me, my enthusiasm evaporated, as I, together with a multitude of boys and girls, were escorted through some double doors into locker rooms and told to change into the waiting uniforms.

In a matter of minutes, I was in the company of fifty other boys. We found ourselves in a room similar to the one I was used to seeing my mom do ballet classes. We all got black trunks, white T-shirts, white socks and black ballet slippers. Here I was, slightly under seven years of age, in a ballet studio taking my first serious ballet audition. The teachers were looking for boys and girls eight years of age and over with slender bodies, good flexibility, good feet, musicality and body coordination.

Right from the beginning the teachers wondered about the tiny, skinny kid in the corner. Not yet seven, I was small and very thin. I was supposed to be eight, the minimum age required, but my mother didn't let this stop her; she registered me as just having turned eight.

Placed in different groups, we were asked to come to the center of the room and jump to the beat of a piano music. All the kids were allowed to jump whichever way they wanted, as long as it was with the music. I had started piano lessons at four, so I was musical. But my mother had been working with me for days before the audition, and I jumped as she had shown me. At the end of what seemed to me a very long day of tests and questions, I was accepted into the school!

I was placed with a group of eleven other kids in the first ever all-boys ballet class in Cuba! We were twelve in total, but I was the only one from a regular home. The other eleven had been picked from an orphanage, since at that time the average Cuban family could not imagine having a boy taking ballet lessons! The boys in our class ranged between eleven to thirteen years of age. I was barely seven!

"*Buenos dias, my name is Joaquin Banegas and I am your ballet teacher...*" That's how we got to meet our teacher for the first time. He immediately put a bunch of nervous and loud boys at ease, for he also had a warm, caring quality about him we all sensed immediately.

Joaquin was a principal dancer with Alicia Alonso's Ballet Nacional de Cuba. Fortunately for us, he was reaching the end of his dancing career, and was ready to move on and become a teacher. He was a tough disciplinarian as well. But Joaquin became as attached to us as we to him, and almost all the boys in his class went on to become principal dancers at some point or another. He cared for us and taught us not only about dance, but about life, and about being responsible human beings.

He had his own method of teaching, which stressed the classical style of dance, but with a definite Cuban feel to the movements, which we all inherited, as well as an athletic approach, and meticulous technical demands of body lines and positions. His teachings stressed a strong upper body posture combined with power and elegance. His favorite pose was the classical fifth position with arms above our heads, faces up, strong legs, stomach in, chest out. We almost always began or ended every exercise like that. Fifth position was meant to be a statement. It showed the audiences who we were. Since all twelve boys were selected because we could stand in perfect fifth positions, with turned-out straight long legs, stretched torsos and long necks, we were encouraged to show off. When at the end of any given combination Joaquin would ask for a fifth position, we made for a very good looking group of boys. Joaquin showed us how to feel proud of ourselves.

When his wife had their first baby, Joaquin immediately brought the tiny newborn to show him to his class. I did not appreciate it then, but now I understand that gesture. Joaquin was sharing his most treasured possession with us. And the reward the kids most enjoyed after a week of hard work at school was to go and spend the weekend with Joaquin, Sylvia and their baby at their home, almost becoming an additional member of his family during those two days. Most of the other kids had no home to go to during the weekends, so for them, going home with Joaquin was heaven. I, in the meantime, was desperate to go home to my mother. But eventually, even I earned a Joaquin weekend, and that was the beginning of my understanding life could be OK, even away from home.

That first year was difficult for me. I would tire easily and lose concentration, while the rest of the class could continue with the exercises. As the classes became more challenging and the combinations more difficult, my mind would start drifting. The more tired I got, the more I clung to the barre. Years later, I realized why. I was always trying to take the weight off my tired legs and feet and leaning on the barre would relieve the exhaustion a bit.

Finally the school year ended, and with it came the end of the year performance. The school had up to five classes of girls and one boys' class. Our teacher had selected Beethoven's Turkish March. All of us boys, dressed as mini-warriors, would march on stage in a single line with each of us carrying a large wooden sword. We then skipped and hopped along in different floor patterns, while raising and lowering the swords to the beat of the music!

I had not given any importance to that first performance, and had not told my mom what we were doing, but the school had invited all parents to come and watch the year's end performance. When she went backstage and saw me - dressed in my costume, with the sword in my hands, she saw a very obvious problem. The sword was as big as I was and I could hardly lift it! I tried to do the step to show her, but failed. Seeing her distress, something inside me told me I had to do the choreography no matter what, and nothing else mattered.

One by one, the different classes did their routines. Finally, the boys' class was announced over the loudspeaker in the theater and Beethoven's Turkish March started. We had been assigned our place in the line by size, and being the smallest, I was the first one. So out I marched on stage, swinging my sword up and down, with the rest of the guys behind me. We were perfect, and got lots of applause from the enthusiastic crowd of parents and friends, who up to that moment had never seen a group of boys in a dance routine. It was also the first time I had been able to swing my sword in unison with the rest, but it took all the strength, willpower and determination I had. It was also the first time I remember the powerful feeling telling me I was going to do something I had not been able to do before. In my innocence, I never thought I could fail!

I shall never forget my professional debut on the stage with my classmates, dancing with the Ballet Nacional de Cuba. Some of us had been chosen for the upcoming performances of the company's new production of "The Sleeping Beauty." That production had a segment titled "The Giant and his Seven Dwarfs." Since I was still the smallest in my group, I was chosen to be "Pulgarcito," the tiniest dwarf. We all did a small dance; the mean giant came in and captured us one by one. All of the dwarfs were now tied up except the tiniest one that escapes between the giant's legs, and hides inside one of his boots.... that was me! Once the giant fell asleep, I, hopping around inside the boot, would untie the other dwarfs and we all escaped. The dance was popular with the public, and we were always cheered, especially after the escape, when we all ran away from the giant.

After our performances we all returned to our training and although success on stage was wonderful, the ballet classes of those days were still an enormous physical and mental challenge for me. One day the older boys killed a lizard and put it inside the piece of chicken on my plate. As I went to bite into the chicken, miraculously I saw the dead lizard before putting the piece of chicken in my mouth. I guess this was a way of the boys to test me... but to this day I still pass on chicken.

If in class I was still the last one trying to catch up, gradually the boys made me feel as if I was truly one of their own. They looked after me, joked with me and at lunch time never hesitated to eat whatever I still had on my plate. Jorge Esquivel, who had a particularly hearty appetite, never lost the opportunity, making sure my lunch dish was clean before it was taken away. Even so, thanks to ballet, my appetite, while still far from great, was getting better. Life at school with the rest of the boys was not as bad as in the beginning.

## CHAPTER 2

# *Leaving Cuba*

**Bay of Pigs, 1961**. I remember clearly the day when the whole thing started. I had stayed home with Zeida and Carmita, my live-in nanny, while mom, by then a playwright with The Children Theater Group, was on tour. I was playing on the front porch of our small apartment, when all of a sudden we heard the sound of big guns or explosions. Zeida and Carmita came running out. We looked into the sky and saw a small military plane flying in circles, firing its guns. Small arms fire from the ground was shooting back at the plane, which disappeared.

Next thing we heard was a loud explosion and the sound of more guns still firing. Everyone in our block was spilling out into the street asking each other what's going on, but we started ducking and running for shelter because the shots sounded much closer. Carmita instinctively pushed me onto the floor and threw herself on top of me to protect me from flying bullets.

At that precise moment, my mother arrived from her trip! She crash-parked her car, ran to the porch where Carmita, Zeida and I were now lying on the floor and ushered all of us into the apartment. We were all stunned. Mom told us while she was driving back home, the roads were filling up with soldiers in combat gear, she could hear sporadic firing coming from different areas, and she drove home as fast as the car could go. The whole country was experiencing the first stages of the unfortunate revolt-invasion known as the "Bay of Pigs" where a group of anti-Castro forces were trying to overthrow the new self-proclaimed communist regime.

The invasion was an attack force headed by a group of exiled Cuban men, who for months had trained in Florida, with the aim to start a counter revolution that would lead to the overthrow of Fidel Castro and his regime. At the last minute, President John F. Kennedy reneged on his pledge to provide the needed support; the invasion failed and many lives were lost.

My father, I later learned, who was already living in the United States, was part of a second wave of men waiting in Key West for their order to join the first assault of the island... an order that never came. As a result, practically the entire first wave of Cubans were either killed or taken prisoners. Communications broke down and the second wave of men were detained in Key West and told to go home, without any explanations as to why this decision had taken place. My father, along with many others, was deeply frustrated. As quickly as the invasion had started, it ended, and with it came the end of Cuba as a wonderful country where people thrived and freedom prevailed... a country where over 250,000 of its people have been killed or just "disappeared," where over a million of its people have gone into exile.

A whole year had already passed. It was now summer of 1963 and I was eight. The ballet classes were becoming increasingly difficult. Joaquin was concerned the more advanced classes in the next grade would be too hard for me to follow. The difference in age and strength between the other boys and myself was still obvious, and he recommended I repeat the first year, which I did. That second year became easier for me, and I slowly started to develop the stamina and concentration to follow the combinations.

As I was to start my third year of ballet, a bigger and more ambitious school was created, this one a direct product of the Cuban National Ballet company, to be directed by Alicia and Fernando Alonso, with the company's principal dancers as teachers. It would be called Cubanacan. This school would have classes tailored to younger boys, and was supposed to be better for me. The decision was made to transfer me. But although Cubanacan was an incredible school, providing students with a great scholastic and artistic education, it never gave me the peace of mind and happiness of L y 19.

In Cubanacan, one learned all the academic studies plus various languages. Spanish, French, English and Russian were in the curriculum; gymnastics, fencing, music and ballet. But the school was too far away from my home, from the surroundings I had grown accustomed to. The atmosphere was very military and it was a boarding school. Students lived there from Monday to Friday. We were picked up by our parents on Saturday morning, to be returned by Sunday night. I began to feel very homesick and even today, I can recall how I would cry on those Sunday evenings, knowing I had to go back to school. It got to the point Cubanacan irritated me.

I shall never forget the morning wake-up calls. Every day at 6 o'clock in the morning, this sergeant-woman in charge of supervising our dormitory, would come with a sandal in her hand, bang the heck out of the dormitory door and scream at the top of her lungs, "Wake up!" The beds were bunk style as in the army, and each student had the choice to sleep either on the lower or upper bed. Since I was one of the last ones to register in Cubanacan, all the lower beds were gone, so I had to settle for an upper bed. Every time the sound of that sandal broke the morning peace, my head would hit the ceiling of our small room!

After the initial human alarm wake-up call, the students would walk like zombies in their underwear to the showers. By 7:30 in the morning we had finished eating a light breakfast and we were on our way to our morning class. The first class at 8 o'clock in the morning was taught by Josefina Mendez, one of the company's principal ballerinas, who also happened to be Zeida's first cousin! Up to that moment, I had been taught by a man, who made it very clear to me he cared for me and my classmates. Now I had new classmates and a very different female teacher, the opposite to what I had been used to.

If the situation in Cubanacan was depressing, the situation in Cuba was starting to be alarming. Cuba, prior to the revolution, had been a splendid island with one of the richest and healthiest economies of all the countries of the Caribbean, Central and South America. Our universities, health care professionals, public schools, sugar, cattle and coffee industries were among the best anywhere. Cuba was a top producer of sugar, nickel ore and textiles. All the top international artists included Cuba in their tours and we enjoyed the great performances of top opera stars, world class orchestras, theater and sporting events. As far back as the 1940's artists of the caliber of Ana Pavlova, Arthur Rubinstein, Tamara Toumanova and so many others, visited Cuba regularly. Cuba had magnificent hotels, casinos, beautiful beaches, a fabulous tourist industry and people from all over the world came to enjoy a real island paradise. I still remember Havana as a beautiful, sparkling city with striking architecture and magnificent parks, modern buildings, theaters, spacious colonial homes and an incredibly gorgeous countryside.

But Cuba was about to go through major political radical changes not even the Cuban people could have ever imagined. The relationship between Cuba and the United States had become far from amicable and day by day more frightening news and events were becoming commonplace.

By late November, 1963, relations between the two countries were at their worst. One day there was a tremendous commotion in Havana. Everyone seemed to be listening to the radio. President John F. Kennedy had been shot! By now the social and political situation in Cuba was horrible and speculations Castro may have been involved in an assassination plot didn't ease up matters. Living conditions in the island were deteriorating, food was scarce. Milk and meat were impossible to find.

As an individual, you had no rights whatsoever to demand or fight for better living conditions. You actually could not even move from the house you were living in. The government however, had every right to demand you volunteer your labor to whatever next enterprise they might assign you to or throw you in jail for dissenting.

If you lived in Cuba, you did what the government told you to do or you risked going to jail. By 1964, mom's plays and short stories started dealing with the reality of life in Cuba as she saw it. Shortly after, she was called to the Ministry of Culture and told she had to change the style of writing and be more positive towards the Cuban revolution. My mother, like so many other Cubans, loved her island, but she was not a woman to be told what to do. The last thing she wanted to write about was the Cuban revolution. She was not about to being manipulated by the government. Life was becoming very difficult.

One Sunday morning in 1964, mom and Zeida drove to my Uncle Abner's farm in Pinar del Rio, the island's farthest province to the west. Mom's brother had told her he was going to slaughter one of his cows and she should arrange to drive out to the farm to pick up some decent pieces of meat. This was completely forbidden by the new government, so it was all done in secrecy. Although my uncle and his family were still living on the farm which he had bought and worked for years, the property was no longer his. Now it belonged to the government, together with everything in it, including livestock and grains. With the help of a few selected friends, my uncle, as everyone else who could, was getting ready to leave the country.

If getting food was a problem in Cuba, culture was not. To distract the people from the lack of food and other ongoing difficulties, the government was making as much art available to everyone as possible, as long as it was not critical of the revolution. As a child I saw many ballet performances for free and became very familiar with the Cuban National Ballet's classical repertory. Balanchine's Apollo was my all time favorite then. I remember mom taking me to watch the stage rehearsal, sitting right behind the conductor, in the empty theater, loving the Stravinsky score and the action on stage. For the first time I saw a male dancer appear onstage as the center of the action and I loved it. My enthusiasm for dance grew by watching full-length classics like Giselle, Swan Lake, La Fille mal Gardee and Coppelia, all staples of the Cuban company.

Some of the great Soviet dancers also came to Havana, with fantastic Pas de Deux programs; Raissa Struchkova, a very young Maris Liepa and Maya Plisetkaya making the most impression on all of us. A year later, they sent Maya's brother, Azari Plisetski to join the Cuban company as a principal dancer and teacher. Gradually a larger influx of Soviet dancers came and went during those first years of the revolution and I never forgot the wonderful music from their ballets, and the energy of their male dancers, since nothing like them had ever before been seen in Cuba. Zeida and I would pour over ballet books from The Bolshoi, the Kirov and the Paris Opera and became very familiar with their productions and dancers through those books.

Early in 1964, the political situation in Cuba was becoming worse and we were increasingly worried about our future. Operation Freedom was born. The first thing mom, Zeida and I needed to do was to keep our future plans completely secret. By mid-1964 Cuba was full of "Revolutionary Defense Committees." These were spying groups on every block encouraged and supported by the government. The "Committees" were people from the local neighborhood. Their goal was to meddle, interfere, be informed, and inform about everything going on among the other residents of their neighborhood. One word from them and you could land in jail... or your car could be impounded, or you could lose everything you owned, including your life. If they accused you of being a "gusano" or worm, you would lose your ration card, or your livelihood. All of a sudden, not even your own home was safe.

If we were planning to leave Cuba for good, we had to bite our tongues and not let anyone know of our plans. The first thing my mother had to figure out was how to leave. By then, it was almost impossible to get out of Cuba. By talking to the underground, she found out people were buying their way out in some cargo ships, with odd destinations such as Morocco. There was one ship available with a cargo of pigs, and we three were invited to hide among them. Even though my mom's desperation was mounting, we all decided against it.

The other was the legal way, applying for a visa to leave Cuba, waiting for an entry visa from the country you were going to, then waiting for the exit visa from the government, and finally a wait for the plane reservation on the Cuban national airline. All this could take over a year or more! At that time, the flights from Havana to Miami were totally booked for well over a year. If you were leaving Cuba for good, you could end up in an unexpected destination. You also had to buy a round-trip ticket, even if everyone knew you were never returning!

To complicate matters, if you had a Cuban passport, the departure visa or special permission was not easily granted. The Cuban government was going to make your departure as difficult and unpleasant as they could. Mom and Zeida had Cuban passports but I only had my birth certificate and a Letter of Citizenship to the United States of America, which legally was all I needed. My mother had never gotten around to getting me a regular passport.

Zeida was by then a corps de ballet dancer with the Lyric Opera Ballet company. She applied for and received permission to continue her ballet training at the Paris Opera for one year. She now had official approval to leave the country, but mom had to find a way for the two of us to leave.

The American Embassy in Havana had long closed its doors, expelled by the Castro regime, and all U.S. business was being processed through the Swiss Embassy. We either had to wait almost a year to qualify for direct Havana-Miami flights which were booked to capacity, or we could buy the extremely expensive but available in three months, Havana-Prague(in Czechoslovakia) flights, and from there, on to Paris, France, from where we would take a connecting flight to the USA. When my mother called her sister Laura and uncle Rudy in Miami and explained the situation, they told her to arrange everything to leave via Czechoslovakia! They would send us the money!

In Cuba, once you request permission to leave, they strip you of your citizenship. They inspect your house or apartment, inventory all your possessions and you are given an estimated time for how long you can remain in your own home. After that time is up, whether you have received your travel confirmations or not, you have to vacate your home, and leave everything behind. You then have to move in with friends or relatives, who have to house you and feed you until you are called to board the plane. This can take days, weeks or months, and you are living in a very stressful condition.

We were able to move in with our dentist, to whom we will be eternally indebted. Eventually, Dr. Justo Gonzalez and his wife Ana Piñón had no choice but to leave themselves; but at that time, they became our island in the middle of the storm.

The government had come up with a new law in Cuba, requiring every child under the age of twelve to be accompanied by one of his/her parents in order to travel anywhere, with a signed affidavit by both parents granting permission for the trip. My parents were divorced when I was one, and my mom had not stayed in direct contact with my father. Fortunately for both of us, I was an American citizen, and at the Swiss consulate, they accepted my birth certificate and issued a Letter of Citizenship which would serve as the necessary paperwork for traveling, based on the fact I was returning to my country of birth, accompanied by my mother, with my father already living in the United States.

The ultimate goal was to get to Miami, where aunt Laura and uncle Rudy were already well established, with my grandma and grandpa and other members of my family. Zeida was ready to leave in two weeks notice for her scholarship at the Paris Opera, and things were very hectic all around, with her selling and giving away as many of her possessions as possible. Mom and I, started taking inventory of all our things knowing that soon enough members of the infamous "defense committees" would start coming to our small apartment like vultures to see what they could take for themselves, since the minute our request to leave became official, a copy was sent to the committee.

Zeida's plan was to get off in Madrid and remain in Spain for a while, since her scholarship in Paris wouldn't start until July. My mother and I would remain in Cuba waiting for our departure. Zeida hoped to join us in Paris and from there we would travel together to Miami. In Paris I would get a real American passport, my mother and Zeida would get their visas, and in time we would all travel to America. The plan was well conceived... but it made no provision for "Murphy's Law!"

Complications started soon enough. Zeida ended up having to leave Cuba in a hurry, by April, 1964, earlier than anticipated, or risk cancellation of her trip, but my mother and I, with our permits and flight tickets on hand, were facing unexplained delays. Our first departure date in June, 1964, was totally ignored by the Cuban government. They just kept putting other people on board and moving us back. This happened twice. Every time we thought our travel day was approaching, we were moved back, and our trip postponed. For three more months we remained under this suspenseful nightmare.

Finally! After many cancellations and months of waiting, August 17, 1964, was the latest date for our trip. We didn't dare believe it and were still fearful at the last minute we would be once again cancelled, or the flight postponed. But this time it was happening. On the morning of August 16, 1964, Cuban officials knocked on the door of Dr. Justo Gonzalez apartment to advise us we should be at the airport the next day at 6 a.m.

We were allowed to leave with just one piece of luggage that would carry the minimum amount of clothing for my mother and myself. We arrived early at the airport, checked our single luggage piece and proceeded towards the control counters where our traveling documents would be inspected. My memory still boils at the sour faces and attitudes of those officials. When my mother and I stood in front of the officer, he gave us an ugly look, as if we were committing a crime, then turned towards me and asked: "What are you carrying there?" I responded, "It's a postcard album of Cuba." The officer took it out of my hands and said, "This stays here... now go!" I had received the album as a gift, and at that time it was my most precious possession, the one thing I did not want to part with. I couldn't help myself and started to cry.

My mother was then separated from me by a female guard, taken to a small room and asked to undress. She was strip searched. The guard walked slowly towards my mom, still naked, looked at the tortoise shell necklace my mother was wearing and took it from her. That necklace had belonged to her mother, who had died the year I was born, and was the only piece of jewelry mom had wanted to take with her. Mom could do nothing, say nothing. This was one more way of Castro's officials to humiliate and degrade those who did not agree with them, stealing one more time what was not rightfully theirs.

The two of us were reunited and herded with other people in the direction of the plane. It was already dusk and as we waited in line to enter the plane, I got a glimpse of the four propellers that would take us across the Atlantic. We entered the plane and it wasn't long before it became full. All of a sudden the roaring sound of motors dominated the quiet atmosphere of the silent passengers, each enveloped in their own private thoughts. People were holding on to their rosaries and we were all praying. The plane started towards the runway, gaining speed. Seconds later, as the plane tilted upwards to the heavens and Cuba remained in the hell beneath us, a heartfelt applause of relief broke out among all passengers and many started crying. We were really on our way, out of there!

I was only nine years old, but my mother and I simultaneously shared an emotion that cannot be described. One has to live it to feel it. The only thing we knew is for months we had lived like caged birds, where even your emotions do not belong to you, and all of a sudden that cage had opened and we were on our way to a better world, in a flight to freedom. But I could see and feel the impact of what my mother was going through, and I felt it with her. We were going to have the right to be ourselves, to talk and act freely, without the constant fear. No more spying from the corners.

No more ration cards. No more fear of retaliation. But we were also leaving behind our homeland, our home, all of our many friends, and a country we loved and could not return to.

Just ninety miles away thousands of exiled Cubans would eventually find a new life, the liberty they sought. For me this flight meant even more. I was on my way to the country where I was born, a country everyone looked up to as the best country in the world, a country that even from a distance, deep inside, always gave me the feeling of security and well being. I will always be proud of my Cuban heritage, but returning to the United States meant returning to the land where I belonged.

## CHAPTER 3

# *Coming to America*

As the plane climbed to its destined altitude, the lights underneath us faded and the silhouette of an island was left further and further behind. What lay ahead? Would we be able to start our lives all over? With all these feelings of insecurity and fear, I wondered if ballet would also be a thing of the past, out of my life.

The voyage ahead was a long one. The flight captain announced our trip would take us through a northerly route. We would be landing first in Gander, Newfoundland, for refueling purposes and then travel across the north Atlantic to Prague, Czechoslovakia. A stewardess came by and asked mom and I, "Would you like to have dinner?" Chicken! Of course! I chose not to eat and fell asleep.

The sun rays peeking through my window woke me up. It was the morning of August 18, and the captain's voice came over the speakers once again to announce our arrival in Gander, Newfoundland! We would have a three-hour stop and then continue to Europe. Where were we? Most of us didn't even know this place existed. Walking through thc airport there was a scent of freshness, as if everything around us was new and untouched.

All of a sudden the pace picked up. Food! There was an oasis of food waiting for us like we hadn't seen before. Was this scene for real or were we hallucinating? Soon enough we were all treated to bacon and eggs, pancakes, all kinds of muffins and donuts, coffee and juices we had forgotten existed! The taste of that delicious breakfast boosted our spirits and encouraged us to look ahead.

As soon as my mother and I finished, she told me to stand up and to follow her. What was mother up to? We took a few steps out of the cafeteria and away from the rest of the Cubans. Mom had an anxious look on her face, while she stared at various men that were standing nearby. These men escorting us were Cuban agents and were keeping an eye on all of us. Mom took my hand and squeezed it. What was she thinking...? A defection there would have saved us having to travel all the way to Czechoslovakia, another communist country. But her intentions remained just a thought, when she noticed one of the men had spotted her anxious looks.

Back in the plane, we found ourselves among a rejuvenated crowd of Cubans, with full stomachs, singing "Guantanamera" and other popular Cuban songs, while we crossed the Atlantic on our way to Europe. It had taken us twelve hours to reach Gander and now it would take at least another twelve hours to get to Prague. By the time we arrived in Czechoslovakia, the sound of those propeller engines in my ears was like a nightmare from the twilight zone. It was the morning of August 19, 1964, my first day on European soil

As we approached the Czech immigration center, I had a deja-vu of Cuba. It just didn't feel good. My mother showed her official documents and was approved, but when she presented mine, the Czech officer shook his head and said affirmatively, *"This not good! Boy cannot pass!" "Why not?"* my mother nervously asked. The officer continued, *"This paper not legal, where is passport?"* My mother explained my birth certificate was my passport and had been officially legalized and approved by the Swiss Consulate in Havana. The Czech officer remained like a stone wall and repeated, *"You need passport!"* My mother became frantic. She went to the other Cuban passengers waiting in line and explained to them the situation we were facing.

In a matter of minutes, all the Cuban passengers standing in line put their carry-on luggage down and said they would not leave Czechoslovakia if one single passenger was left behind. My mother and I were deeply moved. Meanwhile the Czechs, probably realizing they had enough conflicts of their own, decided one child's problem wasn't worth having these crazy Cubans add to their problems. After consulting with another one of his peers, the Czech officer said, *"OK, Everybody go"* and everyone, including me, was allowed through.

I was still exhausted from the trip but anxious to move on. That's exactly what we did, and we boarded a connecting Air France flight to Paris. We would be the only ones boarding that flight, as all our other Cuban companions would continue traveling via Iberia to Madrid. Our farewell departure at the airport was one of profound gratitude as well as anxiety and best wishes for the future. In the very early morning hours of August

20, 1964, mom and I arrived in Paris. We got into a taxi and mom said, "The Cuban Consulate please." We were hoping to find Zeida's address there, as we had previously agreed in Cuba, and fortunately, we did. After finding her address the taxi took us to the small hotel where she was staying and finally, we were all reunited again.

After resting for an hour or so in Zeida's tiny room, mother placed a collect call to Miami, trying to reach her sister, Laura. Much to our surprise, she was told that Laura, her husband Rudy, and daughter Laureen had already traveled to Paris to meet us, and were staying at the Claridge hotel in the Champs Elysees! With the excitement building in us, we tried to contact them, but they must have stepped out because no one answered their room ... We left a message we were coming to the hotel to meet them. Two hours later, we made our way to The Claridge... I remember our incredulous faces as we entered the beautiful lobby of the Claridge with such luxury as we had never seen before. We sat down in the lobby to wait for them doing the best we could to hide the ridiculous pieces of cardboard luggage we had with us and our old looking worn-out clothes.

Suddenly, we saw them coming through the revolving doors. In seconds, the most incredible emotions filled all of us. Tears, hugs, agitation and joyful laughter filled the space, with aunt Laura and mom embracing for the longest time.

We moved into our rooms at the Claridge Hotel, one of the fanciest in Paris! That evening we all had dinner in uncle Rudi's room. In an instant we went from a life of frustrations, deprivations, instability and fear into one of extreme luxury. Next morning we went to the American Embassy in Paris to formally request my U.S. passport, while Zeida and mom applied for their Green Cards to enter the United States. My aunt, uncle and cousin Laureen, would stay in Paris until I got my passport and I would return to the States together with them. Mom and Zeida would probably need to stay a bit longer waiting for their Green Cards. For a whole week I'd wake up to the scent of those wonderful French croissants and a variety of delicious cheeses as we walked down the Avenue des Champs Elysees.

We visited the Louvre Museum, the cathedral of Notre Dame, La Tour Eiffel and Les Invalides, where the tomb of emperor Napoleon Bonaparte rests. In the evenings we dined like kings and queens, took the Bateaux

Mouche down the banks of the Seine river, admiring the architectural wonders of "La Cite de Lumiere." I had never imagined a city with such history and elegance. From any and all angles, there was always a spectacular view. Paris, with its magnificent museums, bridges, and avenues will be forever in my heart. After a week in Paris that seemed to fly, I finally had my American passport in my hands. Was it true I was really going to America? My heart pumped twice as fast with just the thought of it.

On departure day, I gave a farewell kiss to mom and Zeida and boarded the big aircraft that would bring me back across the Atlantic, which I had just crossed in the other direction – finally to arrive at the destination that was only 90 miles away from the island we had left! I must have slept through the whole flight, because the next thing I heard was, "Ladies and Gentlemen, fasten your seat belts as we are beginning our descent into Miami."

Miami! The name sounded to me like an exotic place! In 1964 South Florida was still a very sleepy area. The city of Miami's only downtown skyscraper was the court building; Flagler street was still the best way to move around, turnpikes did not exist and Orlando's Disney World wasn't even in sight. There was, however, Bay Point, a gorgeous residential area that until today exists, and that was where aunt Laura and uncle Rudi had built their new house. Bay Point was a beautiful, peaceful and happy place that slowly erased the fears and bad memories of Cuba. Aunt Laura and uncle Rudi took me in as if I was their own son. With them I shared many humorous and tender moments that sweetened the years of my childhood and made them memorable.

In the mid 60's American television captivated me. The programs were so diversified! In Cuba, after the "revolution" everything became government-controlled and the TV and radio programs became means for official propaganda only. I also discovered sports and fell in love with football. I loved watching the legendary Johnny Unitas with the Baltimore Colts, and became a die-hard fan of the Miami Dolphins.

After living for almost two months in Miami, my mother and Zeida arrived from France. The three of us were together again and moved to an apartment of our own. I began attending Citrus Grove's public elementary school and it didn't take long before the English words began to sound more familiar to my ears.

If learning a new language had been a challenging task, meeting my father for the first time in Miami, was an anxious event. My parents were already separated when I was born and although they had maintained a friendly relationship, he had not been a part of my early life. When we finally met face to face, we both had the same reaction. Are we truly father and son? Dad kept analyzing me and I kept wondering what was he thinking.. Then I met the rest of his family... Dad's second wife Maria Ofelia, two new sisters, Susy and Annette, and a brother Manolito. It would be a memorable day and we had a blast sharing Maria Ofelia's good home cooking. Though not living together, my father and I gradually developed a very good relationship and we shared a solid sense of humor and affection for each other.

Shortly thereafter a German Shepherd puppy came to live with us, which I named Yeller, after the Disney film "Old Yeller." I also joined the school band as a trumpet player. However, that instrument wound up having a short career, because of my neighbors' complaints about the annoying sounds of my practices. Mom bought her first car and Zeida joined a local ballet troupe called Ballet Concerto. The company's leading ballerina was Lydia Diaz Cruz, a wonderful artist who had started her own ballet training in Cuba, as had most of the other members in the company who now were all living in Miami with their families.

Occasionally, I would hear stories of Zeida's rehearsals but I remained aloof. My mind seemed to wander and the thought of continuing with ballet was put on hold. Instead, I started taking piano lessons, because of mother's eternal dream to see me as a concert pianist. The piano lessons served me well, but the dream of becoming a concert pianist never materialized.

One day Zeida came home from her dance rehearsals and said to me: "You know, we need someone to do the role of the little prince in our Nutcracker production. The directors, Sonia Diaz and Marta del Pino are looking for a young boy with some reasonable ballet training. They know about your background and they wanted to know if you could help us out..." , "OK..." I replied and did not think too much more of it...

For their "Nutcracker" performance, Ballet Concerto was bringing in a male guest dancer for the role of "the Cavalier." He was a Hungarian principal dancer from the National Ballet of Washington named Ivan Nagy. There was great expectation in the studio, with all of us waiting for the car that would bring Ivan from the airport. When he arrived, all the girls and their mothers and teachers went crazy. Ivan was a young, very good looking guy. I thought to myself, "If this is the kind of reaction girls have for a male ballet dancer, maybe this is not so bad!" He looked like a prince to me and I started to look up to him.

I started taking ballet classes with the small company and began enjoying the rehearsals for my new role. Soon performance day arrived. It was to be my debut in Miami at the Dade County Auditorium and sitting in the audience were my mother, my father, most of my uncles, aunts and cousins that lived in the city.

The performance turned out to be an exhilarating experience. This time I was fascinated by the magic of the theater, the lights, the music and, of course, the joy of dancing. My small variation, however, had a couple of double pirouettes, some pantomime and small jumps and a double tour at the end. I felt the power of that spotlight while dancing my solo, and couldn't express in words the excitement I felt again, while I stood on the stage and acknowledged the audience's applause. Since all the steps were rather easy for me to do, being nervous never entered my mind. All I wanted to do was enjoy myself and impress my friends and family. After the performance finished, Ivan came up to me and said, "Fernando, that was very nice... real good... congratulations!" I was thrilled.

Backstage Lydia and Ivan were signing autographs and taking pictures with the fans. And then Sonia and Marta came to get me because people wanted to meet me too! I was getting my first taste of childhood stardom! The most touching aspect of the performance that night was it would be the only time Zeida, who danced the Arabian dance beautifully, and I, would ever share the stage together.

The success of the "Nutcracker" motivated me to return to ballet and I started taking classes again. The teachers at Ballet Concerto decided to stage "Peter and The Wolf," and I got the lead role of Peter plus a "pas de trois" with two other young girls. Soon I became popular with the girls and their mothers at the school, so being the only boy had its advantages!

I remember the excitement throughout our little ballet world in Miami when leading companies like American Ballet Theatre came to town. I have clear recollections of a young Eleanor D'Antuono and Royes Fernandez in the vibrant Black Swan Pas de Deux and Ted Kivitt in his very first "Theme and Variations" and Lupe Serrano and Royes Fernandez in the virtuoso "Don Quixote" Pas de Deux. ABT's visits increased my desire to become a classical dancer and I was immediately attracted to the company's classical image and their exciting repertory, which reminded me of some of the similar ballets I had enjoyed in Cuba.

In 1967, I turned twelve and almost three years had gone by since we arrived from Cuba. While I had continued with my grade school classes, my interest in dance was growing and I was willing to spend more time in a ballet studio jumping around.

Mother was also getting involved in the local theater. She had been doing some stage managing and lighting design for Ballet Concerto, and now was invited to do the same for a popular yearly dance event called *Ballet Spectacular*, produced by Miami impresario, Francis Mayville. It consisted of a group of ballet dancers, headed by two of New York City Ballet's principal stars, Melissa Hayden and Jacques D'Amboise. They were some of the celebrated Balanchine dancers, associated with the School of American Ballet, the most renowned dance school in the country. Mom decided to approach them, and went directly to Jacques ... *"I have a son who has been studying ballet for a few years and I was wondering if you could watch him and see what you think of him."* Jacques politely replied: *"Sure! Bring him before the performance and I'll have a look at him."*

The day of the performance, mom and I arrived at the theater and I went immediately into one of the dressing rooms to change. As I came out into the hallway, there was Jacques! His face was known to American audiences from films like "Carousel" and "Seven Brides for Seven Brothers," but what I noticed first about him was his easygoing manner. The man walked towards me and shook my hand as if I was his friend. *"Hi! You must be Fernando... I'm Jacques D'Amboise.... Nice to meet you! Your mother tells me you've been dancing for a while,"* and as he led me towards a corner of the backstage area, said... *"All right, why don't you hold on to these ropes and we'll start with a simple barre."*

He did start simple, but almost immediately he started getting more daring in the combinations, with large sweeping leg movements and strong quick accents. I was being challenged! The more I responded to Jacques directions, the more he wanted. What was supposed to be a short and easy barre, was turning out to be an all out class. He then asked me to come on stage and try some center combinations and encouraged me to do more. When it was finally over I was totally drained. Drenched in sweat, I headed to the dressing rooms, not knowing what to expect. My legs were still shaking when my mother finally walked in... *"You have just received a scholarship to study at the School of American Ballet in New York City for the summer!!!" "Oh my God!"* was my breathless reaction.

Arriving at home, mom and I told Zeida about the latest developments. She was thrilled for me and said, *"This is the most wonderful thing that could happen to you. Now what happens next?" "We are supposed to wait until Jacques gets back to New York City and we get confirmation of all of this..."* mom told her. Every time the phone rang, whoever was in the house would drop everything and run to get the call, just in case, but day in, day out, nothing happened.

Two weeks had passed after my audition, when finally the School of American Ballet called to confirm the arrangements for my trip to the big city. Oh, boy, now it was real! Mom's actions helped me get a dance scholarship in New York, and the opportunity to develop a career as a dancer in a city that would change our future.

## CHAPTER 4

# *The Big Apple*

In Miami, mom and I boarded the train which would take us to New York City. Zeida would stay behind with our dog, Yeller, and wait to hear from us. We were both fascinated with the view from our train window as we saw the American landscape for the first time. As the train approached its final destination, skyscrapers began to appear left and right. What a sight! The buildings were like gigantic dominoes standing as if there were no limits to their height. No question about it, this was New York! Stepping out of the train we sensed a different energy. People moved quicker, the action in the streets was lightning paced. The city captivated me.

Mom and I were to stay at my aunt Otmara's uptown Manhattan apartment for the summer. She had already been living in New York for many years, with her two sons, my older cousins, Frankie and Luis. The morning after our arrival, I woke up early and unusually hyper with the excitement of my first day at SAB. I was anxious to know what the school looked like, what my first day would be like, in which class level I would be placed, how good the other kids would be and who would be my teachers throughout the summer course. All these thoughts and many more were racing through my mind but deep inside I felt good about myself.

In 1967 life on Broadway was so exiting! Yet, nothing in my life had prepared me for this. My first few years in Cuba had been extremely simple. The trauma of leaving our homeland for good was still very present in our lives, but gradually, life in Miami, among all the family, friends and my new-found ballet environment was turning out to be very pleasant. And suddenly, here we were, in New York City!

At the Metropolitan Opera House the electrifying performances of the Royal Ballet with the magical partnership of Rudolf Nureyev and Dame Margot Fonteyn had everyone talking. Mom and I had gotten tickets to see them, and if that wasn't delirium of the highest order, nothing was.

Throughout the city four major classical ballet companies were giving everyone a feverish excitement ... The New York City Ballet, American Ballet Theatre, Harkness Ballet and The Joffrey Ballet, all in their top form. It was a special time to be in New York. And I was coming here to be a dancer!

I knew I was fortunate to have won that summer scholarship at the School of American Ballet (SAB) but I had this feeling I belonged there. So at the age of twelve it became very clear in my mind my future was already decided and it had to do with this city, with dance and the theater.

All of the students who had been accepted at the SAB summer course were to report to the school's location on Broadway and 83rd street. The place where anyone and everyone came, who aspired to a dancing career or hoped to work with George Balanchine, one of the century's most important choreographers, Artistic Director-Resident choreographer of the New York City Ballet company and founding director of the School of American Ballet. Inside, a multitude of students of various ages were waiting along with their parents or teachers for their evaluation class.

Mme. Gleboff, the associate director gave everyone a warm welcome, and told me the school had received good recommendations from Jacques D'Amboise. She introduced all of us to Madame Ouroussow, the school's director, and Madame Molostwoff. These three ladies were responsible for running the school. Mme. Gleboff turned to me and said, *"You can change in the men's dressing room and then you will join the other boys for your evaluation class."*

Coming out of the dressing room, I spotted mom sitting by herself in a corner and as I approached her she gave me a quiet confident grin. She asked me *"How do you feel?" "Excited"* I replied, and with total conviction she replied, *"You'll be fine."* I had been in this situation before and remembered my very first audition but this time I felt more prepared.

There were about a dozen boys in the studio, all dressed in white T-shirts, black tights, white socks and white ballet shoes. There was complete silence, as everyone concentrated on stretching their muscles and pointing their feet. Suddenly the door opened and a robust woman in her 60's with a long skirt entered. She had a strong accent. *"Boys, good morning! We do two grand plies in first position, in second, fourth and fifth, port de bras front and back."* Here was Madame Tumkovsky, a no-nonsense, direct and very honest person, one of the most admired teachers in the school, with a teaching style that recalled the schools of imperial Russia. Most of the school's faculty were products of the great Russian school, although in time, the school was greatly strengthened by teachers from Denmark, England, France and America.

In those days SAB's training was a powerhouse! There were other celebrated teachers like Anatole Oboukhoff, whom Balanchine himself invited to join the faculty. Oboukhoff had studied at the Maryinsky Imperial School and was said to have been a sensational dancer, quite possibly the equal of Vaslav Nijinsky. There was the famed Ballets Russe ballerina, Alexandra Danilova, Premier Danseur Andre Eglevsky, Muriel Stewart and Felia Dubrovska, giving the School of American Ballet the formidable and prestigious reputation it was built on. And there was Stanley Williams.

Back in Madame Tumkovsky's class, the studio door opened again and a younger woman, obviously a ballerina, entered the room. She was holding a notebook and a pen. I would later learn that she was Diana Adams, former ballerina of the New York City Ballet and one of Balanchine's inspirational muses.

The first week of classes at SAB had almost gone by and I was having a great time in New York. There was still one more class left in that first week, the Saturday 12:30 noon Men's class and all I kept hearing was *"We're having Stanley Williams today!"* The buzz was a Stanley Williams class was the ultimate experience in technique and style. His classes were simply glorified by students and professionals. Stanley was a quiet, sensitive man, who enjoyed smoking his pipe while teaching. Born in England, Stanley came from another distinguished dance tradition. He studied at the Royal Danish Ballet school and performed with the company in many of the Royal Danish Ballet's traditional Bournonville works. Since much of the Danish ballet company and school's repertory relied on the ballets of its renowned choreographer Auguste Bournonville, it was no secret that Stanley's knowledge of the Bournonville style and of his works was supreme. I myself had never heard of this Bournonville.

Stanley's class was very musical and highly energetic. This man had the ability to attract our fullest concentration and consume us all with his way of teaching. He was a fascinating teacher. He spoke with a very soft voice, very low, and we all had to really pay attention to hear him. He also made you feel every word he said was especially for you, even if he spoke from the other end of the room. I recall clearly my first class with him and the very first exercise at the barre. The way he wanted us to use our feet, how he made us aware of the muscles inside our legs, took us into another level of learning technique. He told us every step should have a purpose and a special energy, an accent emerged with each musical phrase. In Stanley's class, unlike any other I have ever taken, my body responded in a most natural way.

My eagerness and desire to please in that first class must have amused Stanley. I was like a sponge, absorbing everything. A rapport was born then, that through the years continued to grow throughout our working relationship. Years later after that first encounter, Stanley would comment, "*What impressed me the most when Fernando was 12 years old and he came to the school, was that he already showed this self motivation and the discipline. When he worked, he worked so consistent always, which is rare for a boy that age. He already, at that time, showed that he really wanted it.*" From the start I treasured his teachings and the special teacher-student relationship we gradually developed.

A month had now gone by and I hadn't realized the summer course at SAB was coming to an end. Mom made me aware of it when she came up to me one day and said: "Diana Adams wants to set up a meeting this week with me and the school's directors."

I waited outside while the meeting went on and she finally came out with Madame Ouroussow, Madame Gleboff and Diana Adams. She was glowing as she walked over to me and said: *"The school is very impressed with you and they are interested in extending your scholarship for a full year. They would like you to return this coming September. They asked me if I would let you stay in the care of another family in New York, but I told them that I felt you were too young and that I could not let you come by yourself. The school, however, is very interested in bringing you back and is willing to help us."*

The SAB had a Ford Foundation grant program intended for scholarships to benefit outstanding students who didn't have the financial means for dance training at the school. Not only did we not have the money to pay for the school; we also did not have the means to survive in New York without financial assistance. In addition, my mother, with her very strict Latin background was reluctant to leave me alone in New York at the age of twelve. She discussed with the school's directors what would be our requirements for such an important move and SAB came forward with an incredibly generous offer. A full Ford Foundation scholarship would include all my ballet classes, full academic studies in junior and high school at the Professional Children's School, once a week private piano lessons and a $150.00 dollars monthly allowance for our living expenses. Mom asked: *"What do you think?"* and I replied, *"Wow! New York here we come!"*

That evening mom and I called Zeida in Miami and told her the news. Zeida was proud of me and said, *"I'll start packing right away ..!"* SAB's summer course had come to an end, but for me a new beginning was just starting. I thanked my teachers, the school's directors for the wonderful opportunity they were providing me with and told them that I was really looking forward to coming back for the full year. Back in Miami, we packed all our possessions and a few furniture pieces into a rented U-haul pulled by Zeida's Volkswagen beetle and headed north.

Mom, Zeida, our dog Yeller and myself, packed like sardines, started our three-day driving trip to New York under scorching heat. Along the way somewhere in the Carolinas, we had a flat tire. We had never driven north before and were very unfamiliar with the highways and the road signs. Yeller went nuts, barking at every truck that went by until my mother finally lost it. While refueling the car, she gave the dog a Valium and from that moment on, we had a quiet ride and a sleeping dog that seemed the happiest one of all.

As we approached the beautiful George Washington bridge that connected the state of New Jersey with New York City, we wondered if our small VW beetle –with us inside– would make it across. We had never seen such a huge bridge and were a bit apprehensive to start across. We suddenly realized that we did not know how to get to my aunt Olympia's house in Queens, our destination. We called them from a pay phone right after the bridge and we stayed put until they came to pick us up.

We had less than a month to get settled, as my ballet classes at SAB and at the Professional Children's School would begin the first week of September, right after the Labor Day weekend. We moved quickly and in less than a week we found an apartment in an upper west side building on 98th street, between West End and Broadway. We were home. The three of us would eventually live there for almost a decade where I would spend all my teenage years. It was a great place to live.

My new life in New York started taking a shape of its own. After a shower and a quick breakfast I would leave home by 8:30 a.m., take the bus or the 96th street subway to the Professional Children's School. This school catered to students in the performing arts and gave them the flexibility of structuring their academic hours around their other artistic commitments.

I arrived at PCS by 9 a.m., had three hours of lessons and by noon was on my way to the School of American Ballet for my first ballet class of the day. Every morning as I walked towards the ballet school and passed by the popular Lincoln Center Plaza with its three beautiful theaters and flowing water fountain, I would tell myself... "*One day I will be performing here...*"

Zeida had also received a half scholarship at the American Ballet Theater school and she took daily classes there. In New York City, there were at that time some other very interesting dance studios with well known teachers and Zeida did not waste time in exploring some of them. She also took classes at the Joffrey School, and at the Richard Thomas and Barbara Fallis Ballet School. It was there she took me that first year to see the magnificent Toni Lander, who was a regular at their studios.

By the spring of 1969, I was fourteen, and SAB decided to move me up to the advanced Men's class. Even though I was a bit young for the advanced level, the school had been monitoring my progress and decided to try me out in the new level. SAB's plan was to motivate me further. They felt a class that included professional and advanced students would create a healthy competition and challenge me more. And what a challenge we all had whenever New York City Ballet principal dancers Edward Villella, Jacques D'Amboise, or ABT's principal danseur Erik Bruhn came to take class with us!

The time arrived for the school's late spring workshop performance and Stanley decided to use me in his restaging of the "Napoli Divertissements" a work by choreographer Auguste Bournonville, a classic of the Royal Danish Ballet company. This would be the first of various workshop performances in which I would perform while at the school.

The experience of performing in "Napoli" turned out to be a real wake-up call for me. This work had three important male solos and I was given the longest and possibly the toughest one. Maybe Stanley had more confidence in me than I had in myself, but all I know was that I never felt so challenged as in that solo. The performance went well but the end result was both gratifying and frustrating. I felt satisfied enough with my dancing and received compliments from Stanley, SAB students and friends. However, when I asked Zeida's opinion about the performance, her reaction was quite different from everyone else.

Zeida had seen the performance, with an objective eye like no one else. After the performance, she too came backstage. "*...Look, you have good coordination and a natural gift, but your dancing lacks strength and attack. There is not enough muscle tone in your legs and you need to start developing them. Until now you have managed with your childhood gifts, but you are now entering the crucial years of development for a dancer and you won't make real progress unless your work has a lot more strength...a strength that is missing right now. Dancing is not easy! You need to develop muscles in your legs, in your back and chest, your knees need to stretch to their fullest, your feet have to point with strength ... the muscles in your back and stomach need to hold you when landing from the high jumps and they are not.. You are just falling down from the jumps... You are not* landing... *your dancing lacks strength overall because your body is still not strong... you have to start working seriously now...*"

I listened and remained silent. I was not happy to hear what she was saying and I remember thinking *"What does she want from me... everyone is raving about my dancing and she is mentioning all these problems..."* But her words hit home.

All this time I had been enjoying the praises coming my way. However, after that "Napoli" performance Zeida's words put the truth right in front of my eyes. She addressed those points that others still were not even mentioning. She detected a pattern of work I had fallen into. A routine that was too comfortable for me to take me past the point of an ordinary level. Zeida threw at me a challenge. For the first time I realized I was no longer the child prodigy I had been since I was seven, used to receiving compliments from everyone who saw me dance. Now I was fourteen, and criticized and I did not like it. I told Zeida if she wanted to help me, I was ready!

From that day on she and I began to work together. We developed a relationship that would last until the final days of my dancing career. She was to be a turning point in my dancing and went on to become the coach of my life. She was determined to make me the best dancer I could be, and I became obsessed with the idea of being nothing but the best.

CHAPTER 5

# *The Will to Excel*

Zeida's words kept ringing in my ears and there wasn't a day or a moment in my daily classes that I was not thinking about straightening my knees and pointing my feet to the maximum. Every night, at home, I would show her what I had done in class. Then she would add accents to the steps that really brought out a sharper definition to those movements. I started working on stronger push-offs for my jumps and on deeper plies for my landings.

Two weeks after that first SAB workshop performance, Zeida returned to watch me in class. I remember I started sweating even before the class had begun. Midway through the barre, I sneaked a quick glance at her. She had a tiny grin visible only to me. I knew that look! Zeida's expression was one of approval. It had taken me fourteen days of intense work but my body was slowly showing what she wanted. Even Stanley noticed. After the barre, he came over to me, pipe in hand and said in his soft, half-grinning way: *"Yeah, yeah! You know, your body is really coming along now. I'm seeing muscles working and more body definition."* I smiled at him and went on with the class. Zeida was right!

Another teacher who taught the Men's advanced classes was Andre Eglevsky, whose big jumps and multiple pirouettes had made him a top dancer in his time. Andre would alternate with Stanley and teach the advanced men's classes twice a week. The first time he saw me he walked towards me pacing from one side to the other, with his head up and hands behind his back. He was inspecting me.

By the end of the class he was asking me all kinds of questions. Where did I come from? Whom had I studied with before SAB? He was pleased to know I had trained in Cuba, as he knew about the Cuban company and had actually danced with them, partnering Alicia Alonso. Andre was not above showing admiration to a younger dancer; he himself had been a very popular principal dancer. He loved to show us some of the tricks and steps that made him famous, and he truly felt a complete joy working with those of us who could absorb his teachings. His words of encouragement meant a lot to me. His sense of humor endeared him to his students, boys and girls, and we were all very lucky to have had him as our teacher.

One day he said to me: *I've invited a special guest to come and see you in my next class."* I asked him, *"Who is it?" "Patricia Barnes, the wife of the New York Times' dance critic, Clive Barnes, so you have to be good in class that day."*

When the day came I dressed in my favorite V-shape black leotard top, white tights and white ballet shoes. Fortunately I wound up having a good class. Afterwards Mrs. Barnes, in her warm and polite manner, complimented me on my work and my dancing. More importantly, following that initial meeting, Trish, as I affectionately called her, became an ardent follower of my career and a loyal friend for life. Years later, she told me her side of the story of our first encounter. It was Andre who had called her and alerted her to come and see the "wonder boy" he had in his class. She proceeded to tell her husband, Clive Barnes, then the dance critic of The New York Times, that she was going to see this wonder boy at SAB Andre was making such a fuss about. When she returned home, Clive curiously asked her: "So how was this wonder boy?" And Trish answered "A wonder!" Since that time a lot has happened in my life, but one thing that hasn't changed is the special friendship Trish and I have shared through the years.

It was already spring of 1970 and I was fifteen years old. That year I did my professional performing debut with the Andre Eglevsky Ballet company in Long Island, New York as part of a group that included Conrad Ludlow and Violette Verdy, Eddy Villella and Patty McBride, all principal dancers with the New York City Ballet. Andre had a special arrangement with SAB that allowed him to use some of the advanced students for his company's performances and he extended an invitation to me. I was to dance my first Don Quixote Pas de Deux with Gelsey Kirkland, the prodigious young soloist from the New York City Ballet! I only knew her from watching her in classes and performances and now I would get the chance to partner her!

In preparation for the performance, I asked Zeida to coach us. We rented a rehearsal studio on Broadway and for two weeks the three of us spent hours drilling the steps and combinations, polishing the technical and artistic nuances. Gelsey and I were technically matched. She was as intent and obsessed as I was on being nothing but the best, but with her 16 years and my 15 years, we still looked and occasionally behaved somewhat immaturely.

During one of those private rehearsals of my solo variation, I became rather neurotic.... I was having difficulty with a combination of right and left double tours into arabesque which I had seen Nureyev do. Zeida stopped the tape recorder and said: *"Change the step"* but I insisted *"I want to do them." "Then do them in a diagonal to the left side only,"* Zeida said knowing I was a left turner. *"No, I want to do them right and left"* I stubbornly answered. I couldn't accept the fact I didn't have the control to execute the double tours to the right and land in arabesque without hopping...and because of it I was sacrificing the end of the variation.

*"You will do this combination when you show me you can do it well, consistently. Keep working on it for the future, but for this performance let's go with the more secure version"* Zeida replied. *"No!"* I strongly shouted, as my nerves began to catch up and I started to work myself up into a frenzy. Zeida wasted no time. She picked up her bag and said: *"When you calm down and listen, I'll come back"* and with those words she left the studio.

I stayed there alone, for the next two hours working persistently on the combination that was making my life so miserable. Slowly, it started to come together as my body gradually understood what it took to control the steps. I managed to execute it properly enough times that I called it quits for the day.

Three days later, we had another scheduled rehearsal with Zeida. I was on my best behavior and did my variation with the easier ending we had both worked out before. After Gelsey left I mentioned to Zeida that I had a surprise to show her. She sort of knew what I meant. I showed her my double-double version and it worked. She smiled and said: *"Good for you, but I still prefer the other version for the performance."* In the end I had to agree it would be better to be safe than sorry for the performance, but I did prove to Zeida I was persistent when presented with a challenge.

The entire rehearsal period with Gelsey was very special and it resulted in a new experience for the two of us. Along the way I learned a lot about partnering and style from her, for she had a natural instinct for them. She was very particular and demanding and because of it I became a better partner. We also began to enjoy the fact that we would be performing together for the first time.

The performance turned out to be a big success for the two of us. Afterwards mom told me that backstage Andre walked over to her and said, *"What are you doing here?"* My mother answered him, *"What do you mean?'* and he replied: *"You should be having more babies like him!"* My mom had the last word: *"Andre, someone like him can be produced only once."*

Perhaps one of the reasons our performance had gone so well and why Gelsey and I had enjoyed performing with each other was because we were also experiencing a different kind of feeling not related to dance; In her book "Dancing on my Grave" she writes about them.... *"A mad and prolonged infatuation drove me to distraction. I fell for a promising dancer at the school. A dreamboat named Fernando Bujones, who initially returned my feelings in kind."*

At the time we first met I was fifteen and Gelsey was a year older and I felt like she was always one step ahead of me. She was anxious for a sexual involvement but I never did get the courage then. In her book she continues: *"I went to absurd extremes in my vain effort to lure my reluctant sweetheart, Fernando Bujones into promiscuity."* I must admit I was cautious of her adventurous spirit, but we always maintained a great admiration for each other as our careers developed in such different but fantastic ways.

Back at SAB my main focus remained in the ballet studio where the school was preparing for its 1970 spring workshop performance. I had been cast in the lead roles of Madame Danilova's excerpts from "Coppelia " and Stanley's restaging of "Konservatoriet," this last piece, a traditional and much loved work from the Danish school of ballet, by the great choreographer August Bournonville. This meant lots of work for me. As excited as that made me, it also scared me. I did not really know if I could do those two works in the same night! Both ballets were very different and each one was highly demanding technically.

Zeida's coaching did much to help me develop the necessary stamina and artistic nuances of each role; Zeida would take her ballet class at American Ballet Theatre, then come over to watch mine at SAB. After class, we would review my daily progress, on technique, on my lines, on my jumping and turning... And slowly both Coppelia and Konservatoriet started coming along, each with its own different style.

*Zeida Remembers:*

*"For me it was always a pleasure and a challenge working with Fernando. He was so committed to dance and so obviously talented. He always wanted to do everything just right and would practice and practice until he was happy with the way the steps or combinations were coming along. Sometimes, what he thought was right fell a bit under his ability and he couldn't feel it, but I could see that there was still room for improvement, more he could get out of the step. So I would push him a bit... and he being, after all, human, would complain because he thought he already had it right. Many mornings, we would leave the house for our respective classes and he would tell Mary excitedly: "Today we'll be late because I'm working with Zeida on my variations..." in which case, Mary would keep our dinner warm. When we finally arrived at about 8 pm, Mary would ask him how it went... "That woman is never satisfied with anything I do!" So in the mornings I was "Zeida." At home that night I was "that woman." But he was always ready to join me again next day at the studio!*

*Fernando had a photographic memory. He would go to watch ballet films at the Lincoln Center library and come home and show me the entire pas de deux and variations of whatever he had seen. He memorized choreography as if he had a notebook in his mind. It was that easy for him. He would also memorize football scores, the dates of spectacular games and plays, the names of every player on every team; he had an incredible memory. It was the same with dance. He was also a great lover of history, and Greek and Roman mythology fascinated him. He was a fanatic follower of Alexander the Great and knew by memory all of his battles."*

Madame Alexandra Danilova was one of the most colorful personalities at SAB. The students used to say *"If you want to see Madame Danilova at her best, just get her an audience for her classes or rehearsals."* She could be hilarious but also sarcastic and nasty, particularly with some of the girls. At times she would say, *"You know girl, it may be better for you to be a wife, stay in kitchen and cook."* She was somehow easier on the boys.

It was in one of Madame Danilova's "Coppelia" rehearsals that I had my first encounter with Mr. Balanchine. Without warning, he suddenly showed up. Except Mme. Danilova, we all froze, but Mme. just went on with the rehearsal. He probably wanted to see how we all were doing, but that rehearsal turned out to be a challenge for Mr. B (as everyone called him), for the pianist, Mme. Danilova and myself. Mr. B insisted the music for my variation was too slow and he wanted the pianist to speed it up. His idea was if I moved quicker I would be seen more in the air than on the ground. While his demands might have been musically exciting, they were not to my advantage.

When I started ballet lessons for the very first time in Cuba, our boys' class was taught by Joaquin Banegas, principal dancer from Alicia Alonso's Ballet Nacional de Cuba, and his teachings reflected Fernando and Alberto Alonso's ideas on technique and style. The Cuban school of ballet was a combination of the English school of classical dance, devoid of mannerisms, greatly influenced by the Vaganova pedagogical method with special emphasis on placement. The more bombastic Russian style was not much appreciated.

Cuban technique consisted of correct placement of the body for each and every step and the class was designed to help you achieve this placement. Correct turnout was an all-special goal, for here was the key to how you could hold and push your body without getting injured. The daily class was instrumental in helping everyone achieve this correct placement, gradually developing and preparing your muscles so they could meet the demands of the infinite variety of steps that formed the classical vocabulary, and still dance pain free. From my earliest start, I was taught to go slow, precise and clean, and thus I never experienced any pain while training or dancing, except when injured! So far, my ballet training had focused on developing a clear and strong technique, using all the right muscles in my legs, back, torso and feet to their fullest. To this day, all Cuban dancers still follow the same strict discipline and style.

But now, Mr. Balanchine's dancing style demanded an almost blurred vision of this technique and he favored speed and fluidity over precision. He always asked for the music to be played fast and faster. Many of Balanchine dancers suffered from chronic injuries like tendonitis and damaged Achilles tendons, back and hip problems and feet problems, all because of this need for speed and neglect of placement. I feared I could hurt myself if I did what he wanted.

So I spoke up and suggested maybe I could have a medium tempo that would be satisfactory for everyone. There was silence in the room, for no one ever dared to talk back to Mr. B. but at that time I did not know any better. Madame Danilova, old fox and shrewd as she was, quickly said: *"We do plie and move quicker"*... and with those words she wasted no time in signaling to the pianist to go on with the rehearsal. But it never pleased Mr. B. who wanted to see me change over to his style of dancing.

My rehearsals with Stanley Williams in "Konservatoriet" were just as challenging, but in a different way. Here I would be partnering Lisa de Ribere and Marianna Tcherkassky, two beautiful and talented SAB students in my same class. Stanley was introducing me to a new and superb style of dancing. Through his teachings and coaching I learned the Danish Bournonville style and technique with its intricate footwork and beautiful jumps, and from day one I loved it. The Bournonville technique and style is also known for speed, but the speed came in the marvelous combinations of steps, most of them including very fast beats or "battus," and not by rushing the tempo to do those beats. I could easily do "entrechat-sis," and of course, loved to show them off... I loved to upgrade the difficulty of my steps with all kinds of beats, and that was at the very core of the Bournonville choreography. That's why I loved it so. In the following years I became a well-known interpreter of the Bournonville style, and this technique eventually became an asset to my dancing which throughout my career would serve me well.

The SAB workshop's performance of that year was a big success, and in particular, "Konservatoriet." My name became known in the NY dance circles because the next day, June 13, 1970, **Clive Barnes**, dance critic of **The New York Times** wrote:

> ***"...Young dancers should never be praised too much or too early-it is bad for their souls. But it is impossible to ignore the remarkable promise of a 15 year old boy of the most unusual talent... He has a style that is unmistakable, his feet are perfect and his manner has the authority of a born classicist."***

Backstage after the performance, Zeida was nowhere to be seen. I was talking to everyone and enjoying the moment, but my eyes were everywhere, looking for her. Finally, I glanced to one dark corner, and there she was, by herself, waiting. We had worked so hard for this performance. From across the distance, my eyes found hers... and she made the tiny face and head gesture that by now I knew so well. She was pleased. My heart exploded in happiness, and I knew all that hard work was starting to pay off.

One the most remarkable aspects of the SAB performance of that year was the incredible group of talented students the school had. By the time I came to the School of American Ballet, Balanchine was no longer teaching classes at the school, but the school had a roster of top-rated teachers. I was basically studying with Madame Tumkovsky, Andre Eglevsky, Stanley Williams, Diana Adams, Felia Dubrovska and Alexandra Danilova. They taught the traditional classical discipline, not the dancing style that Mr. B now insisted on for his company dancers. So during my five years at SAB, my classical technique and style continued to thrive and develop properly. I was also being closely coached and trained by Zeida.

Ironically, Mr. B's best works, his earlier ones, such as Apollo, Serenade, Themes and Variations, Concerto Barocco, Ballet imperial, Four Temperaments, Night Shadow, La Valse, Firebird, Scotch Symphony, Raymonda Variations, Allegro Brilliante, Western Symphony, Square Dance, Midsummer Night's Dream, were created on dancers that had been trained elsewhere, and were not necessarily the newly minted "Balanchine dancers."

It was one of my greatest pleasures to dance "Themes and Variations" with ABT since he created it for Lucia's company when Alicia Alonso and

Igor Youskevitch were principal dancers there and it has remained in ABT's repertoire until now.

Mr. B. gradually started changing his "style" into a more modern neo-classicism. He no longer wanted to see the steps themselves, much less the preparations for executing them; rather he was focused on blending steps together to achieve a fluidity of movement as he saw fit. In the process, body placement was no longer a priority, preparations were rushed, and new requirements were being placed on his dancers' bodies. This newly found style of "blending" the steps and "speeding up" were getting the dancers injured often, sometimes with dire consequences to them.

With the success of the school's presentation came the first official invitation from Mr. Balanchine for me to join the New York City ballet company. I was honored by his invitation, but after serious consideration from my mother, Zeida and myself, we decided not to accept it. At fifteen, I was still too young to join a professional ballet company... But there was still the business of telling "no thank you" to Mr. B. I spoke to the school's directors and explained to them my mother wanted me to finish high school as well as complete my ballet training before she would let me become a professional. And Mr. B accepted to wait for me one more year.

One thing was clear to me then, if I wasn't going to join a company yet, I was going to get as much dance knowledge from every opportunity I could. I was growing up surrounded by fantastic role models. Our teachers were all deeply rooted in wonderful traditions and backgrounds. I truly loved dance history and was fortunate to have access to that wonderful place, the Lincoln Center Library for the Performing Arts, where I read books, magazines, reviews, and studied numerous dance films of the great artists from the past. I was always aware of what companies were performing in New York City and whenever I had the opportunity to catch a performance, I was there.

While a student, we saw The Royal Ballet with their incredible roster of great dancers; The Stuttgart Ballet with Marcia Haydee, Richard Cragun and Egon Madsen, among others; The New York City Ballet with Suzanne Farrell, Jacques D'Amboise, Patricia McBride, Edward Villella and Violette Verdy, Connie Ludlow, Arthur Mitchell and others with their unique style of Americana dancing at their best... We saw all of the performances of City Ballet and I became very acquainted with Mr. B's choreography.

There were two particular ballerinas which I thought were fabulous and I enjoyed seeing them dance. Mimi Paul and Kay Mazzo. Even though they were typical Balanchine dancers, tall, thin and long legged, they also had a serene beauty and poise about them that made them glow. We saw the Harkness Ballet during their brilliant and unforgettable first opening season in New York, where I saw Helgi Thomasson and Lawrence Rhodes dance in Variations for Four for the first time, and what excitement they created. They were excellent!

We never missed ABT performances whenever they were in town and will never forget seeing "Etudes" performed by Toni Lander herself! We saw performances of "Giselle" and "La Sylphide" with Carla Fracci and Erik Bruhn during their glorious partnership years. I was blessed to see Maya Plisetskaya still in top form with the "Stars of the Bolshoi Ballet" in her legendary solo from the "Dying Swan." I got to see the incredible performance when Rudolph Nureyev danced "James" in "La Sylphide" and Erik Bruhn was "Madge" the Witch!

It was also lots of fun to be recruited by the Bolshoi Ballet when they came to town, to participate as one of the students in their production of "Ballet School" – sort of a Russian version of "Etudes" and I loved it. When The Royal Ballet came to town to perform "Sleeping Beauty" and "Coppelia" they always recruited students from SAB as extras in the background. I was always selected and could see their performances for free. Everything I experienced whether it was inside a ballet studio or outside was a learning event. I was living in the right city at the right time.

The one event that ranks the highest in my mind was to see my first Royal Ballet performance with Rudolf Nureyev and Dame Margot Fonteyn in the "Le Corsaire Pas de Deux" and "Marguerite and Armand" at the Metropolitan Opera House. Dame Margot, that evening was an exquisite jewel.

But it was Nureyev, with what seemed to me panther-like movements who had the charisma and the power to captivate everyone at all times. He danced with a strength, beauty, passion and virility that I had never seen before. Now it became clear in my mind that ballet was an extraordinary form of expression, and the stage the perfect place to express yourself. Until today, I can hear the scream of a fan behind me when Nureyev took the first leap in his variation from "Le Corsaire." When the pas de deux finished, a rainstorm of flowers and bravos fell upon them as they stepped in front of the curtain at the Met. It was a glorious sight to see and I was filled with raw emotions. I instantly memorized his variation and coda and practiced it every time I could.

*Zeida Remembers:*

*"Every summer vacation, as soon as classes were over at PCS and at the School of American Ballet, Mary, our dog Yeller, Fernando and myself would immediately pack our bags, get in the car and drive home to Florida. We had bought a small beach house in Anna Maria Island on the West Coast of Florida, and would go there for some well needed relaxation and time in the sun. He had memorized the variation from Le Corsair, but there were still some steps that challenged him. So we started working in the sand, where it was no problem if he fell during the landings. The take-off for the jumps in the sand were doubly hard, since there was no hard surface he could push off from, so he would practice those opening jumps over and over. I would get tired just by watching him, but he would enjoy every single moment, despite the sand in his hair, in his eyebrows, his eyes, everywhere. We would jump in the ocean, swim for a bit, and out he went again to continue practicing the steps.*

*We did this routine daily and gradually his muscles grew stronger and the steps started to take shape. By the end of the summer, now back in New York City, he told me he wanted to do the pas de deux from Le Corsair the next time the Eglevsky Ballet invited him! But one thing is being able to do the steps; another is understanding what you are dancing and being able to convey those feelings and emotions while you dance. I told him he could not do that pas de deux at all until he had experienced the raw attraction and desire between a man and a woman, until after he had his first sexual encounter. He threw a fit but I was firm."*

The following week I saw Nureyev perform in his own restaging of The Kingdom of the Shades from "La Bayadere." From the moment I heard the overture music, I was mesmerized and fell in love with the ballet. But it was again Nureyev who brought joy to my soul and made me realize the kind of dancer I wanted to be and the kind of ballets I wanted to dance.

After seeing him perform that night, Nureyev became the most influential male dancer in my career.

I started meeting lots of people who would eventually become friends for life, whose encouragement and support never failed to sustain me. My friendship with Trish Barnes became a very special source of joy for me. She had tremendous knowledge about dance, was practically a dance encyclopedia all by herself and I would spend endless hours benefiting from this knowledge that she so graciously shared with me. I also spent many hours with her and her children. Her constant encouragement and words of wisdom guided me and motivated me during all my growing up years.

*Trish Barnes Remembers:*

*"Following my first meeting with Fernando at the School of American Ballet made possible by the kind invitation of Andre Eglevsky, our friendship grew, not least through the initiative of Fernando who, recognizing a true balletomane when he saw one, made sure that I was always aware of the varied performances he was soon to undertake with the Eglevsky Ballet and the School of American Ballet. It was a thrill to watch him in class and rehearsals for it enabled me to watch at close quarters the development of what I knew would become a major talent.*

*"Never before had such a unique opportunity come my way! Even better were the opportunities to see him perform on stage at a very young age in partnership with the wonderful Gelsey Kirkland. The years rolled by and whenever possible, I saw him dance. There can be few roles I missed out on. What a pleasure his dancing always brought me."*

All my life dance and determination have walked alongside each other. In my teenage years you would always find me doing a ballet class somewhere around New York. If there wasn't a time conflict with any of my ballet classes at SAB, I would be taking a class somewhere else. I started taking lessons with other well known teachers around the city, primarily those from the American Ballet Theatre School.

Three teachers I thoroughly enjoyed there were Leon Danielian, William Griffith and the rigid, brilliant and unique Valentina Pereyslavec. It was to her classes that all the big-name professionals came while their companies were in New York. That's where you would find Dame Margot, Nureyev, Erik Bruhn, Carla Fracci, all the dancers from The Royal Ballet, the Australian Ballet, and whatever other company was there for the season... junior students like myself were usually not allowed in her professional classes...

Tiny as she was, Madame Pereyslavec always wore high heel boots, and called out the combinations and corrections with a booming voice that could intimidate any newcomer. Zeida, who was a regular student in her class, had asked Madame's permission for me to join them. Her classes were so huge she always had to divide them in two groups. After finishing her terribly slow "8-count grand plies" combination in every position at the barre, my legs were shaking and I was soaked in sweat. There was no oxygen in the cramped studio, so I leaned towards the window above the barre to catch a breath of fresh air, grabbed my small towel to wipe off the sweat from my forehead. From the corner of her eye Madame caught my action and screamed across the studio *"Boy! What you doing?... this is ballet class... not Chinese laundry! In my class nobody use towel!"* I was so embarrassed I never touched that towel again.

At the end of the barre, we all moved to the center. She had the habit of assigning places to each of the dancers as she saw fit, and she placed me at the center in the front line. She had a unique way of intimidating dancers by throwing her head back a bit, with eyes almost closed, and would then pretend to look away from you, but she didn't miss a thing! Then her voice would boom *"Valia, music! And one..and two..!"* and her long time pianist would bang away the most grandiose Russian melodies from all the well known ballets, as Madame Pere counted, clapping her hands so hard it was ear shattering! Mme. Pere gave me one sly look out of the corner of her eyes... I know because I never let her out of my sight. She then proceeded to give the most difficult and complex center combinations... However, I was enjoying myself, and I loved how challenging her classes were. For the end, Madame always requested a jumping combination, and from the men, she asked for sixteen entrechat-sis (leg beats). As I started the jumps with the entrechat sis, she came up to me and stood right in front, watching me with her head thrown back, eyes almost closed, and boomed: *"Look class! Beautiful!"* As we all were leaving, I went up to her and gave her a kiss and thanked her for a great class.

Needless to say, I took many more of her classes. Whenever the Royal Ballet was in town, I would go and take her class, because I knew Nureyev and Fonteyn would be there. Zeida and I took many of those incredible classes standing right next to so many of those same dancers we idolized on stage! Madame would then come up with her beautiful and grandiose combinations, those big, sweeping Russian adagios and grand jumps, which I loved.

By the summer of 1970 my vacation weeks were getting shorter. The "Don Quixote Pas de Deux" performance with Gelsey Kirkland and the Eglevsky Ballet Company, plus the end-of-year SAB workshop performance had had repercussions throughout the dance community and thanks to them I began receiving invitations to perform with different groups. SAB was very flexible and allowed its students the opportunity to perform... So at this point I welcomed all the stage experience I could get and accepted everything that came my way.

With the Eglevsky Company we toured upstate New York. It was mostly a family affair, but I was getting to learn a varied repertory of new ballets. Andre let me dance the lead in Balanchine's "Allegro Brilliante," "Raymonda Variations," "Glinka Pas de Trois" and "A la Francaise." The two latter ballets were created by Mr. Balanchine for Andre himself and Andre taught them to me personally, which I cherished.

The spring of 1971 I turned sixteen, and another wonderful opportunity came along. I was given the leading role of James in Stanley Williams' restaging of "La Sylphide" for the SAB year-end workshop performance. "James" was to be my first big acting role in a ballet. "La Sylphide" is the classic story of impossible love. James, a young, romantic Scotsman, is seduced on his wedding night by an alluring Sylph which appears to him as he sleeps, and he is prompted to leave his fiancée Effie. He follows the Sylph into her mythical world and swears to her eternal love. But the Sylph will not be his to have, and his very attempts to keep her end up killing her, leaving his world shattered.

My "Sylph" was going to be Nina Brzorad, the young, very talented student from my same class. She had all the qualities, the beautiful face, light but powerful jump and that almost untouchable feeling... She was just right in her role as the Sylph.

Once again, Zeida, Nina and I went to work. We rehearsed that role to the point I *became* James and Nina *was* the Sylph. The choreography and the steps became second nature for both of us... we worked on the stamina and interpretation. We talked at length about our characters, about the story itself. The music of this ballet is haunting and eloquent, and it helps to get you into the mood. Under Zeida's coaching, we slowly but surely, developed the stamina for the entire work and came to understand our characters completely. I identified very closely with James' poetic and romantic character, and loved it. We started adding nuances, small gestures here and there that would reveal James' real feelings for the Sylph. Every single pantomime gesture became very real for me and I started to understand how to really express sentiments and feelings through my dancing. To this day, the role of James is one I will forever cherish.

*Zeida Remembers*

*"When we started working on La Sylphide, neither Fernando or Nina had any major problems with the technique or the steps. What they were lacking was the stamina. This was also their very first attempt at a typical story-ballet, where pantomime was an essential part of the dancing and here they had no experience. In Cuba, I had also studied acting, appeared in some major theatrical productions, and was very familiar with the Stanislavsky sense-memory technique. So I devised a plan. We would start working after they finished their daily class, when both were fully warmed up and ready. From the very beginning, where James is asleep in the chair and The Sylph first appears, I would ask them to show me the pantomime for that particular section. At first, they*

*made "gestures" and "faces" which they thought were telling the story. But if I asked them what were they thinking during those "gestures" they had difficulty in establishing and vocalizing the exact reasons for them. So I started building a very clear narrative for each section, asking them to think of the reasons and understand their actions and why they were doing them...*

*"I made them re-create their surroundings and tell me exactly how they "saw" their enchanted forest, what was around them and what reactions they expected from their actions. After we all got a clear picture of where they were, I made them tell me who they were, what were they like, what was happening to them and how they were reacting to each other. I started to tone down their "gestures" asking them to be natural about their feelings and reactions. Both fully understood the reasons for doing this and gradually they started getting really involved in the story. Now they not only knew what and why they were doing, but they also started to "feel" it. When Fernando (James) gets an imaginary little bird's nest and brings it as a gift to Nina (The Sylph), you could see him believe in what he was doing... he knew exactly what he had in his hands. When he goes to the small running creek and gets a handful of water to quell her thirst, you felt the tenderness and care in his gestures, for that is what he felt and believed.*

*Each section was worked out this way, with the pantomime slowly evolving; then I would ask them to do a non-stop dance run-through of that section. I would make the necessary corrections, and ask them to do it immediately right away again, for stamina. In that way, in pieces, we would do the entire ballet. Then we did two and three sections at a time, twice. Their stamina and the pantomime were improving. They both started to grasp the concept of pantomime and how to still be natural about the way you can feel and tell a story. When their own beautiful personalities started to come through, that was the most wonderful part for me, because they were gradually morphing into their roles. We followed this same pattern for all his future roles. He loved it, because it gave him the opportunity to create his roles from the inside out."*

The performance went very well. During the first intermission someone came to tell me that Erik Bruhn was in the audience watching. My heart made a double flip and this gave me the biggest rush of adrenaline. Erik came to take class with Stanley Williams whenever he was in New York City, and he was here now to set his own version of "La Sylphide" for American Ballet Theater and dance it with Natasha Makarova and Carla Fracci. Now he was in the audience watching us!

Nina and I were comfortable with the Bournonville style, thanks to all our years with Stanley. I had already seen both Bruhn and Nureyev in the role of James and was impressed by the strength of Rudy's dancing. My "James" was not a carbon copy of either one; yet I was putting all of my sixteen years and all my love for dancing into that role and under Stanley's and Zeida's guidance, it felt very good. Our SAB workshop performance as a whole got reviewed and **Clive Barnes**, from **The New York Times** wrote:

> ***"The couple at the first performance were Nina Brzorad and Fernando Bujones who both danced exquisitely. Miss Brzorad has just the right elusively Romantic air for the role, a fugitive and Taglioni look and Mr. Bujones danced outstandingly. This young man, as I have noticed on other occasions, although still a student, is already a major talent..."***

After the performance, Stanley came backstage to congratulate Nina and I. He also casually mentioned I had received compliments from two celebrities that had come to watch the performance; none other than Lucia Chase, the Artistic Director of American Ballet Theatre and her company's principal dancer, Erik Bruhn. They had been very favorably impressed. Erik told Lucia afterwards *"This young Bujones is magnificent, like nothing he had ever seen and Lucia should not lose sight of him."* Lucia herself told me this story when years later she was the one who presented me with the Dance Magazine Award.

In February, 1972, just a month away from my turning seventeen, I was invited to participate as part of the group for that year's "Ballet Spectacular" in Miami, the familiar troupe I had grown up seeing. This time the group was going to be led by the legendary Dame Margot Fonteyn, partnered by Karl Musil. I was going to dance excerpts from "La Bayadere" and asked Nina Brzorad to be my partner again.

Nina and I were second on the program. I was already on stage warming up and the curtain was getting ready to go up for my number when from the corner of my eye I saw Dame Margot in her robe picking up a chair and sitting down between the wings. My heart started to race. I don't even remember how I danced, for all I could think of was Dame Margot in her chair in the wings watching me. But I do remember what happened afterwards. Someone came over to me and said that Dame Margot would like to see me in her dressing room. I knocked at her door and I heard *"Come in"*... She was sitting down and fixing her hair getting ready for her own appearance in the "Romeo and Juliet Pas de Deux." Dame Margot was already in her mid fifties, and here she was, as gorgeous as ever, with that magic of hers, still dancing, though no longer with Nureyev.

In her very simple, friendly and joyful way she said: *"Sit down...it was beautiful to watch you dance... your dancing is so clean and you remind me so much of Rudy... I can see some similarities in your dancing."* Imagine how that made me feel... Dame Margot gave me her compliment without realizing to what extent I admired her and her celebrated partner.

I told her of my admiration for her and Nureyev and their legendary partnership which had given us, especially me, so many remarkable moments to remember. I excused myself then, knowing she had to get ready for her performance. However those precious minutes with her will always live inside of me and aside from her great artistry, I shall never forget her caring qualities and the time she took to speak to me.

With the Miami performances over and back in class at SAB, we are all getting ready for Eglevsky's advanced men's class. We had already started the "grand plies" combination when the door to the studio slowly opened. A face we all knew too well by then looked in and nodded to Andre. Rudolf Nureyev! He had come to take Eglevsky's class! Nureyev looked for a place at the barre, and by one of those turns of fate he chose to stand right in front of me. Throughout the entire barre he was focused deeply on his work, his concentration like steel.

When the class moved to the center and we began to work in different groups he started to relax a little and look around. About five minutes before the class ended, he walked towards Andre and leaning against the mirror watched us finish the class. He left the studio just before the class was over. I stayed practicing a while longer as was my custom until Andre called me. *"Nureyev is very impressed with you. He says that you are a first class dancer and he hopes you join a company where your talents can be properly used."*

After I changed to my street clothes, I walked over to the water fountain and was taking a sip, when I heard the sound of clicking boots behind me and a strong accented voice saying to me: *"Boy, you are too good for me."* I nearly choked with the water but slowly looked up at Nureyev, who had a slight grin on his face and said: *"...It was a pleasure to watch you dance." "It was my pleasure to watch you."* He must have noticed how excited I was so he added: *"I wish you all the best and I hope you make the proper decisions in your career."* He shook my hand and walked off down the school's long corridor, wearing his unmistakable leather cap and boots. From the next day on, some of the boys in that class started to show up wearing leather caps and boots... all pretending to be like Rudy, me included.

That first encounter with Nureyev continued to help shape a decision that already was very much in my mind. More and more I was moving away from the idea of joining the New York City Ballet company even though Mr. Balanchine had already issued a second invitation for me to join his company. Along with his second offer, another had come from Celia Franca, the founding artistic director of The National Ballet of Canada. And the word was out there that Lucia Chase, ABT's founding artistic director, was also interested. This was now my last year at SAB. The moment to join a ballet company was approaching and I knew that last call was up to me.

Having studied all those years at SAB, the official school of the New York City Ballet, I felt like I had an obligation towards them. I also knew that many dancers who also studied at SAB by the end of their training moved on to other companies around the world. I was ever so grateful for how marvelous SAB had been to me, that without their commitment to my development as a dancer I would not be who I was, but the New York City Ballet *was* Mr. Balanchine. He was the figure head, the leader, the main choreographer and absolute authority; he believed that "ballet is

Woman" and all his attention was focused on them. All his dancers had to commit to Balanchine's personal style. A magnificent style at that, but I wanted to dance a more varied and different repertory. And I kept thinking of Nureyev's words... *"I hope you make the right decision for your career..."*

Mr. Balanchine's ballets are exquisite, musical gems that shine with glorious choreography. Almost all his ballets are plotless and mostly favor the ballerina. His company classes are also designed as a process, in preparation to perform his works. During that last year, obviously in preparation of what was to come, we started to have New York City Ballet dancers come to teach us. They even acted as if they were Mr. B themselves and would include in the exercises some of the ideas and mannerisms that characterized Mr. B's choreography. If there was one thing that was very clear to me, it was my style of dancing, and I wasn't going to change or compromise the kind of dancer I knew I wanted to be. And clearly enough, I did not fit into the pattern.

Balanchine discouraged individualism in his dancers. In his company you were an instrument that matched the music and colored his creations. With the exception of his version of "The Nutcracker," there were few opportunities to perform the much loved full-length classics like "Giselle," "The Sleeping Beauty," "Romeo and Juliet," "Coppelia," "Fille Mal Gardee," "La Bayadere," and other ballets as a child and later as a student I grew up to love...

The New York City Ballet had some wonderful works in its repertory. I loved "Apollo," which I had seen for the first time when I was still 8 years old in Cuba but as much as I admired Mr. B as a choreographer, I also wanted to be something more than an instrument for his ballets or a support for his ballerinas. I wanted to interpret different characters and emotionally reach out and connect with the audiences. I wanted to express myself, my passions, through dancing and wanted a company that would let me be myself. There aren't two dancers that look or move alike and real artistry does not blossom from trying to be like everybody else, or trying to be someone you're not. It must come from within oneself. I knew I would not be satisfied just to dance with my legs, I wanted to dance with my heart and my soul.

*Trish Barnes Remembers:*

*"When he was about 16 years old, Fernando telephoned me and asked if we could meet, as he had something to discuss. I was about to take my children, Maya and Christopher boating on the Central Park lake and when I suggested Fernando join us, he gladly accepted. The "something to discuss" turned out to concern his future career and whether he should join American Ballet Theater or New York City Ballet. Both companies were eager to take him on. I think he had already made up his mind, but he needed reassurance that his decision was the right one. I tried to present a fair case for both companies, but in any event I am sure Fernando could sense that my preference would be Ballet Theatre for the greater opportunities and diversity of repertory it presented for a dancer of Fernando's star potential."*

After discussing my final decision with mom and Zeida, a contact was established with ABT and an appointment was made for me to meet with Lucia Chase, the company's artistic director. Now the next step was for me to meet with the School of American Ballet directors. This was not an easy thing to do.

We arranged to meet with the school's directors. Looking straight at Madame Ouroussow and Madame Gleboff I began the conversation by saying, *"I want you to know how grateful my mother and I are to SAB for the dance education and benefits the school has provided me with. I will always treasure the training I received here, but with all respect to Mr. Balanchine, who I admire tremendously, I have decided to join the American Ballet Theatre company."*

A few seconds of silence followed and then Madame Ouroussow replied with a calm voice, *"You know Fernando, we are very proud of you and the school would of course love to see you join the New York City Ballet, but SAB is an international ballet school that also develops dancers for other companies around the world. You are entitled to choose the company you want and we must respect your decision. It has been a pleasure to have you at SAB and we wish you the very best in your future career."*

Madame Ouroussow's words sounded comforting and understanding and I replied: *"I shall never forget everything the school gave me and in the future I promise to come back to the school and take classes here whenever I can."*

It was now June of 1972. SAB was preparing for their upcoming annual workshop presentation and at age seventeen this would be my last and graduating workshop performance with the school. I was cast in the leading role as Prince Siegfried in Madame Danilova's restaging of "Swan Lake Act I Divertissements." Our entire class prepared and rehearsed as hard as possible, for this would be our ballet school's graduation workshop. After that, we would all become professionals.

CHAPTER 6

# *First Year with ABT*

1972 was my last year as a student at SAB. I saw all of ABT's summer season at the Met. I was taking two and sometimes even three classes per day at SAB or at the ABT School. Then towards the end of April, 1972, I finally got a date to meet with Lucia Chase. I was just about to finish ballet school, just about to graduate from high school, and was now ready to look for my first job. Zeida thought it would be nice if I showed up for my first interview at ABT dressed up for the occasion and she went out and bought me my first three-piece suit. I took a taxi and headed down Broadway to meet with Ms. Chase at her office.

I introduced myself to her assistant, Florence Pettan, who told me to sit and wait for Ms. Chase, who was interviewing other dancers. That immediately put the fear in me. What if by the time she sees me, she has already hired all the dancers she needs and there is no longer room for me? I remember my hands getting clammy and I held on to the armrests. All of a sudden, I felt very vulnerable and nervous. Then I heard, *"Ms. Chase will see you now... follow me..."*

Upon meeting Ms. Chase in person, I thought to myself she was such an elderly lady... but she instantly proved me wrong. She was all business and super sharp! Her first words to me were *"Hello there... why, I thought you were blond... your hair looked so much lighter on stage!"* Slightly surprised by her words, I giggled and replied: *"I was very blond as a kid but my hair got darker as I grew up."* Later I found out Lucia loved dancers with blond hair. She ignored my answer and instead asked me to sit across from her. She then started to look for something in her briefcase. *"Well, here it is! I hope this is what you want... Here is your contract! Just look it over and if you have any questions, let me know..."*

She went on about her business as I sat there looking at my first ABT contract, thinking the writing on this agreement was secondary to the joy

I was feeling. I had just been handed an ABT contract without having to audition for it. The gesture in itself was saying a lot about Lucia. She always knew what she wanted, and got it. If she was that confident, then I did not have to read any further... and quickly signed on the dotted line. That's how on May, 1972, at age seventeen, I officially became a member of the American Ballet Theatre corps de ballet. After signing the contract I gave it back to Lucia who said: *"Congratulations! You are certainly one of my youngest dancers... Now go see my secretary and she will give you a schedule of the company's classes and rehearsals."*

Lucia made it a point not to make any fuss over me then. She was not making any idle conversation to humor me either, but sitting speechless in front of her in my new suit, I was getting more and more excited knowing I was now part of ABT. I don't even remember what I said to her as I got up to leave, but suddenly I was out of the building, with a contract and a rehearsal schedule in my hand, and a smile from ear to ear. I looked up at a splendid blue sky and laughed out loud. I had a job! I was now part of the major leagues, with a weekly salary and a place in the corps de ballet of a company that to me, was already a legend!

Before I could start my rehearsal period with ABT there was still the final SAB workshop performance I was scheduled to dance; Prince Siegfried in Madame Danilova's "Swan Lake-Act I." SAB's workshop performance took place on June 4, 1972. Madame Danilova herself had cast me as the Prince and I wanted to do my best to honor her production. She had always been very supportive of me and even now was encouraging me to give the performance of my SAB life. Not everyone had been in agreement with my decision to join ABT, but Madame respected it and encouraged me with the words, "*We must do in life what our heart says."* And it was from the heart I performed that last workshop performance of the school. The next day, **Clive Barnes** of **The New York Times** wrote:

> ***"... First and foremost there is Fernando Bujones, who is already at 17 technically and stylistically the most sensational male dancer to emerge from the school since Edward Villela. Probably only Mikhail Baryshnikov in Leningrad has a technique of this equal at his age....Mr.***

***Bujones is easily picked out. He is already one of the dance stylists of our generation..."***

All the top brass from ABT came to watch the performance. My decision was already made. At SAB, the school directors had been hoping by the end of the last workshop I would reconsider and stay on with the New York City Ballet. But I already had my ABT contract and I decided I better speak to them again. This time they really understood my heart was indeed with ABT. I reiterated to them how indebted I was to SAB, to my teachers and to all who had helped me along during my five years, and I would always be a proud part of SAB and come back continuously to take classes there. Little did I know my intentions were not shared by the one person who could do something about it. I was to find out soon enough.

*Trish Barnes Remembers:*

*"From the beginning I was impressed with the maturity, courtesy and single-minded discipline that characterized his personality, as well as the strong sense of justice and fair play and an often unexpected sense of humor. Some may have found in him a certain arrogance. If so, they were wrong. Fernando's belief in himself was as necessary a part of his preparation for the life of a dancer as was the daily class. He wanted to be not just any dancer, but the best. And he did indeed become "the best" to be ranked with the leading dancers of the 19th Century. Yet always there was a certain humility to his manner, though never any false modesty. He knew just how good he was and I admired him for it!*

*"More importantly, Fernando's teachers and others at the School of American Ballet were well aware of the exceptionally talented student in their care. I remember on one occasion talking about Fernando with Mme. Danilova at an event celebrating Diaghilev's 100th Anniversary. She began by telling how pleased she was with the rehearsals at the*

*School for the forthcoming workshop performance of "Swan Lake" in which Fernando was dancing the principal male part.... She was clearly proud of her pupils but was particularly enthusiastic in her praise for young Fernando."*

Within a week of my last performance with SAB, I was scheduled to start rehearsals with ABT. Every morning I'd wake up at 8 a.m. and take the bus to get to the New York City Center, where company class started at 10 a.m. The class would run for about an hour and a half. We'd have a fifteen minute break and then a full rehearsal schedule followed that lasted anywhere from five to six hours a day. By 7 p.m. I was back home, taking a quick shower, eating a good dinner which my mother had ready for me and studying until late at night for my final high school exams at the Professional Children's School.

I had given more priority to my ballet training than to my academic studies and I was still one credit short to graduate, which had me extremely distressed. But my wonderful teacher, knowing the rehearsing schedule I was already into as a new corps de ballet member of ABT, recommended I take an intense summer correspondence course. This I did, and if I was disciplined enough, by the end of the summer I could take the final exam again, allowing me to receive my high school certificate.

On graduation day, however, I found myself standing on stage with my fellow classmates from the senior class and heard my name being called. I walked up to the podium and stood next to Mrs. Lewis. She shook my hand, handed me a diploma and winked at me while offering her "congratulations." No one in the audience ever knew, but the diploma I received was a blank piece of paper. The real one was on hold.

Mrs. Lewis continued to help me throughout the summer with my English courses, and I finished all the reading and homework I needed. Three weeks later, Mrs. Lewis asked me to meet her in her office and said: *"You did it! I don't know how, but you passed your English course!"* And just in time, for in July, ABT's full season would be starting and I would no longer have a moment to spare. When Mrs. Lewis gave me the real diploma, I rushed back home and gave it to my mother. *"Here is your diploma..."* And she replied... *"You see, if you want it real enough, you can do anything. Now go be a dancer!"* Thanks to SAB, I had finished my basic education, was groomed to excel in my career of choice, and already had a job. I was on my way.

Twenty-five years later, on June 13, 1997, I returned to the Professional Children's School (PCS) to receive an "Honorary Alumni's Achievement Award " for my artistic accomplishments and I was pleased to present the diplomas to the 1997 PCS graduating class. As I handed the certificates to each one of them, I saw their joyful expressions and knew exactly what they were feeling.

~

## American Ballet Theatre!

In 1972 this ballet company founded in 1940 was at its peak, capturing the attention of audiences, critics and dancers all over the globe. In my mind, ABT stood out from the rest because it had the most exciting repertory of them all... this is where the great classical masterpieces were. Some of these works had been performed for decades by legendary dancers, and they were the heart and soul of the company. I was fully aware the company's wealth was its heritage and its stars.

Royes Fernandez and Lupe Serrano, Erik Bruhn and Carla Fracci, Toni Lander and Bruce Marks, Eleanor D'Antuono, Ted Kivitt, Michael Denard, Paolo Bortoluzzi, Sally Wilson, Karina Brock, Dennis Nahat, Christine Sarry, Gayle Young, Scott Douglas, Roni Mahler, Cynthia Gregory, Natalia Makarova, Ivan Nagy, Michael Smuin, John Prinz, Jonas Kage, Bill Carter... those were only some of the names that were making Ballet Theatre such an exciting company! ABT had the history, the magic and the inspiration that made me want to dance. American Ballet Theatre was where I wanted to be. Our ballet masters and regisseurs, Enrique Martinez, Michael Lland,

Scott Douglas, Patricia Wilde, Dimitri Romanoff, themselves had fantastic backgrounds, having danced with some of the legendary ballet companies. Choreographers like Anthony Tudor, Agnes DeMille, Eugene Loring and Glenn Tetley, Eliot Feld, Jerome Robbins, Jose Limon, Alvin Ailey, were also part of the company's great strength, adding depth and a new dimension to the existing classical repertory.

Without a doubt, there was one person at the helm of this remarkable ballet company, Lucia Chase. At the time I didn't know much about this woman, but as the years went by, I came to admire her greatly. Lucia had the kind of courage and commitment you need to pursue your life's dream, and even more, to make it come true. She had it, and American Ballet Theatre was the culmination of her dream, her magnificent obsession. ABT lived through Lucia Chase. I am sure her vision and stubborn determination to keep her company alive through good and bad times has earned her the brightest star in ballet heaven. Without her, the most glorious ballet seasons our country has ever seen would never have happened, and because of her, that company secured its place in history.

From the beginning, my rehearsals with ABT were very challenging. Soon we would be opening our summer season at Lincoln Center's New York State Theatre. I had been cast in six full-length works, and had to learn all those parts in less than one month's time! I was dancing in the First Act "Peasants" and Third Act "Neapolitan Dance" of the full-length "Swan Lake." I was a warrior in David Lichine's "Helen of Troy," the Drummer Boy in "Graduation Ball," a Cow Roper in Agnes de Mille's "Rodeo," in the corps of Jerome Robbins' "Interplay," and in the corps of Harald Lander's magnificent "Etudes." It was a repertory of dreams.

During the company rehearsal period I had gotten a taste of what "corps de ballet" work was all about and now I realized the days ahead meant long hours of classes, rehearsals and performances.

My first time on stage with ABT came during a performance of "Swan Lake." That evening, Prince Siegfried was being danced by Bruce Marks. Right before the curtain opened, he walked to me, shook my hand and said: *"Good luck! I wish you the best in your career."* Some of the older dancers embraced me and wished me good luck and as the State Theater's curtain rose and I heard the applause of the audience, I felt the adrenaline rush and excitement of knowing I was now part of that great company.

As ABT's summer season progressed I realized how much I still had to learn about being a corps member. During my years at the School of American Ballet I was always cast in the lead role. So when I joined ABT, formations and counts were new to me. That season during one of the "Swan Lake" performances I got carried away while listening to the beautiful music and lost my concentration. All of us male peasants had to hold a pose in a large circle formation and I'm supposed to wait eight counts before starting the next combination. But I lost the count, and started the next turning combination while all the others were still motionless. All of a sudden I am the only one turning and making it seem like I am dancing by myself. To the audience it was obvious there was one lost soul on that stage who would have given anything to simply disappear. I had learned a valuable lesson, the importance of corps de ballet work – the concentration, focus, and precision required by a group to move as one.

I began to make the most of every company class. If the combination required a simple jump I would add beats to it. If it was a single turn in the air I would make it a double turn. No matter what combination the ballet master gave I would always add that extra beat or turn to make it harder without sacrificing quality.

During that first season in New York, Lucia came to watch a class and right after it she called me into her office. *"You know dear, one of the company's soloists has left and we need someone to replace him... We're so pleased with your progress that we think you can do it... It is in Anton Dolin's "Variations for Four" and the performance will be in January at the City Center Theater."* My mind was racing. "Variations for Four!"... I knew the work! Dolin had created it for four men. It is sort of a male version of "The Grand Pas de Quatre" for four ballerinas. I had already seen it beautifully performed by the Harkness Ballet and knew that it was an exciting classical virtuoso showpiece for four men.

At ABT "Variations for Four" had always been performed by either principal or soloist dancers. And here I was having just joined ABT five months ago and Lucia was offering me the role! It was a tempting challenge and a risk. The other three dancers were seasoned company principals. Each variation was a showpiece!

The day after Lucia spoke to me, my name already appeared for rehearsals under "Variations for Four." The other dancers were John Prinz, Terry Orr and Paolo Bortoluzzi who was guesting with ABT for the winter season in New York; all of them company principals and myself.

I learned "Variations" in four days. But the company had an extremely large repertory to rehearse and I never got enough time to work in my new role because I had so many other roles to learn and rehearse. I knew I needed coaching and there was only one person I really could trust. Zeida and I started to work on my variation and coda.

Now when I look back at those early months with ABT, I see the huge difference our work together brought to my dancing... and the incredible impact her remarkable coaching had in my career. She had a great instinct and an extraordinary eye for detail. As a coach, she truly understood my strengths and weaknesses. And she succeeded more than anyone else in making me think and work with an energy and understanding that pushed me beyond my limits. She knew how far to push me and when to stop me. Perhaps it was the combination of our personalities, or our similar ways of thinking, but our work always seemed to generate new challenges and with them came the excitement to conquer them.

*Zeida Remembers:*

*"At seventeen, with only five months of having joined ABT as a corps de ballet member, Fernando was still transitioning from being a student to becoming a professional dancer. He had lots of new roles to learn and not enough time to continue the type of work we had established in class so far, through which his body was becoming stronger and his technique more defined. So the solution was to incorporate our kind of work into every single variation or combination that he was to dance on stage, making sure to preserve the attention to the technique involved, proper placement of each step, and continue to improve his jumps and turns."*

At times she was so very demanding, I would start thinking she could never be pleased no matter what I did. But deep inside of me I had a feeling if she kept asking for more, it was because she knew I could be better. And she knew I responded to that. I loved being challenged. I was never satisfied with less. We had many an argument about particular steps or combinations, or maybe that day it would be my behavior, or my temper tantrums... either way, they all worked out for the best, and in the end, after I finally got to do what she was asking for, I could feel and see the improvement in my dancing, sharper, more in focus, more radiant and assured because of her.

The first day we got together to work on my "Variations" solo I showed her the steps. She began to laugh and said: *"Your variation is composed around one main jumping step but you are making it look like a leaping frog..."* I became defensive. *"Very funny! And what am I supposed to do with this variation? I got the worst one of them all."* I was cast in the third variation of the ballet.

Mr. Dolin had choreographed the third variation around a step called a "pas de chat," which literally means "a cat's jump." You jump with both legs in a tucked position under your body in the air. Zeida was right. If the jump is not done properly and is repeated continuously, one can easily look like a jumping frog. But she also saw the beauty of the step. By creating the illusion of suspension in the air, by pushing off the floor quicker and holding the pose in the air for a split second longer, arms at the sides, it seemed the dancer was sitting in mid-air...and it was a striking effect nobody expected! Of course, it was also much more difficult to achieve this illusion.

When the idea was put into action, the variation gained another dimension. But the real challenge was getting to the point where we were both satisfied. This jump had to be repeated throughout the solo more than twelve times and on my first rehearsal day with Zeida, it felt like I had done it a hundred times. We were almost at the end of the rehearsal time and she was still not happy with my jumps. I looked at her with my hands on my hips and asked: *"Does anything please you?"* She answered, *"Not yet, but I'll let you know when it does."* I continued, *"By the time you let me know you will have to bury me."*

*Zeida Remembers:*

*"The third variation was so simple that it was actually dangerous. It was also the shortest If you messed up, there was barely any time for the dancer to make good after the mistake. That's all the audience would remember. In its simplicity, it really showed the dancer's gifts. If you had it, you could shine. There were not many steps or choreographic patterns into which you could hide, twist, turn or fumble your way through. When I asked Fernando to jump in the pas the chat and sit in the air, he thought I was crazy. Many dancers, when doing this step, take off with one leg first and the second leg follows... and it looks funny. With Fernando's elevation and powerful legs and feet, he could get off the floor with both legs at almost the same time; then I suggested holding the position in the air for a split second longer. He tried it a couple of times and with a quick glance at the mirror saw maybe he could push the jump a bit more and stay up. I saw he could do it if we worked at it.*

*"When you work with and coach an outstanding athlete, whether it be a horse, a ball player, a boxer, a sprinter, a swimmer, and you have that kind of talent in your hands, you know it, and there is a different thrill in the air during the workouts, because you know you are pushing boundaries, you know you are reaching for something intangible, something that doesn't exist yet. We decided to make the short variation a memorable one."*

Deep down inside of me I loved her demanding rehearsals. As hard as it was to please her, I also knew if she was pleased, the chances were pretty good the audiences were going to love it! And throughout my career this proved to be right. Ours became a caring, trusting and lasting working relationship during which she and I shared some very precious times.

The evening of my performance for "Variations for Four" came on a cold snowy night in the month of January, 1973. When the curtain opens all four men are on stage and they go through some sequences together. Then one by one, the solo variations come along. Terry Orr did the first variation

... Then John Prinz did his... These were two dancers very familiar to the New York audiences, who had seen them many times before. Then came my solo.

I waited until there was total silence in the audience and walked slowly unto the farthest stage right corner for my first "pas de chat" jump. Then my music started. As I pushed off, I put all my concentration and energy into sustaining the tucked legs position for the longest possible moment, with my arms fully extended to my side, and for a second I really felt suspended in the air. At the peak of the jump, I hear a loud "Aaaah!" coming from the entire audience... It gave me a big lift!

The applause as I finished my variation was the reward for the many hours Zeida and I had worked together. Paolo Bortoluzzi followed with his variation. After that came the four codas and the finale, after which we all took our bows together. The Third Variation got a very strong round of applause!

A week after that performance Zeida and I were taking a class with William Griffith, one of the principal teachers of the ABT School. Mr. Griffith had seen my performance at City Center and was very happy with my success. He mentioned some dancers were commenting I was lucky because I had been born with beautiful legs and feet and everything was natural for me. Zeida and I exchanged quiet looks. We knew better. Sure, it helped to have individual gifts like a good physique, feet, flexibility, coordination and other qualities, but there is something more important. It's called hard work and the will to excel. By now, Zeida and I had well over five years to prove it.....

By the end of January, 1973, ABT's New York City Center season came to an end and now the company was about to start its yearly three-months national tour. We were to perform in Los Angeles, San Francisco, Portland, Seattle, Denver, Milwaukee, Chicago and Washington D.C. My mother was instantly concerned. For all of my seventeen years I had always lived at home. But now I was really embarking in my new life as an adult. Being a dancer with American Ballet Theatre meant living close to five months out of the year on the road. It was sort of a gypsy life, but mostly that is the life of a dancer.

On our travel day all ABT dancers were to meet outside the New York State Theater, where various buses would transport us to Kennedy airport. When I got to the State Theater, the scene there surprised me. I had done some touring while a student with SAB, but this was different. This was a large company about to go on the road and I had never seen anything like it. The amount of suitcases, black company theater cases and dancer's pets that were being loaded, plus all the dancers, ballet masters, coaches, pianists... It was quite a sight. Finally, everyone boarded the buses and we headed for the airport.

I had never before traveled outside of New York and Miami and that night in Los Angeles I hit the sack early and slept like a rock. All of a sudden there is a rumbling sound that wakes me up... it's about 6 in the morning and it starts getting stronger. I am slightly awake but not fully and my first thought is... I've never heard anything like this. Then the bed starts shaking. By this time I'm totally confused, apprehensive and even annoyed. I covered myself with my bed sheets. Then the room begins to sway a bit and when I look up to the roof I see a chandelier swinging from side to side. In seconds I am sitting on my bed fully awake and finally it hit me... my first earthquake!

After breakfast I joined the rest of the dancers at the Dorothy Chandler Pavilion where the company would be performing for the next two weeks. This is the same theater where the annual Academy Awards ceremony is held.

In Los Angeles I made some very special friendships that have lasted through the years, among them Larry and Clara Yust and the late Shirley Birnbaum. During our second week there the company was scheduled to tape a series of performances for the "Dance in America" series for PBS. This became a special presentation titled: "ABT--A Close Up in Time," and it was shown on national television. It has a special meaning for me because it is the only recording that exists of me with ABT as a corp de ballet member performing in such wonderful ballets like Agnes de Mille's "Rodeo" and Harald Lander "Etudes."

Our next stop on the tour was San Francisco, at the War Memorial Opera house. Right away I fell in love with this city and it became one of my favorite places to perform. I turned eighteen in San Francisco and it was my very first birthday away from home but I thoroughly enjoyed myself in the company of some good new ABT friends.

We arrived in Portland on March 14, 1973, five days after my birthday. That afternoon Enrique Martinez, the company's regisseur, called me aside to tell me that Ted Kivitt, one of the company's principal male dancers, had suffered a metatarsal bone fracture in his foot while filming the special in Los Angeles. *"Ted will not be able to continue with us the rest of the tour and Eleanor D'Antuono is without a partner. She is scheduled to perform the "Don Quixote Pas de Deux" and full-length "Swan Lake" and has asked for you. "Don Quixote" would be in five days time and Swan Lake a week later...."*

I am surprised beyond belief and speechless. After a brief silence, Enrique asks, "How do you feel about performing the two ballets?" .... I replied, "Wow! This is incredible!" Don Quixote Pas de Deux and Swan Lake! "I think I can do the Don Quixote... I would like to think about Swan Lake and I'll give you an answer tomorrow." As I walked away I thought, is this a break or what? I was also sorry to hear about Ted's injury. But Swan Lake was a different matter. I kept thinking I had just turned eighteen and had never ever done the full-length Swan, had not studied the role of Prince Siegfried the way I was used to working my characters, and would not be able to spend any time working at it, since I still had to dance my regular corps de ballet rep and deep inside had big reservations about my being able to do Swan Lake properly. But it was so tempting... I knew that technically, I could do it, but again, I had never partnered Eleanor... what was she going to be like? After all she was a principal ballerina and I was extremely nervous I could fail as her partner...

That evening I called home and discussed with mom and Zeida the whole thing. Even though I was delighted and pleased with the idea of myself as Prince Siegfried, mom and Zeida made a very strong case against it. We all finally agreed artistically I wasn't mature enough for the role and I wasn't going to have enough time to prepare the right way. I wanted my Swan Lake debut to be something special. Swan Lake would have to wait.

The next morning I told Enrique I was honored with Eleanor's request, but for the time being I only felt up to "Don Quixote Pas de Deux"...

Fortunately, he understood. That afternoon I had my first rehearsal with Eleanor D'Antuono. This was the same ballerina I had seen just a few years ago in the "Black Swan Pas de Deux" when ABT came to Miami! She was a technical firecracker! Eleanor and I greeted each other and then she said to me, *"This is exciting. It's going to be fine."*

*Eleanor D'Antuono Remembers:*

*"When Ted got hurt, Lucia came to me and said: "I want you to come and look at this young man. He is still in the corps, but I think you may be interested.." So I went to one of his rehearsals to look. And he was incredible. I urgently needed a partner and I thought he could work out. First, I was used to dancing with different partners, and had also worked a lot with Rudolf (Nureyev). He taught me a lot, how to communicate, and how a most important part of dancing was making a performance together. So I told Enrique I would have Fernando as my partner. And we went to work. Fernando was so receptive, and eager, and even though he was very young, he understood what I was doing..."*

From the first moment, Eleanor made me feel completely comfortable with her... She was very secure in her technique and had performed that work many, many times. She showed me her version of the pas de deux... and taught me little tricks that would help me partner her better. After the adagio finished, Enrique who was in charge of the rehearsal stood from his chair and said to me: "Now I'll teach you the variation..." and proceeded to show me a couple of his steps... Before he could continue further, I said: *"Enrique can I show you* my *version of the variation that I've already performed...?"* Rather surprised he went back to his chair.

When preparing to dance this pas de deux with Gelsey Kirkland for the first time, I studied films of my favorite dancers. I put together a variation then that was as technically demanding and comparable to the best known Soviet versions. From my first leap across the studio in a "coupe jete" I could see Enrique's face. He was stunned. When I finished, Eleanor broke into applause! I asked Enrique *"Is that okay?"* Enrique, blinking his eyes rapidly, managed to answer *"Oh well, yes!"* trying to sound as casual as possible.

The night of the performance, company dancers were packed backstage in the wings. They all wanted to see what was going to happen. A corps de ballet member getting a lucky break to perform with a principal ballerina on one of the company's firework pas de deux! Would I make it or would I fail? My legs trembled for the first few seconds while I stood next to Eleanor on stage in our opening pose, right before the curtain opened. I kept thinking ... relax, you can do it.

When the curtain opened and the music started, the hours of rehearsals and Eleanor's confidence in me took over. Eleanor and I danced our hearts out and by the end of the performance all the dancers in the wings were cheering as much as the audience. They all stormed the stage and congratulated us. But the night was hardly over for me. I dashed up the stairs to make a costume change for my second ballet of the evening and twenty minutes later I was changing into a third costume for the third ballet of the evening, back in my corps de ballet roles.

After the performance I was still so keyed up I decided to call mom back in New York. It was around midnight my time, and about 3 a.m. her time. But this was one call I had to make. When my mother answered, I was already shouting to a sleepy mom the details of the performance. The following day March 19, 1973, **Martin Clark** of **The Oregon Journal** wrote:

> ***"Star Born Saturday Night"***
>
> ***"American Ballet Theater's record breaking run in Portland at the Civic Auditorium came to a climactic conclusion over the weekend with a superb Swanilda by Natalia Makarova in "Coppelia" Sunday afternoon, and what many balletomanes feel was a history-making debut by a young unknown Saturday night. In fiction it may be a trifle backneyed when the big name performer breaks a leg and the young unknown steps in and becomes a star overnight. But when it happens right in front of your eyes, there's nothing***

***hackneyed about the unmistakable thrill most members of the audience feel.***

***When Ted Kivitt, one of the American Ballet Theater's brightest stars, broke a bone in his foot last week, he was thoughtful enough to do it early enough in the week so that management could notify his replacements anywhere from one to three days in advance. They had an eye for some time on a young member of the corps de ballet, Fernando Bujones, an 18 year old Miami born dancer who had studied in Cuba... Bujones was asked if he felt he would be ready to do the "Don Quixote" grand pas de deux with Eleanor D'Antuono by Saturday night. As the reaction of the audience Saturday night indicated -- he was ready.***

***What a spectacular series of leaps and turns he gave that audience. Members of the ABT were at the back of the auditorium cheering their protégée on, but the roar of acclaim came from the entire audience... the most enthusiastic response in the entire run of ABT here. He has a purity of form seen only in the likes of such a dancer as Erik Bruhn. Yes, a star was born in Portland Saturday night."***

After that night I felt that ABT's artistic direction knew they could count on me. That "Don Quixote Pas de Deux" was about to open the way to more solo and principal role opportunities and I would soon be dancing a full repertory of corps, soloist and principal parts, all during my first year.

The following day ABT traveled from Portland to Seattle by bus and I was able to admire the beautiful landscapes. Thanks to a clear day we were fortunate to see from a distance Mount Hood all covered with snow. During the ride I found some time to read, I learned how to play poker, and even found myself betting with some of the guys.... I was now accepted.

My memories of those long trips as the company toured are forever etched in my mind. For me these times were about maturing in life. It was then we made friends, romance bloomed, and I bonded with other dancers, sharing and speaking about our experiences, our anxieties, our feelings and our goals. And the most beautiful thing about the company was the camaraderie that existed during those long trips. We were a fun company on the road.

I became very good friends with ballerina Cynthia Gregory and her husband, Terry Orr. Many nights, there were parties after the performances we needed to attend, and I would go with Cynthia and Terry. This gave me the opportunity to meet some wonderful people all around the country. Finally, after the snow and chilling temperatures in Colorado, Milwaukee and Chicago, we arrived in Washington DC. The cherry blossoms were in full bloom and I was looking forward to dancing at the Kennedy Center.

Aside from my regular corps de ballet roles, I was now cast in soloist roles. I was to appear in another "Don Quixote Pas de Deux" with Eleanor; in "Variations for Four" and in "The Turning Boy," one of the three leading roles of Harald Lander's "Etudes" one of the most technically difficult ballets in ABT's repertory.

In Washington, DC, the company's principal dancers, as well as the company management and artistic staff, stayed at the luxurious Watergate hotel. The majority of the company dancers stayed at other various more affordable places. I convinced two other dancers to share the cost for a two-bedroom suite with me so we could also stay at the glamorous Watergate. I had also asked mom and Zeida to come to Washington to see the season here, since I was being featured more prominently and was anxious to have their reactions to my "new" self! I was thrilled to see them arrive. They had come at a moment when I needed a boost. The "Etudes" rehearsals were more difficult than expected and were driving me up the wall. I was edgy and felt more nervous about this ballet than any other I had performed. I asked Zeida to watch one of the rehearsals. "Well, we've got work to do!" was all she said. My performance of "Don Quixote Pas de Deux" was in two days time and "Etudes" was a week later.

The day for my first "Don Quixote Pas de Deux" at the Kennedy Center arrived. Eleanor and I had by now performed it together several times on tour and we were feeling more confident. Our performance went very well. **Clive Barnes**, the dance critic for **The New York Times**, had come down to see the company over the weekend. He wrote:

***"Bujones Shows His Style"***

***"For about four years, cognoscenti in the American dance have been watching and commenting on the quite unusual promise of young Fernando Bujones. Last year, at the age of 17, he graduated from the School of American Ballet and joined the corps de ballet of American Ballet Theater. During the current tour he is still in the corps de ballet, but now he is starting to dance more and more leading roles, and to dance them sensationally. Sunday night at the Opera House of Kennedy Center he appeared in the "Don Quixote Pas de Deux" opposite Eleanor D'Antuono. Ms. D'Antuono confident and exciting was at her best, and Mr. Bujones, particularly in the coda, showed just the kind of form that is having people predict him to be a future world-beater.***

***He has both technique and style. His jumps are clean, his line is impeccable and--for this is particularly important for a male dancer--his line is never impaired in the air. He has attack, a certain necessary forcefulness in phrasing and a modest but not unassertive personality. He is well-built, with the long legs of the classic male dancer, and his head is exceptionally well set on his shoulders."***

*Eleanor d'Antuono Remembers:*

*"First of all, Fernando had the natural equipment… I mean, he had an incredible technique and we could really dance and enjoy each other. He was also very polite, very eager to learn, to work, to try… and since I was also obsessive – I always thought if I could do something one more time, it would turn out better and he was always willing to go along… to do it again, just for me."*

~

But now I was facing "Etudes." Zeida and I started working by ourselves for hours on end. We concentrated on one passage at a time. We took every single step apart, fine-tuning and repeating each one until they became second nature and only then we would put them back together as part of their sequence. We repeated and cleaned the sequences, before moving on to the next ones... We did this for several days until we had gone through the entire ballet... Then we focused on the stamina I still needed in some critical sections...

With the days getting closer to the performance, I finally felt my dancing getting stronger. When we got to the Mazurka, I had already caught my second wind, and felt in good form. The two of us searched for ways to highlight the jumps that were part of the ballets' most exciting choreography.... The Mazurka begins with a series of single back "cabrioles" to both sides, jumps where you beat your legs behind you, once.

I told Zeida: *"Why don't I do double cabrioles instead of singles"* (as it was originally choreographed) She agreed. It would be a more powerful way to start the Mazurka and visually, of much more impact. We drilled every single move, refining it until my dancing really showed off the wonderful choreography of Harald Lander with absolute precision... That was the quality we were looking for.

The Sunday before my first performance was my last day off, yet Zeida and I were at the studio by ten in the morning, working away. Sometime around noon, Christine Sarry, one of the company's top soloists, came by and was very surprised to find us there. *"My... you are really serious about this one, aren't you...?"* She was also very encouraging and before leaving said: *"You'll be very good in it... don't worry, just enjoy it!"* The night of the performance, I was nervous but ready. And enjoy it I did.

As usual, Zeida was nowhere to be seen, but by now I knew she would be the last one to appear. When she and mom finally joined me in my dressing room, we all got very emotional. She finally said *"Well, it paid off, didn't it?"* "Etudes" marked a point in my dancing when I felt my technique was consolidating, reaching a level we had been striving for. The day after the performance I ran to buy a newspaper and sat down in the Watergate's cafeteria to have breakfast. I started reading the review by **Jean Batty-Lewis** from **The Washington Post**, April 30, 1973, which read:

***"Some Impressive New Faces"***

***"Most notable was Fernando Bujones' debut in the demanding male lead in "Etudes" Saturday night. At 18 he is a real wunderkind in dance. His technique is so perfectly schooled that connoisseurs gasp at its refinement; his leaps are straight, clean and high vaulting and he already commands the stage. The Kennedy Center has a special distinction for being the place where the incomparable Erik Bruhn gave his last performances before his retirement last year. It can now also be remembered as the stage where Bujones danced some of his first important roles with a major company."***

By mid-April, 1973, ABT's tour had ended and I was glad to be heading home. Mom, Zeida and I, along with my dog Yeller, (he also came to Washington) drove back to New York. Along the way, all I could think of was how much I had experienced since I left home, just three months before. I had seen so many wonderful sights around the United States, but more important, during this first tour with ABT I had begun to learn about life, about being on my own and about assuming responsibility. That first tour put me in touch with myself, with my character, at times testing my will, at other times, adding strength to it. I proudly told Zeida a bit of news that she already suspected... I lost my virginity! From now on I was ready and able to dance the pas de deux from "Le Corsair."

CHAPTER 7

# *My First Season at the Met*

We were back in New York again and after three months on the road it felt good to be home. As much as I loved discovering the new cities around America on my first national tour with the company, New York was still for me the extraordinary and unique city where anything and everything happened. Working and living there was exciting but also a constant challenge.

I knew how important it was to dance in the big city. On tour I had gained some respect from the company's artistic direction, staff and dancers and my dancing had been praised by the national press, but I knew the success I had achieved on tour and the new confidence I had in my dancing would have to be tested in the Big Apple. I was feeling the pressure.

That spring of 1973, ABT's rehearsal period for the summer season at the Met began immediately after we returned from the tour and I was cast in some new leading roles. My name appeared on the cast list for "Fancy Free," a sailor's romp choreographed by Jerome Robbins, sharing the cast with Buddy Balough and Terry Orr, and as the Transgressor in "Undertow," one of the many works of legendary choreographer Antony Tudor, who at the time was ABT's choreographer in residence.

I had just turned eighteen and was very impressed by him. I wondered how one could work with a legend. Tudor chose me to understudy the role of the "Transgressor." The ballet had not been performed for years and was now being revived for the upcoming New York season. I did not know whether to be flattered or petrified. Mr. Tudor himself and Hugh Laing, on whom the ballet had been originally set, were going to coach me.

Tudor was known for his extraordinary theatrical ballets like Jardin aux "Lilas," "Pillar of Fire," "Shadowplay," "Romeo and Juliet" and others. His ballets were technically difficult, yet nobody noticed except the dancers, because they didn't look difficult. They were also composed at a highly intellectual level. His ballets were intelligent and significant. They all had a meaning and it was up to us to convey it to the audiences. Tudor was also known for the way he intimidated his dancers. He was spontaneous and unpredictable. He scrutinized and berated the dancers if they did not understand his sequences or if they could not do them to his liking. He always got what he wanted, even if he had to embarrass a dancer in the studio. At times he was meticulous and intense; other times he could be mischievous or cynical. He had no patience with mediocrity. Whatever his mood, Tudor had a wicked way of challenging the dancers.

When I showed up for my first "Undertow" rehearsal, I found out I would be paired with ABT's principal ballerina, the brilliant Cynthia Gregory, who was cast in the demanding role of Medusa. I was still a corps de ballet dancer, gradually taking on some soloists roles but dancing with Cynthia was another matter. I was totally floored.

Everyone in the company was in awe of Cynthia, and now here she was right in front of me. Rehearsals started smoothly enough, with Tudor himself showing us the sequences. Cynthia is not only an extraordinary dancer; she is also very beautiful, almost like a Greek goddess. There is a very physical sequence where Medusa keeps taunting me and I murder her. The first time we had this close contact, it was electrical for me. Somehow I started to fall under Cynthia's spell and I thought I was falling in love. Dancing with Cynthia pushed me up to a much higher level than what I had experienced so far.

*Cynthia Gregory Remembers:*

*"The first time I saw Fernando I remember seeing this young, gorgeous colt, I mean, unbelievable legs and feet and the smile... that wonderful smile... someone so eager to learn and so eager to be part of this fantastic world of ballet... he was just beaming over with excitement and love of the dance...By now I had already done "Undertow" many times and was very familiar with the role and was sort of curious as to how this new, young corps de ballet dancer would react to Mr. Tudor's very difficult demands..."*

I had learned the sequences and knew the steps and I thought things were going smoothly. On our third rehearsal, Tudor suddenly stopped me: *"Young man do you have the slightest idea what that clenching fist gesture behind your back means?" "I think so."* I replied. *"You think so? ... You better know darn well what it means!"* Cynthia started to giggle, while Tudor walked towards me.. Standing face to face with me he asked, *"What do you think of this gorgeous woman beside you?.. . Do you like her?" "Yes... Sure!"* I answered ... Tudor screamed at me: *"Then close those fists even tighter and show me through those closed fists that you've got a hard-on!"* Cynthia couldn't hold it anymore and burst out laughing, while my face turned beet red, I tensed up, started feeling very hot and began to sweat. Tudor smiled and said: *"Oh, now I'm seeing some of the emotions I want to see."*

All of a sudden I realized his choreography was not only about steps, it was also about emotions, feelings and the human drama between two or more people. Here was something to dance about! To dance Tudor you had to know what he meant when he created the steps, otherwise you were just doing empty steps.

Tudor liked me and he liked my dancing. So he pushed me... and he finally got what he wanted out of me. By the end of the rehearsals I was emotionally drained, but Tudor's ballets were so interesting because of his powerful physical language. Eventually I learned how to work with Tudor and not take his cynical remarks seriously; I could relate to his dark sense of humor and he appreciated that. Soon he was casting me in all of his ballets. At times, some of his choreography simply went by me as when I started learning "Jardin aux Lilas." I simply stared at the beautiful choreographic designs but just couldn't grasp them. I turned to one of the company's principal dancers, Gayle Young, who was rehearsing with me and mouthed, "Help!" Gayle knew the work inside out and explained the sequences to me. When I finally understood "Jardin," I felt very much at home in it. It is such a jewel of a ballet!

In time I would perform other Tudor works like "Shadowplay" and "Romeo and Juliet." Each one of them added something to my growth as a dancer. At that time I was not so aware of the importance of working with a choreographer of Tudor's stature, but today I know how fortunate I was to have had such an opportunity. Tudor was to be the first of the great choreographers with whom I worked. It is an honor for me to know I was part of the celebrated group of dancers who performed Tudor's ballets.

"Fancy Free" was another first for me that New York season. Choreographed by Jerome Robbins, this was his first work for ABT when he created it in 1944. I instantly loved this ballet. I was cast as the Latin sailor dancing the "Rhumba" variation, the same part that Robbins created for himself. "Fancy" was one of those ABT ballets you couldn't help but love performing. The dancers loved it and the audiences loved it. It was a hit every time it was performed and I couldn't wait to dance in it.

During that rehearsal period, I received a phone call with a message from principal ballerina Natalia Makarova, or Natasha, as we all called her. She had seen my first performance of "Don Quixote Pas de Deux" with Eleanor on tour. Now her regular partner, Ivan Nagy was hospitalized because of an injury and she was requesting me to partner her in her upcoming "Don Q" performance. This news electrified not only me, but the rest of the company as well. Lucia granted Makarova her wish, but a day later, my name was removed from the "Don Q" rehearsal and a guest principal dancer was flown in from Europe to dance with Natasha. Imagine my disappointment! But I heard through the grapevine several of the principal male dancers at ABT were upset Natasha was passing them over and requesting a corps newcomer as her partner. Lucia had no choice but to replace me.

However, several performances of the "Don Quixote" Pas de Deux were scheduled for the Met and ballerina Eleanor D'Antuono immediately requested me again. Again she took me under her wing, showed me all kinds of nuances and we rehearsed to death. Ours was to be the last of the "Don Q" pas de deux performed that spring. She inspired and provoked me to go all out. We were scheduled to dance August 12, two days after my mother's birthday. I had told my mom that my birthday present for her would be my first performance of "Don Quixote" at the Met.

Ever since we moved to New York for my dance scholarship, my mother dedicated her life to make sure I lacked nothing, that I could concentrate on my career while she cooked all my dinners, washed my tights, helped with school homework and made sure I kept my head on my shoulders and my feet on the ground. She was my strongest supporter and cheerleader. Her strength gave me strength. Her belief in me and dedication to me was total. She worked wherever she could so I could have the best of everything. She was a cashier at Brentano's Bookstore, then in Bergdorf Goodman and Lord & Taylor. Even though she had been an upcoming playwright and an actress in Cuba, once we arrived in New York City she left all her ambitions behind. It was my career that counted. She loved the theater, music and ballet. A woman of tremendous culture, she passed her love of the arts on to me. Her comments and suggestions were invaluable to me and we were very close. She became a well known visitor at ABT and backstage at the Met.

Finally it was the night of our performance. Eleanor was in top form that night. She was "on" and doing incredible technical feats. And her performance turned me "on." It became such a thrilling performance because the audience at the Met went wild. They were cheering us on. It was my first pas de deux at the Met, I was dancing with a principal ballerina and we brought the house down. In the audience were two of my favorite teachers from SAB, Stanley Williams and Andre Eglevsky and almost all my old classmates. Some came to cheer me on, some to see if I was going to make it. During the final bows, Eleanor was presented with a huge bouquet of roses. She graciously took one out and with a beautiful gesture gave it to me and pushed me forward while she took a step back and the audience roared. After innumerable curtain calls I spotted my mother in one of the first rows, and threw my rose and a kiss to her.

*Eleanor D'Antuono Remembers:*

*"It was astounding, an astounding performance... The New York public loved us. They reacted as only the New York public can and their reaction to us was incredible. It was a performance forever etched in my mind, and it is the one that everyone who saw us dance always remembers. That was really the beginning of our many, many performances together..."*

That was my introduction to the Met. **Don McDonagh** of **The New York Times** was there to review the night, and on August 13, 1973, he wrote:

***"...As a farewell bouquet, American Ballet Theater offered an array of cast changes at the State Theater over the weekend. Among the more notable was Fernando Bujones***

> ***dancing Saturday evening in the "Don Quixote" pas de deux with Eleanor D'Antuono... As an emerging dancer Mr. Bujones is one upon whom the gods have looked with favor. He has that special quality in a jump that gives it a soaring look, that fractional second in which gravity is defied past its lawful grasp... It was a thoroughly memorable performance."***

The 1973 summer season was coming to an end. I was very happy with the many opportunities the company had given me, with the warm reception from the audiences and the wonderful reviews I had received from the press. Rumors were going around that I was going to be promoted to soloist. Before the season finished Lucia called me to her office and handed me a new contract *"I have good news for you... you are now a soloist with the company"* ...she said...and I signed my second-year contract!

After my success at the Met, Mr. Balanchine decided I would no longer be welcomed at SAB, and I was forbidden to go and take classes there. I was heartbroken, for no longer would I be able to attend Stanley Williams' wonderful classes. I am sure Stanley felt the same way but he was in no position to contradict Mr. B. As he knew, Mr. B. had a very jealous nature.

It was now fall of 1973. I was eighteen years old and a soloist with the most wonderful ballet company in the world. The casting started for the upcoming season's repertory. I got the lead in the Flower Festival Pas de Deux of the "Napoli Divertissements" that was being staged by Hans Brenna, Headmaster from the Royal Danish Ballet who was setting the work for ABT. My partner was again to be Eleanor D'Antuono, and I was looking forward to another very exciting season. The entire company traveled to Washington. One week before the opening at Kennedy Center, after a morning class I stayed in the studio practicing some of the steps of the Flower Festival variations. Into the studio came corps de ballet member and friend Rhodie Jorgensen to watch my rehearsal.

I continued dancing while talking to her and the next thing I knew I was on the floor with my left foot twisted underneath me. I felt an excruciating pain and I knew I was in trouble. I kept feeling more frustrated, angry and depressed. It was what I called a stupid injury and I felt like crying. All I could think was, *"there goes my "Napoli Divertissements" opening night performance at the Kennedy Center."*

In dance all it takes is a second of a mental lapse or losing your concentration for a moment and the body might not forgive you for it. That was to be my first injury as a dancer and because of it I would miss the entire two week season at the Kennedy Center. Next morning the company staff sent me to see Dr. Alfred Kagan a well-known orthopedic doctor. Various ABT dancers had already been treated by him. Once in his office all I remember is Dr. Kagan massaging my foot while speaking on the telephone. I wanted to kill him for being so casual while I was in such pain. It was then that I felt a hand on my back, a gentle touch.

The hand came from Dr. Kagan's assistant, a Mexican gentleman named Armando Zetina. Doctor Kagan finished his therapy and bandaged my foot; *"Try not to put any weight on the foot... it is a serious sprain and you overstretched various ligaments... it will take about a month before you can really begin to dance on it again."* I was crushed as I kept thinking of a whole month without dancing and the loss of an opening night principal role at the Kennedy Center.

That evening I received a call from Armando Zetina. *"Fernando, I know how you must be feeling...if you want I can come to your house every day next week after I finish work here and we can work on your foot. It's possible that we can get you going faster than you think if we care for it every day."* I immediately accepted. In one week he had me on my two feet with minimal pain and full mobility on my foot. Armando's caring and his concern for me developed into a loyal friendship that has lasted all these years, and he became my official masseur throughout my twenty-eight years as a dancer.

After a week of Armando's therapy, Zeida took over. We would go daily to ABT studios in New York City and holding on to the barre she would have me doing strength exercises for the foot. My foot trembled and felt extremely weak. But Zeida's watchful eye and my desire to get well worked fine, and we managed to strengthen that darned foot. In less than a month I was pushing off from both feet and jumping again. By the time ABT was back in New York I was ready to join them in company class and ready to pick up where I had left off, learning and rehearsing various new roles.

For the upcoming season, the company was also bringing back "Les Rendezvous" and "Les Patineurs" by the English choreographer Frederick Ashton. These works were fun, lighthearted short ballets, like "Graduation Ball." But there was one juicy role, that of the "Green Boy" or the "Green Skater"…and I got it! There is no story to "Les Patineurs," just a group of boys and girls out for a night of ice skating fun. Terry Orr had been the most recent "Green Skater" and he was in charge of teaching me the role. Mostly, the dancers hopped everywhere, simulating skaters, whether spinning or jumping. Zeida and I started working on a gliding step that would give the illusion of skating, better than the hops. It was very tiring on the legs, because the standing leg had to remain in "plie" at all times, but it really did the trick. And I kept repeating to myself I could feel the cold breeze in my face from the skating rink to the point I convinced myself I was skating! I enjoyed this role a lot and was the dancer selected to be the "Green Skater" when the ballet was videotaped at the Grand Ole Opry in Tennessee for the "Dance in America" series.

Another one of the new roles was the challenging and exciting "Bluebird Pas de Deux" in the company's new production of "Aurora's Wedding" from the Third act of "The Sleeping Beauty" staged by David Blair, a former principal dancer from The Royal Ballet who had just restaged ABT's "Swan Lake" and "Giselle." I was second cast in the "Bluebird Pas de Deux," but when I started learning it, I never imagined what awaited me in the upcoming company tour.

ABT's 1974 national winter tour would once again begin in Los Angeles. The entire company traveled to LA and rehearsals started. The third afternoon I was warming up in the wings watching the first cast of Bluebird rehearse on stage. Then I heard a loud sound...like a loud pop! Next thing I hear is a scream and I see the commotion on stage with everyone running to the center. I ran too and saw principal dancer John Prinz on the floor grabbing his calf muscle with the most agonizing expression on his face. He had just torn his Achilles tendon! John was an ex-Balanchine dancer. He and his wife Nannette Glushak left City Ballet in order to join ABT, where they immediately expanded their dancing roles and became excellent Tudor dancers. Some company members began to embrace each other, others began to cry and I was horrified. I felt nervous and scared. An injury of this kind traumatizes the entire company. This was the dancer that weeks ago had comforted me when I was on the ground injured, and now I was feeling very much for him.

Not even ten minutes after they had taken John to a doctor, I was told I would be performing the opening night "Bluebird Pas de Deux" in Los Angeles' first "Sleeping Beauty" with Christine Sarry. And that performance was the next day! That was hardly the news I wanted to hear at the moment. All I remember was feeling very ill and worried about my own health. This was the second time I was replacing an injured principal dancer in a lead role. As a result of John's injury I wound up dancing "Bluebird" in all the opening night performances on tour. The one in Seattle, Washington went especially well. The next day, **Carole Beers**' review in **The Seattle Times** read:

> ***"Ballet Theater lacks sparkle"***
>
> ***"...The whole concert was saved by a Bluebird, in the third act from "The Sleeping Beauty." Fernando Bujones that just-turned-19 prodigy, earned bravos for his flawless footwork and snappy turns."***

The role brought me much success and I was scheduled to dance the opening night performance as the Bluebird, partnering ballerina Natalia Makarova at the New York State Theater summer season. I would also learn and dance the Peasant Pas de Deux in "Giselle" with Zhandra Rodriguez. I learned and was cast as Benno in "Swan Lake" first act Pas de Trois, with partners Christine Sarry and Marianna Tcherkassky. Dance critic **Frank Gagnard**, wrote in **The New Orleans Times-Picayune** of March 25, 1974...

> ***"...An exception was Fernando Bujones who did have the capacity to thrill. The smart seasoned dancer would do well to avoid appearing with Bujones, as veteran actors refuse to share with child stars and trained animals. Young Bujones, only recently turned 19, danced the role of Benno and had***

> ***only the first act Pas de Trois to strut his stuff, but he proved a memorable scene stealer....He gives the impression of leaping higher, staying longer, and landing lighter than any one since Rudi what's his name. An astonishing physical thrust is followed by an amazingly poised lyric resolution. The smile is composed but a rival might see "So there!" written into it. What the audience sees, most likely, is a great big star in the making."***

Finally it was the first week of April and the tour had finished. We were back home. Mom and Zeida welcomed me with the news there was an invitation to perform in a Gala in London, England. Lady Anya Sainsbury, a former Royal Ballet ballerina, together with another former Royal Ballet dancer, Petrus Bosman, were organizing a Royal Gala benefit performance that would take place at the Palladium Theater in London. ABT was in a layoff period, so I was free to go and quickly accepted and invited mom to come with me.

My first trip abroad! They wanted me to perform two pas deux and I could choose my ballerina. I asked my most frequent ABT partner, Eleanor D'Antuono to perform with me the "Don Quixote" Pas de Deux and the pas de deux from "Diana and Acteon." These were two really demanding pieces, but it was to be my European debut and I didn't want to play it safe.

The performance was scheduled for April 28, so my mother, Eleanor and I traveled a few days earlier to get used to the city and the time change. Waiting for us in London was Trish Barnes' twin sister, Rosemary Winckley who proved to be a wonderful host and friend and we got to know that wonderful city through her thoroughly informed eyes. She was also a confirmed balletomane with an incredible knowledge of dance and dancers and knew everybody, everywhere. Also in London at that time was Dina Makarova, a photographer and friend of all of us, as well as the personal assistant to Natasha Makarova (no relation), and together between rehearsals, we would all run from one museum to the next, from one gallery to the next, from one fabulous boutique shop and restaurant to the next, wanting to cram as much as possible of that fantastic and historic city. I loved London.

After a few days of rehearsals, the evening of the performance finally arrived. Eleanor and I were very excited and could not wait to perform our two pas de deux. The gala's roster of artists performing that night was impressive. Natalia Makarova, Ivan Nagy, Anthony Dowell, Merle Park, Heinz Bosl, Wilfride Piollet, Jean Guizerix, Ann Jenner and Wayne Sleep. In the audience was choreographer Sir Frederick Ashton as well as principal dancers Frank Augustyn and Peter Schaufuss. To add to the excitement of the evening, all the dancers were told prior to the performance that Princess Margaret, sister of the Queen of England, and a ballet lover, would be attending the event. Eleanor and I were electrified. We had never performed in such an incredible event before.

*Eleanor D'Antuono Remembers:*

*"London was such an exciting event... I remember I didn't really want to do Diana and Acteon because I had not been pleased with the way it had gone for me before.. But Fernando was convinced that it would be a stunner and I agreed to try. So I got help and I got it back. Fernando and I went to work with the choreography and things started really working for me too. He was simply spectacular in that role... and he was right, the London audiences loved us!"*

The evening turned out to be a success, with everyone dancing beautifully. After the final curtain came down, we were all advised to stay on stage and to line up. Princess Margaret would be coming on stage to congratulate the artists. When the princess finally got to me I was so nervous I could barely breathe, but I will never forget her words. *"Congratulations...you were simply breathtaking...Is this the first time you are dancing in London?"... "Yes your Highness,"* I answered. *"Well I'm sure there will be many more occasions in the future and I look forward to them."* I treasure our meeting as one of the most extraordinary moments of my life. The next day, **The Evening Standard** on April 29, 1974 had a picture of me with Princess Margaret, and **Sydney Edwards** wrote:

***"Backstage at the Palladium, America's 18 year old ballet superstar Fernando Bujones meets Princess Margaret after giving a remarkable performance for her and his first London audience at a royal gala last night. Bujones trained in Cuba but now dances with the American Ballet Theatre. His reputation had preceded him across the Atlantic and last night he won an ovation after dancing with splendid Spanish fire the male role of the Don Quixote pas de deux."***

Back in New York, The Royal Ballet was performing at the Met and I wanted to see all their performances, especially the ones with Rudolph Nureyev. One night I got there early, went backstage and knocked on Rudy's dressing room. We already knew each other back from my student days and he welcomed me into his dressing room. He had already heard of my London debut... and he says to *me "So you are following my footsteps? Well, don't follow them too close..."* And we both laughed.

It was May of 1974 and ABT was about to start the rehearsal period for the upcoming New York State Theatre season in July. But I was also involved in a separate series of rehearsals because I had a private, personal goal I had not shared with the company yet, which had been a part of me for several years now and it was about to become a reality.

CHAPTER 8

# *Varna*

Varna! A name that will always warm my heart. The memories of winning the most coveted prize, the Gold Medal at the 1974 International Ballet Competition in Varna, Bulgaria together with the excitement of the unforgettable, chaotic, draining but emotionally rewarding artistic event known as "the Olympics of Dance" will eternally light my soul!

It all started when I first learned there was such a competition. From that moment on I knew I had to go. It was in 1970, I was fifteen and still a student at the School of American Ballet. One day I was glancing through a Dance Magazine issue when I spotted a familiar face; it was Jorge Esquivel in the "Don Quixote" Pas de Deux at the Varna Ballet Competitions! That was the very first time I had seen or read anything about any of the boys with whom I had started my ballet training in Cuba.

Seeing his picture aroused all kinds of feelings in me! "*He must be twenty-four by now...*" I thought to myself... "*Of course he was the one they picked to represent Cuba!*" I kept wondering who else might have gone to Varna from my class. Was my first ballet teacher Joaquin with them? All of a sudden I longed to connect again with those first memories and long lost friends of my first ballet class.

When I went home that day, I brought the magazine with me and showed it to Zeida and my mom and told them I wanted to go to Varna. My competitive spirit received a cold shower! Both of them explained to me at length that to compete at Varna you needed a lot of money and how were we going to pay for the trip? My mom and Zeida both worked, mom as a cashier, Zeida as a part-time typist and photographer's assistant. Zeida also had a half scholarship at the American Ballet Theater School and went to her dance classes every day in the afternoon. Their small income was supplemented by the allowance the School of American Ballet gave my mom as part of my scholarship, which paid the rent for our apartment. Part of the deal with my school was my mom would also agree to have another student living with us, which she did.

Throughout my years at SAB I shared my room with several ballet students; Gerry Ebitz, Dennis Marshall and Michael Owen, all of them coming from different parts of the country. Gladly for me, they filled the void for the brother I never had, and my life with many funny, endearing and unforgettable moments throughout my teenage years in New York. In the meantime the question was still how was I going to get to Varna? SAB paid for my ballet training and my scholastic studies at the Professional Children's School, but finding money to go to Varna was a different story.

Most of the dancers who competed in Varna were from the Eastern socialist countries, as were the judges, and their respective governments paid for their expenses. I was only fifteen then and even if they did have a "junior" category, my mother said if we could ever put together the effort for me to go to Varna, we should wait until I could compete as a "senior." My body would be stronger; I would be more mature, able to dance a more challenging repertory with the right style and interpretation. Of course, I did not like to hear what mom and Zeida had just explained, but I agreed to wait and we decided in four more years, the year I turned 19 would be the right time to go. They thought in the coming years I would be too busy and would eventually forget about the competitions, but for the next four years the thought of being a part of such an event motivated me. I worked hard in every class, every rehearsal and all I could think of, dream of, was to go to Varna. It became my obsession.

In the meantime, Zeida had enrolled in a Motion Pictures Production class at the New York Institute of Photography and was well on her way to becoming a professional filmmaker, although she still was taking all her ballet classes and working with me on a daily basis. She wrote and directed a small film about a day in the life of a ballet student, for the PBS children's series "Vegetable Soup" with Hilda Morales, an ABT soloist, as the ballerina. The entire film was shot at the ABT studios. Films and dance were her two passions and she decided if I ever got to Varna, she would make a film of the competition.

I had four years to prepare, so I researched and learned as much as I could about the competitions. They started for the first time in 1964 and took place every four years. The next ones would take place in 1974. Most of the time, the Russian dancers were the dominant force. The judges were mostly from the communist block countries like Russia, Poland, Czechoslovakia, Hungary, Romania, Bulgaria, Cuba and it was no secret they had their favorite dancers. I was aware politics would be playing a major role. Still such a competition appealed to me. I wanted to compete and I wanted it badly. Deep inside, I loved the idea of representing my country in an international competition. I also hoped to see some of my old classmates.

You could compete with a partner as a couple, or by yourself as a solo dancer. The couples had to perform three different classical pas de deux, with variations and codas and one contemporary piece. The solo dancers had to dance seven different variations. The competition was divided in three stages and you had to pass stage one to continue into the second and so on.

1974 finally arrived and I turned nineteen. It was my second year with ABT, and I had just been promoted to soloist. When I first mentioned my desire to go to Varna representing the United States, company members asked me why should I bother since I was already a soloist in a good company... But I still focused on finding a partner. I asked every possible ABT ballerina and then some, and found out none of them wanted to go. After weeks of frantic search, I realized if I were to go, I would have to go alone!

The 1974 Varna competition was to start on July 8 through July 24. These dates were conflicting with ABT's New York summer season. I needed special permission from the company; and after much worrying, I went directly to Lucia Chase since she would be the final voice. To my surprise, she was all for it and even offered to help me financially! I couldn't believe it! My company was now officially sponsoring me to go to Varna. This was no longer a dream, this was now real!

That night when I told my mother and Zeida of Lucia's conversation, our trip to Varna took its first tiny steps. Then two more sponsors came forward: Sheldon and Helen Atlas (she was Editor of Dance News) and Brent Orcutt and Enid K. Botsford, directors of the Enid K. Bostsford Ballet

School in Rochester, New York, very generously volunteered to help out. They not only contributed financially to my trip, but organized a group called "The Friends of ABT" who traveled to Varna to see me compete and offer much needed support. Mr. and Mrs. Orcutt were also helping Zeida financially with her filming of the competitions. I will be forever indebted to them and to Lucia for believing in me.

We were now about three months away from Varna. For the past four years, Zeida and I had already discussed at length the possibilities of the competition and we had developed a general idea of the type of repertory I should dance. Of course, she would be my coach, and she was as challenged and excited as I was. At that time, very few dancers in the United States had private coaches. This was standard procedure in the eastern countries and Europe, but in the American schools, there was no individual coaching or training.

Zeida believed dance was the purest form for self-expression and the human body had to be fine-tuned and sculpted to such a degree as to become the unique instrument through which beauty and passion could flow. I learned to believe the same. And now we were to have our own Olympics of Dance! We went to work.

My repertory had to consist of seven solos during three different nights. We came up with some we hoped would be technically exciting, with contrasting styles to show versatility and depth. For Stage One, my first solo would be Colas' variation from "La Fille mal Gardee," a youthful, carefree, happy-go-lucky variation. Exactly ten minutes later, I had to perform the second variation of that first night. For that we chose Prince Siegfried's variation from "Swan Lake's Black Swan Pas de Deux ," a total reversal from "Fille." I was to show a mature Prince and aristocratic demeanor.

For the Second Stage we chose James' technically brilliant Scottish variation from "La Sylphide" - Act II, followed by the spectacular bravura variation from "Le Corsaire" Pas de Deux, and I would finish with the fun-filled Rhumba variation from Jerome Robbins' "Fancy Free." The Rhumba variation was to be my required contemporary solo. This second stage with three almost back-to-back solos was to be the hardest of my appearances.

For the third and last stage I saved two of the best and most exciting male solos in the classical repertory; Solor's Variation from "La Bayadere" and Basil's third act variation from "Don Quixote."

Two months prior to leaving for Varna our work intensified. My day started at 10 a.m. with a company class. I would do the barre only and leave. Zeida was already waiting in another room and for the next hour, it was all Varna, five days a week. We would work on two variations per day. We would practice over and over working on the technical aspects of each variation until each and every step was executed the best it could be. We rehearsed for stamina, repeating the variation twice in a row without stopping, then three times in a row until I thought I could no longer breathe and I would die. *" ... use your plie... travel your grand jetés... hold those arabesques! Don't STOP!"* she would call out. I could feel my legs shaking. But Zeida would not let me stop.... *"hang on...finish!"* Somehow she knew how to push me to the edge without injuring me and she certainly motivated me.

After the intense Varna hourly rehearsal with Zeida, I would rush to start a regular day of company rehearsals for the roles I would perform with ABT upon my return from the competition, starting from 11:30 in the morning until 5:00 or 6:00 in the afternoon. By the end of the day I was totally exhausted but once back home I would get so excited explaining to mom all the combinations and details that Zeida and I had worked on, I would forget how tired I was... It seemed like I never had enough of practicing and on many occasions my mom would yell, "Fernando your dinner is getting cold!"

Now we needed to start thinking about my costumes and the music. ABT graciously gave me permission to take the costumes I normally used when dancing those roles, so I had beautiful jackets for all my variations. The music was a different story. Most of the European dancers arrived with their own pianists or musicians. Zeida approached a pianist friend of ours, who agreed to play the music for all my variations. I got the scores from ABT and one afternoon, Juan Pirez came to our apartment. We had our faithful Sony tape recorder, one of the older 2-reel models, a huge, bulky square black box that weighed 15 pounds with equally huge speakers hanging from either side with which I used to rehearse, but the sound quality was excellent. Juan sat at my mom's piano and there, he played the music for all my variations as we recorded them. Only the music for "La Sylphide" was taped from an original record.

Then, to my horror, Zeida starts asking Juan to slow down the tempos of the variations. I screamed in protest. This would make it so much more difficult for me, to dance to the slower tempos. She refused, and after ten minutes of heated arguments, she got what she wanted. I could already feel my legs burning from trying to keep up with those tempos. We finally got all the music on tape and made three sets of copies to take with us. Thank God for those extra sets!

By mid June, two weeks prior to our trip to Varna, Zeida invited Lucia Chase, all the ABT dancers, company Regisseurs and Ballet Masters to watch one of our rehearsals. She did not tell me. The large rehearsal studio at ABT was packed. As I entered the studio, then she told me. I must say very few times in my life I have felt as nervous as I did then. Zeida knew this and her reason for arranging such a rehearsal was to start preparing my nerves for what I was about to face. That particular rehearsal felt different from any other rehearsal I had ever done in front of my colleagues.

My nerves let me down, the rehearsal was a mess and the overall picture, after weeks of good private rehearsals, was a disheartening day for me. Nothing seemed to work! I was not able to be in full control of my nerves and it showed. After the rehearsal a lack of confidence in myself and in my dancing began to creep into my mind. I realized in order for me to be at my best in Varna, I would need to be in control of my nerves... and we started to work on that as well.

On the first week of July, 1974, and one day prior to my departure to Varna, ABT opened its summer season at the New York State Theater with its new production of the "Sleeping Beauty." I was scheduled to dance the "Bluebird Pas de Deux" with ballerina Natalia Makarova. It was the very first time I would be dancing with her.

*Zeida Remembers:*

*"This new production of "Beauty" staged by Royal Ballet's David Blair was getting the royal treatment from ABT. New sets and costumes for everyone. Fernando immediately wanted to see his costume, and went to the design department to check it out. The body dress was fine, but the*

*head piece seemed strange to him. We had been working long and hard on details to make his head, arms, and torso movements like those of a real bird. We had been studying videos of birds in flight, birds resting and especially the bluebirds. Even during the partnering, if he was holding Natasha with one hand, his other arm would still be moving with a very subtle flutter… if he was in a static pose, his head would move with the tiny, nervous bird-like movement and he really enjoyed doing such a characterizations.*

*"Now, the new head piece was a sort of crown, which had nothing to do with a bird. When Fernando mentioned it to me, we decided to have our own seamstress (my aunt) make a small head piece that fit very tight around his head with real blue feathers. It turned out just right.*

*"The night of the performance, he stayed in his dressing room until it was time to go on stage. Then someone noticed that he was not wearing the costume headpiece and all hell broke loose! ABT staff was summoned backstage in a rush, to make Fernando change the head piece. He refused. The production designer came backstage to complain that no one could change his costumes. Fernando did not budge. Out in the audience, we were all treated to a slight unusual delay when the curtain would not open, the kind of delay that makes you wonder if there is something different happening backstage. All of a sudden, the music started, the curtain opened, and the performance began. The second Fernando came out on stage as the Bluebird, I noticed a strange tension on his face and thought to myself, there is something wrong… but almost immediately, it disappeared. His dancing was pure joy and my nerves gradually relaxed. Only after the performance, when we joined him in his dressing room, he told us of the incident about the head piece with the feathers. I was livid. But he overcame that moment and focused on his dancing."*

It was a happy night for me because the performance went really well and the audience gave Natasha and me a roaring ovation. But the next day the review from the New York Times praised her performance and blasted me, criticizing the choreographic version I performed assuming it was I who had selected the steps, and compared my version to some older Russian one, describing the double diagonal of beats in my coda as "vulgar." I was disappointed by Clive's comments, but realized you can never please everyone. Still, Clive did not criticize my dancing, but the variation. So I wrote him a little note explaining it was David Blair from England's own Royal Ballet who was responsible for the choreography I was asked to perform. The next morning I was on the plane for Varna!

Just before leaving for the airport, I received a reassuring phone call from my friend Trish and another one from Makarova herself. Both of them understood how I must have been feeling, so they encouraged me and wished me good luck. I never got to dance the Bluebird again. From then on, I would dance the role of the Prince!

On the evening of July 5, 1974, my mother, Zeida and I flew into London's Heathrow airport on our way to Varna, Bulgaria. Throughout the flight I was in a very pensive mood, but I managed to keep my spirits up and remained focused on the challenges that lay ahead.

After arriving in London we changed to a second plane, destination Sofia, Bulgaria. On that flight an older gentleman sitting in front of me turned to me and said: *"You look very familiar to me ...what is your name?" "Fernando Bujones," I answered. "Oh you're Bujones! ... I am Anton Dolin."* When he said his name my heart jumped! Here was one of ballet's great Premier Danseurs, whose legendary partnership with Dame Alicia Markova earned him a place in dance history! Anton Dolin was also on his way to Varna and he was to be one of the judges representing England! Excited, I replied *"It is an honor to meet you"* ... Dolin continued *"So you are the young man that Clive Barnes has been ringing my ears about! He told me to look out for you, so you better be as good as he said."* I smiled to myself.

Dolin himself described our first meeting, writing in his Varna diary in the September, 1974, issue of **Dance and Dancers**:

> ***"We are all seated when within a few moments, three other lost passengers got to their seats behind us. The young man was Fernando Bujones, as I soon found out by his mother and a most charming girl and her movie camera. He is to compete in the competition. I had heard much about his great talent from Clive Barnes and knew he had been dancing with American Ballet Theatre in my "Variations for Four"...***

We arrived in Sofia, the capital of Bulgaria early on the afternoon of July 6, but we still had to take a third plane to get to Varna. It was a very hot and humid day and the exhaustion of a long trip was showing in our faces. The three of us got into our third and smallest plane followed by Sir Anton Dolin and his companions. Just as we got into our seats, another group of people started boarding the plane. The faces looked familiar... Suddenly Zeida says in almost a whisper... *"Oh my God, they are speaking in Spanish... these are the Cubans...! This is the entire Cuban team!... and we are all on the same plane!"* All of a sudden, things were getting exciting and tense very fast.

Chaos! The hotel to which we had been assigned in Varna was understaffed. More than fifty dancers with family members, teachers, coaches, pianists and friends from all over the world, speaking different languages were pushing their way to the reception desk. There was a lot of shouting in the small lobby and all of them were trying to understand or at least trying to make themselves understood. Some had already been there for at least an hour and were still waiting for rooms. In the meantime mom and Zeida were told family members, teachers and coaches could not stay in the same hotel with the dancers. They were checked into a separate hotel.

About an hour after both had finally checked into their room, they received a frantic call from me! *"They have put me in the same room with four other Cuban dancers! They are calling me a traitor because I'm representing the United States and they are telling everyone that I am a Cuban also! Can you come and get me out of here?"* I did not need the extra tension at this point. The competition itself was going to be hard enough. My mother and Zeida rushed back in a Bulgarian taxi. After a shouting match with the reservation people, they finally made the staff understand I was in fact an American competitor and changed me to a different room. For four days, I had the room all for myself. On the fifth day a young Belgian dancer opened the door of my room and introduced himself as my new roommate.

The competition had two categories: Juniors -- from 15 to 20 years old -- and Seniors -- from 20 to 28 years old. Even though I was legally still a Junior, I had registered to compete in the Senior category. All dancers had to submit their entry photographs with their registration, and these photographs were then blown up to poster size and displayed all over the small town of Varna. Once we arrived in Varna, Zeida and my mom noticed the posters all around town, and they immediately searched for mine. They could not find one. Zeida went to the Competition's Office to complain, only to be told an equal number of my posters had been put up, but dance fans were taking them for themselves as soon as they were put up. More posters had to be printed, only to disappear again. Zeida was unable to find and save even one poster to take back to America! These posters were made of photos Zeida had taken of me back at the ABT studios, so in the end, it did not matter.

Throughout the hotel, on all the floors and in the lobby, schedules were posted with the different class times, the names of the teachers, rehearsal times for the different teams of dancers, the performance days and starting times. I was assigned a number and became Candidate #78 from the United States of America.

There were 115 contestants from 24 different countries competing that year. Their official number was determined by alphabetical order of the countries they represented. When I heard I was #78, my stomach cramped. "Oh no! I get to go towards the end..." Candidate #78 meant I would not be competing until the third day of Stage One. I was already anxious and the feeling of sitting and waiting around until the third day didn't do any favors to my nerves, but Zeida convinced me it didn't hurt to have two days where we could have a good look at the dancers I would be competing against.

Up until this year, no other American dancer had shown any interest in coming to the Varna competitions... but now not only myself, but two more American couples were here. Right after breakfast we headed for the rehearsal hall where our small American contingent had been assigned. We all introduced ourselves and felt much better to know there were several of us here. Mom and Zeida rented a tiny Russian car, and now we had our own transportation.

Mom went to the Competition's Office to turn in the required set of my taped music. Zeida and I went right to work. The Bulgarians had assigned a tape recorder for my rehearsals and we used the second copy of the music tape for those. I ran through the two variations of my first program.

After the rehearsal mom, Zeida and I decided to check out the open theater where the competition would take place -- and our hearts flipped!

What a magnificent sight! A big outdoor amphitheater, with beautiful trees all around, with huge, beautiful stone arches covered with ivy surrounding the stage. From where the audience sat one could clearly see to the right of the stage the staircase that led to the "Olympic" torch, still waiting to be lit.

Mom and I sat down to watch a rehearsal that was going on while Zeida set up her camera and began to film the beautiful surroundings. On stage, a lovely young ballerina by the name of Eva Evdokimova was rehearsing the second act pas de deux from "Giselle." Evdokimova had already won a gold medal at the 1970 Varna competition and she was now competing for the Grand Prix. This was a special prize that had been presented in 1968 for the first time to the Russian ballet dancer Vladimir Vassiliev.

While sitting there admiring Evdokimova, a lady from the competition's committee approached me: *"Excuse me Mr. Bujones, we have noticed that in your application you ask to compete in the senior category with dancers that are 20 to 28 years of age, but you are only 19 years old. You do not need to compete against them and you can compete in the junior category, ages fifteen to nineteen years old. Are you sure you want to compete in the senior level?"* I never had a second thought. *"I have decided to remain in the senior category."* She looked at me with a smile and replied: *"Very well, good luck."*

Finally, the first day of the competition arrived but now the weather was not cooperating. For the last two days it had been raining quite a bit, jeopardizing the performances in the outdoor theater, but the opening ceremony went on as scheduled. The flags were raised, the orchestra played, and with flowers and the torch bearer lighting the competition's torch the VII Varna International Dance Festival officially opened. The jury members were introduced, among them the president of the competition, Yuri Grigorovich, Artistic Director of the Bolshoi Ballet, Alicia Alonso from Cuba, Anton Dolin from England, Walter Terry from the USA, as well as many other illustrious names from the Dance world.

Then an announcer explained due to the weather, the performances would be postponed until tomorrow. The next day, July 9, the weather continued to be nasty. Only at lunch time did the rain stop. The outdoor stage is like a swamp; certainly not dry enough to dance on and as Anton Dolin pointed out in his Varna Diary: ***"They (the Bulgarians) could***

***learn something from Wimbledon by getting out the waterproof covers."*** After an emergency meeting the organizers decided to move the competitions inside into the huge Sports Hall and remain there for the entire First Stage to avoid any unfairness to those performing on the first night. The decision was a great relief to me!

When Zeida and I saw the open-air amphitheater, we immediately noticed the stage was raked, with a noticeable forward slant! Back in America, we never thought about rehearsing in such a way. A raked floor throws off a dancer's sense of balance if one is not used to working in it. Many of the older theaters in Europe as well as the dance studios all have raked floors, so most European dancers train that way. In the U.S. the dance schools and theaters have normal, flat floors and I was not used to the incline. I was overjoyed to hear the stage at the Sports Hall was as flat as they come. It was important for me to feel as comfortable as possible for my first appearance. Then if all went well, I would deal with the next stage and the raked floor.

Stage One began July 9, 1974. It started at around 8:30 p.m. and it lasted over four hours! We saw dozens of dancers! Most of them insisted on performing the "Don Quixote" and "Le Corsaire" pas de deux and variations. This made Zeida and me feel good, for we realized that my choice of variations from "Fille Mal Gardee" and "Swan Lake" were right on target. Those two variations were rarely being performed, so I would be giving the judges some fresh material to start with. The real highlight of that first day came when the very last pair performed well past midnight! They were a Japanese couple; she by the name of Yoko Morishita and her partner Tetsutaro Shimizu. The moment they stepped on stage, everyone knew they were seeing something special. We were all instantly captivated by their presence. I fell in love with her technical strength, musicality and sense of style.

Two days later, July 11, was my turn. Before I danced, Lazaro Carreño a Cuban dancer, whose name I knew well but had never met, performed a strong "Don Quixote" Pas de Deux with his partner. Lazaro was one of the many Cuban dancers competing that year and he was a favorite to win a medal. I remembered hearing about how he was one of the better older students at the Cubanacan ballet school while I had been there.

Inside the small room that leads out to the stage, I was one more dancer in a group of others that were warming up, but I was already as warm as I could be. I was bouncing around, hyper and ready to go. I could feel the blood in my veins, part excitement, part "I'll show you!" Then I heard a voice through the microphone call out "Fernando Bujones, candidate number #78, United States of America, in the variation from La Fille Mal Gardee" and I started to run towards the stage... I was possessed and something bigger than me was in control...

I stepped out at the left back corner of the huge stage with the first musical chords of my variation and ran across the entire stage to start from the right! That run caused audience applause and got me hyped up!

My variation started with a double tour en l'air to fifth position into an arabesque en-releve. I feel weightless and I'm airborne and all my steps are coming out perfectly without me having to think. Towards the middle of the solo come the bigger jumps and a diagonal of revoltades, a sort of spectacular leap which so far has not been performed by any other dancer. The audience begins to shout "bravo." I get the feeling that my body is in total command of the steps as they unravel and I don't need to worry.

The Sports Hall, filled to capacity with spectators, is now cheering every single step I do and clapping to the beat of my variation. I can barely hear the music. Their enthusiasm is exhilarating and I'm flying. The final step of my variation is a double tour to the knee. I nailed it. I hold that final pose for a few seconds to tell myself that indeed I'd done it! Then the roar of the audience made me jump up like a spring. Four years of dreaming about this moment, so much planning, so much work, so much sacrifice, but after the two and a half minutes of that first solo, the smile on my face could not contain the range of emotions that were just pouring out of me. I continued taking bows, and for as long as the audience kept applauding and cheering.

*"My God, in ten minutes I have to do my second variation... hurry up and get ready..."*

With just ten minutes to change I ran backstage to the dressing rooms taking my costume off as I ran. There, waiting for me is my mother with a Bulgarian dresser holding my Prince Siegfried's costume, a beautiful jacket that had belonged to the great Premier Danseur, Igor Youskevitch and was given to me as a good luck gift by Tom Adair, the director of the Poughkeepsie Ballet company from New York State after my guest appearance with them in Swan Lake two months before. I changed into the white tights for Swan Lake and the Bulgarian dresser slips the jacket on me. In the rush to get me ready, he pulls the zipper much too hard and now the zipper is in his hand! My mother is beyond herself. The dresser doesn't speak a word of English and my mom did not know Bulgarian, but she made herself very clear somehow. The next minute two more dressers are sewing shut the back of my jacket. They are still sewing, when we all hear through the loudspeakers...

"Candidate # 78, Fernando Bujones...United States of America" ...

*"Oh, my God, run! Wait for me, don't start the music!"*

The unmistakable first few chords of the Black Swan variation fill the air, and I'm not on stage yet.

*"What if this jacket tears open in the middle of a jump? Forget it and go. I'm late!"*

In the audience, Zeida has been filming the competition. Around her are the ABT friends with Brent and Enid Orcutt, who paid their way to Varna to see me compete. Also in the audience are the other four American dancers who were not appearing tonight. Zeida has her eyes glued to the viewfinder making sure she will not miss my entrance. But the music has started and I am nowhere in sight... Somebody whispers "Where is he?" and she takes her eyes off the viewfinder and looks into a huge empty stage. All of a sudden, like a bolt, in a huge glissade jump I made my entrance, making as if the variation had started from behind the wings... and desperately tried to catch up with the music.

A lack of initial focus blurs my mind momentarily, but instantly I catch myself and some incredible things begin to happen. My nerves started calming down and I begin to deliver what other dancers would later describe as "technical wonders," multiple slow pirouettes ending in total balance, holding it for a few seconds. A sequence of entrechats and double tours into arabesques both left and right that landed perfectly, astounding everyone, most of all myself... I was dancing effortlessly in slow motion as if in a dream. I was to experience that feeling again several times during my career, but I will never forget that first time in Varna.

Someone else seemed to have been equally impressed. A man had been standing in the lower corner of the stage watching me perform. Joaquin Banegas, Zeida's and my very first ballet teacher from Cuba. We knew he was there, but the Cuban team was closely guarded by their own security personnel in case anyone wanted to defect, and no Cuban was allowed to talk to us, the exiled Cubans, now Americans. He was one of the coaches for the Cuban team! I had caught a glimpse of him during my first variation, and he was still there for the second one. I wondered what must have been going through his mind. Twelve years had gone by and I am sure Joaquin would have loved to get together with Zeida, my mom and myself, and speak to us freely, for we had been very close in Cuba. But freedom of speech or any other kind of freedom was not something the Cubans were allowed. Joaquin, like all the other Cubans, was being constantly watched by the Cuban secret police.

For mom, Zeida and me there was a lot to rejoice because it had been a solid first round. **Anton Dolin** described it in his Varna Diary, in the September, 1974 issue of **Dance & Dancers'** Magazine:

> ***"The real sensation was Fernando Bujones. Born in the USA of Cuban parents. First variation from "La Fille mal Gardee." Second variation from "Swan Lake." There is only one word -- perfect. Bujones is everything Barnes told me he is. Extraordinary presence, intelligent and a simplicity of showmanship. One must hope and pray he will not be spoiled, for there is no doubt he is the public's favorite."***

**Janet Sinclair** and **Leo Kersley**, dance reviewers that were covering the Competitions, wrote:

> ***"... And there was (the audience's darling from his first step) Fernando Bujones from American Ballet Theatre, young enough to be a Junior but entered by his own choice in the Senior Section; he had everyone eating out of his hand by the time the First Stage was over."***

**Anton Dolin**, in his Varna Diaries, continues to report:

> ***"July 13, 1974... Big luncheon hosted by Ann Barzel and 36 members of the friends of American Ballet Theatre. (Alicia Alonso at one head of the table, me at the other.) So many old and new friends. I was asked to propose a toast for the health of Lucia Chase and introduce Alonso... A most happy***

***get-together of energetic ladies and gentlemen, who are our ballet public and who truly carry the force of Terpsichore. Not to spoil him, but I must admit a main topic of conversation is this phenomenal youngster, Bujones."***

There was a day off after the end of the First Round. Now that the "qualifying round" had been completed, and I had done well, mom, Zeida and I were much relieved. Other dancers were not as fortunate. Some were crying, others along with their teachers or coaches could not hide their feelings of frustration and discontent when they saw their names were not on the list of second round dancers that had already been posted in the lobby of the hotel. My heart went out to so many of them who had traveled from such far away countries to get to Varna.

> ***"With such a large number of dancers competing, it was no wonder that so many fell by the wayside ... over 40 per cent eliminated after Stage One..."*** wrote **Janet Sinclair** and **Leo Kersley** in their 1974 Varna Competition dance article.

In the meantime the weather had improved and the competition was moved back to the beautiful open air amphitheater. All stage rehearsals had to be scheduled at night, since during the day the heat was extreme.

I was shocked to learn my stage rehearsal had been scheduled for 3 a.m.! That day mom, Zeida and I slept during the day so we could stay awake later. I received a wake-up call at 1 a.m. in order to get ready for my 3 a.m. scheduled rehearsal. And there I was in the middle of the night putting on my Scottish kilt for the second act variation from "La Sylphide." The next day I had an 11 a.m. rehearsal for the variation from "Le Corsaire" and for Jerome Robbins' "Fancy Free." I'd hardly slept the night before, and with this new rehearsal during mid-morning, I was really feeling wiped out.

My mother spent most of her Bulgarian hours in Varna looking for food for me. This was not an easy feat. To find a cold Coke was a miracle. She had to bribe the cooks in the better restaurants to get a glass of milk for me. Bulgarian food was not the best for my stomach and every day she would visit every available grocery store and stand patiently in line in order to get something for me to eat in between the strictly regulated breakfast, lunch and dinner hours of my hotel. Fortunately, Bulgarian yogurt is delicious and highly nutritious, and I devoured tons of it.

July 14 was the first day of the Second Stage. Once again the most exciting dancers of the evening were the Japanese dancers, Yoko Morishita and Tetsutaro Shimizu in a lovely version of the "Le Corsaire" Pas de Deux. During the next two days some outstanding male dancers began to emerge and now this competition was becoming a real battle. Among the standouts was Mikhail Tsivin, a strong Russian dancer with an impressive variation from Spartacus.

Then there is a brilliant Hungarian dancer, Gabor Kevehazi, shining in the variation from "Flames of Paris." Ramazzan Bapov from the Soviet Union with one of the softest demi plie landings I had ever seen in a male dancer and another excellent Rumanian dancer, Marin Boieru. The competition suddenly is being dominated by the power and virtuosity of the male dancers and all these men are much older than I. I start to feel the pressure. I wondered out loud if I should have stayed in the junior category... No matter now, it is too late.

One hour before the start of the performances, an older Bulgarian who worked backstage comes to the dressing rooms looking for me. I am doing my warm-up bar and he tells me that the music tape for my second round is nowhere to be found. I scream something unprintable at him and run out looking for mom or Zeida. They can't believe it, but both run out to our little car, and in the trunk, where we kept all our important papers and possessions under lock and key, was our last backup tape. They ran back and gave it to the sound people. The tape had three different cues, clearly marked, where each of my variations started and stopped. The Bulgarian sound guy was unhappy with the markings and said he would not be responsible. Mom stood next to him the entire time and made sure he would start and stop when he had to. Zeida was again up front, filming the competition.

For this second round, Zeida and I had selected three solos, very different in content and style. The first variation was the brilliant solo from "La Sylphide," choreographed by August Bournonville, very seldom seen in the countries from the eastern block, with lots of quick footwork and leg beats, both strong points of mine, and I was wearing a kilt, which again was not typical.

My second solo was the athletically demanding variation from "Le Corsair," to show I could compete head-to-head with any of the Russians at their own game. And last but not least, was the "Rhumba" from Fancy Free, a sailor on shore leave dancing up a storm. This last piece was my non-classical repertory. My three solos couldn't have been more different in choreography, style and interpretation. We knew if I danced them well, I would get extra points for the diversity. I passed into the third round.

By now, less than forty dancers remained from the original one hundred and fifteen and a real nail biting finale was in the works. Zeida and I continued rehearsing more intensely than ever. Back in the rehearsal studio we continued working out, improving artistic details and technically beefing up my two remaining variations from "La Bayadere" and "Don Quixote."

We agreed we needed to strengthen my last round and decided to add the *coda* to the "Don Quixote" variation. After the end of the variation, I would not leave, but stand in my place as if watching my (absent) ballerina in her variation while her music played! Then I would begin the coda. This would give me the opportunity to breathe and perform combinations and steps which I had not shown before.

Before the last round began, the young Bulgarian woman translator assigned to us mentioned to mom, Zeida and me that strong rumors were spreading around the city that I was the favorite candidate for a Gold medal and she asked if she could watch me rehearse. By this time, rehearsals are being done in total privacy, in secret, so that competing dancers can't get wind of another one's variation! We told our interpreter we were sorry, but my rehearsals were private. We sensed she was more than just a translator. She was spying for the Bulgarians. We had noticed how every time we were together for breakfast, lunch or dinner or sightseeing, she would excuse herself for five minutes to make a phone call. The girl wore dark sunglasses and a trench coat. She even *looked* like a Hollywood spy! We started calling her Mata, as in Mata Hari.

Suddenly, my rehearsal room became unavailable to me, and I had no place to rehearse. We will never know how or why that happened, but I could not get a place to rehearse! Now, two days before my Round Three performance, I had no studio to practice in. Fortunately the Japanese dancers learned about this situation, and invited me to rehearse in their assigned room! That is how I got to meet Yoko Morishita and Tetsu Shimitzu and his parents, Mr. & Mrs. Shimitzu. They owned a ballet studio in Tokyo and were very respected in the dance community in Japan. A beautiful friendship was born, one that saw me dancing in Japan with Yoko a year later and I reciprocated by bringing Yoko to ABT to perform with me many more times again.

The Third Round was now in full swing and once again my performance day arrived. I remember warming up in the backstage room at the amphitheater already wearing my dark red Spanish matador costume from "Don Quixote." As I looked left I saw another dancer dressed in a similar "Don Quixote" matador costume starting to warm up next to me. A few minutes later a third dancer in yet one more Spanish matador jacket joins us. We all looked at each other and laughed. Then I said *"I guess this is what a competition is all about."*

During the afternoon, right before the 7 p.m. performance time, there had been some heavy rain downpours and thunderstorms and the stage was still wet and slippery. To speed up the drying process the Bulgarians poured gasoline on the stage and then proceeded to set it on fire. Zeida, who had been filming outside, rushed on stage and tried to stop this, explaining gasoline would make the stage even more slippery, but the stage workers told her every competition they did the same thing. She could do nothing but watch incredulously as the stage burned. The result of this bizarre experiment helped to dry parts of the stage, but it also left some very slippery spots all around. Seven dancers slipped and fell that night, Mijail Tsivin and myself included. Fortunately the jury did not take any points away from a condition we all had to endure.

My first variation in the Third round was the solo from "La Bayadere," and I did not miss. I felt and danced in top form. So did Mijail Tsivin, dancing the same solo! Only our styles were different, but technically we both danced very strong variations worthy of Solor. Then came my second and final variation in the competition... "Don Quixote Variation and Coda."

I finished my variation to thunderous applause, but surprise!... the music did not stop! It continued playing the ballerina's variation while I stood in place and caught my breath. When the music for my coda started, I was on fire! I finished my Varna competitions with a full heart.

Once more, **Anton Dolin** wrote in his Varna Diaries:

> ***July 22, 1974 - "The long awaited Bujones lit up the stage with a superb solo from Don Quixote, and greater still on artistry; the girl's solo was played while he prepared to dance the coda. For the first time the dancer stood still, yet in his vision he was watching the absent solo. This was real art, and now for me (and many others, I know), this boy of 19 years old, had more, much more than the phenomenal technique he had shown us in his previous solos. This was dancing with no tricks. John Gilpin had it, Rudolf Nureyev has it, and tonight Fernando Bujones showed us all, jury and spectators, he has it. This boy is an artist. Not since Anna Pavlova in The Fairy Doll, when the curtain revealed her presence and all she did for those magical moments was to stand still, the curtain closed to an applause as though she had danced the most perfect solo - not since, have I witnessed such presence, such true magic from a male dancer."***

It was over! It had been a trial for the body and nerves. That night, we all stayed up very late with our ABT friends and supporters and fellow dancers. When I finally went to sleep, I was totally exhausted. I slept until very late next day. Then sometime in the early afternoon my mother woke me up and said: *"Congratulations! You won the bronze medal."* Still half asleep, I looked up but her words were already sinking in. I was disappointed to say the least. *"Bronze medal?"* Zeida, who was also just starting to wake up, heard the same thing, and was so stunned she did not dare say a word. The pained expression on our faces was too much for my mother, who then embraced me proudly and declared, *"No! It's the Gold Medal! You won the gold!"* Oh my God! Yes! I felt delirious. I wanted to scream, but I had no energy. I looked at mom and just kept smiling as I tried to wake up fully. Zeida was feeling just as proud. This moment of victory was the realization of a long-held dream, an achievement only the two of us knew how it really felt... one we will savor for the rest of our lives. Then we all said at once... *"Let's go!"* We all started hugging each other and jumping up and down, got dressed in seconds and ran down to the hotel lobby where notices of the winners were posted everywhere. And there it was, the confirmation! It was true. I had won the Gold Medal.

It was 1974 and politics still played a big part in everything. A second Gold Medal was awarded to Mikail Tsivin, the 28 year old Russian dancer. But the judges decided to also award me with a Special Certificate for the Highest Technical Achievement as a clear indication my Gold Medal was indeed the top honor of the competition. I became the first American dancer to win a medal at an international competition.

The official ceremony and medal presentations came finally the night of July 24. The stage was beautifully lit and glowing with flowers and torches. A small orchestra played the competition theme and we were all thrilled to be there to receive our prizes. All the judges were on stage, as well as all the dancers who were to receive their medals. One by one our names were called. First, the junior categories, female and male Bronze, Silver and Gold medals were awarded. Then, the senior categories; again female and male. Yoko Morishita won the Gold Medal in her category and she went up to receive her medal dressed elegantly in her traditional Japanese kimono. My name was the very last one called. For one last time I heard "Candidate #78 Fernando Bujones, United States of America"... And I walked towards the podium where the president of the competition, Yuri Grigorovich, director of the Russia's Bolshoi Ballet shook my hand and congratulated me. He pinned the Gold Medal on my lapel and handed me the Certificate. I returned to my seat with a huge smile on my face. Zeida was filming the entire ceremony.

The first person to hear about my Gold Medal was ABT's Artistic Director, Lucia Chase. I sent her a telegram with the one word that said it all – "GOLD!"

I made many great friends in Varna. Teachers, choreographers and judges got to know of me, as well as many other international dancers. We all received invitations to perform in many different countries. It was a memorable experience.

In 1983 a book titled *"Varna Ballet Olympiad, the story of a great ballet contest"* was written by **John Gregory** and published in Great Britain by **Newsome and Associates**. He writes:

> ***"In the general contest one personality stood out - that of the Florida born Cuban, Fernando Bujones (US passport) and soloist with the American Ballet Theatre. He came well prepared, with his mother, his attractive cousin and was highly organized. No competitor has been more assured than Bujones; it was as though he had written all over him in large letters; 'I AM THE CHAMPION!' And champion he was."***

My success, however, was also a result of Zeida's extraordinary coaching. No one could have prepared me better and my triumph was as much hers as mine! It is true I had been well prepared for the competition. Whether I felt I was a champion before I won is another story. The knowledge I gained by watching dancers from all over the world working with their teachers and coaches, and the opportunity that the competition offered in exposing my dancing to an international panel of judges, artistic directors, teachers and audiences from around the globe made it all a priceless experience in my life.

Preparing to return home I held the Gold medal one last time in my hand before packing it and I felt a chill down my spine. On the plane back to America I had time to think, to look back and to realize this medal meant more than just winning the competition's highest prize. I was looking forward to returning to ABT, feeling real good ... one could say "as good as Gold." I had tremendous expectations. I was in top form and I wanted to share my experiences with everyone. But most of all, I wanted to dance.

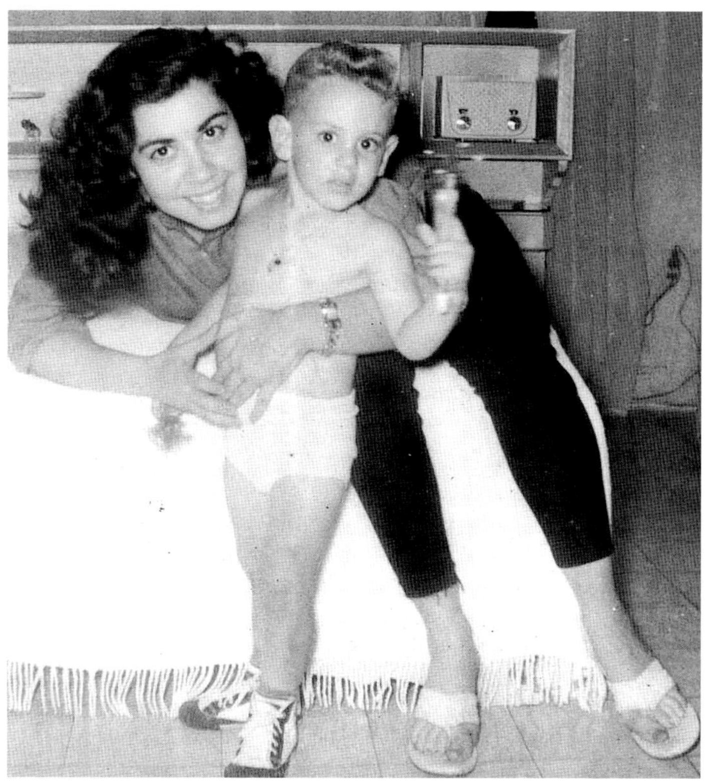

Mom and I, 2 years old, taking my first ballet steps at home.

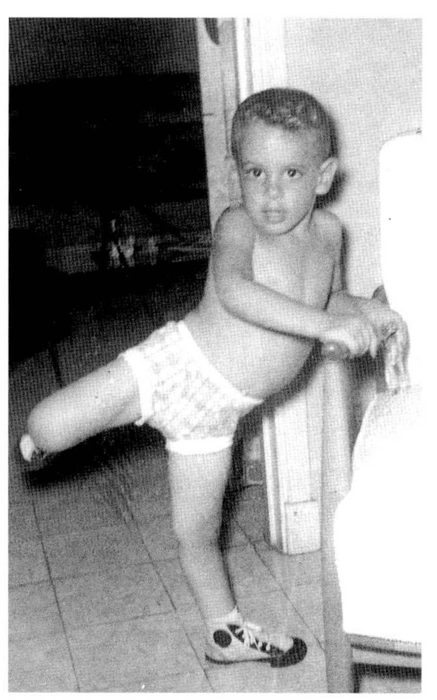

9 years old at the beach in Havana, Cuba, practicing with Zeida.

Just arrived in Paris, France, from Cuba. Mom behind me, Uncle Rudy and Aunt Laura, Zeida and my cousin Laureen at the Moulin Rouge nightclub.

Ballet Concerto

My second performance with Ballet Concerto in Miami, as Peter in "Peter & the Wolf"

Ballet Concerto

My first "pas de trois."

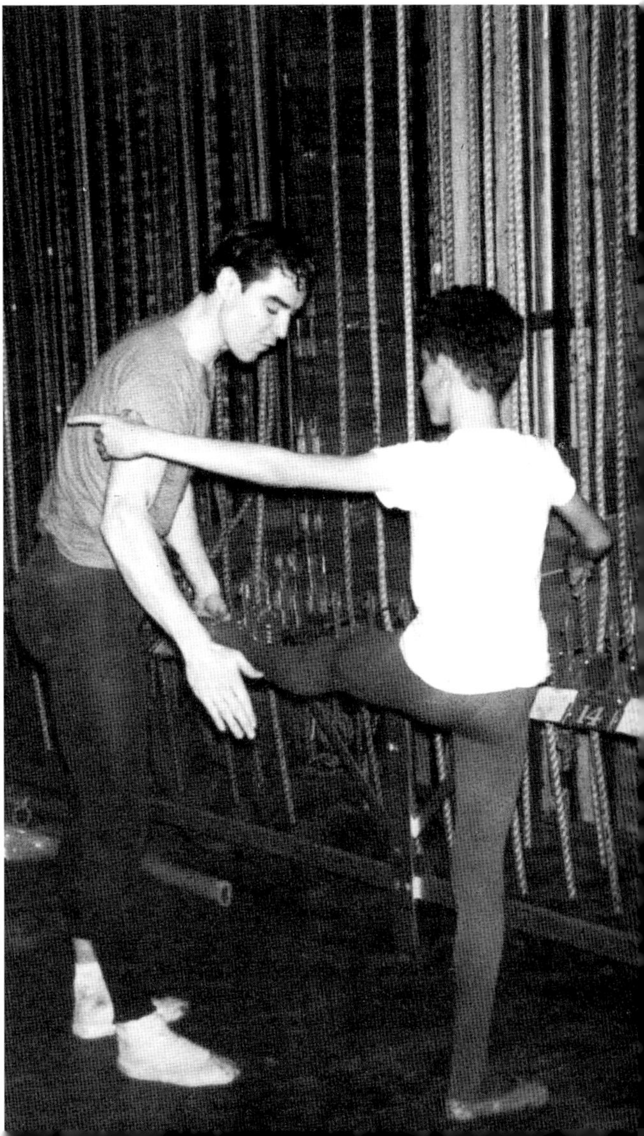

Z.Cecilia-Méndez

Backstage at the Dade County Auditorium in Miami, auditioning for Jacques D'Amboise for a possible scholarship at School of American Ballet in New York City.

Z.Cecilia-Méndez

In New York City, taking class with Toni Lander and Bruce Marks.

Relaxing at Riverside Park.

By the fountain at Lincoln Center on my way to ballet class.

Martha Swope

End-of-year SAB workshop with Lisa De Ribere, in "Konservatoriet."

Z.Cecilia-Méndez

At fifteen, rehearsing with sixteen year old Gelsey Kirkland in our first "Don Quixote" Pas de Deux together.

At our New York City apartment, Mom, Zeida and me.

Mom and I, enjoying the snow in Riverside Park.

Graduation Day at Professional Children School. I'm the fourth from the right.

Z.Cecilia-Méndez

Third year-end workshop at SAB, as James, in "La Sylphide," with Nina Brzorad.

Dina Makarova

With Trish Barnes in Ottawa, Canada, to see the Cuban National Ballet on tour.

Z.Cecilia-Méndez

Rehearsing the "Flower Festival" pas de deux with Nina.

In class at the School of American Ballet.

Judy Cameron

First season with ABT as corps de ballet member, 17 years old, suddenly cast in my first solo role, Anton Dolin's "Variations for Four."

Martha Swope

Rhumba sailor in "Fancy Free."

Z.Cecilia-Méndez

As the Bluebird in "Sleeping Beauty."

Z.Cecilia-Méndez

Sharing moments backstage with Dame Margot Fonteyn.

Z.Cecilia-Méndez

Dina Makarova

In London for my first appearance there.

Daily Express

Congratulated by Princess Margaret after the "Don Q" Gala.

Louis Peres

First tour with ABT, 18 years old, and my second solo role, in the "Don Quixote" Pas de Deux with Eleanor D'Antuono at The Met.

Martha Swope

Again with Eleanor in the "Flower Festival" Pas de Deux.

Linda Vartoogian

Second year with ABT, Promoted to Soloist, 18 years old, as The Green Skater in "Les Patineurs."

Martha Swope

The Jungle Boy in "Shadowplay."

Martha Swope

The Lover in "Jardin Aux Lilas" with Cynthia Gregory.

Rehearsing a new work with Anthony Tudor.

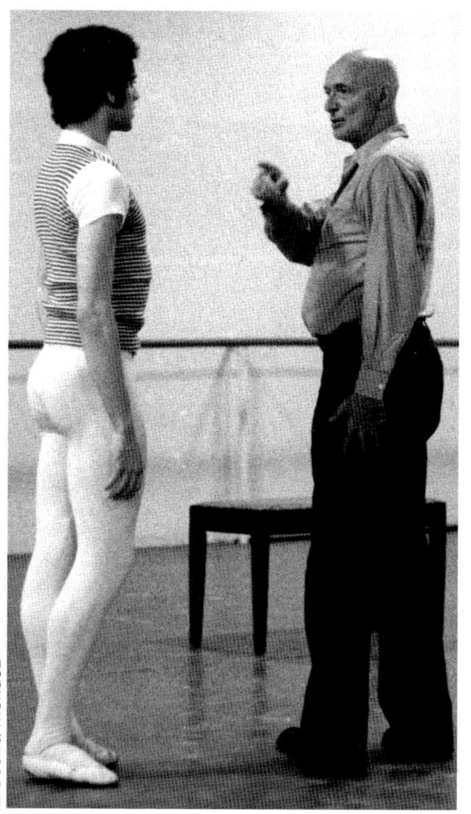

Z.Cecilia-Méndez

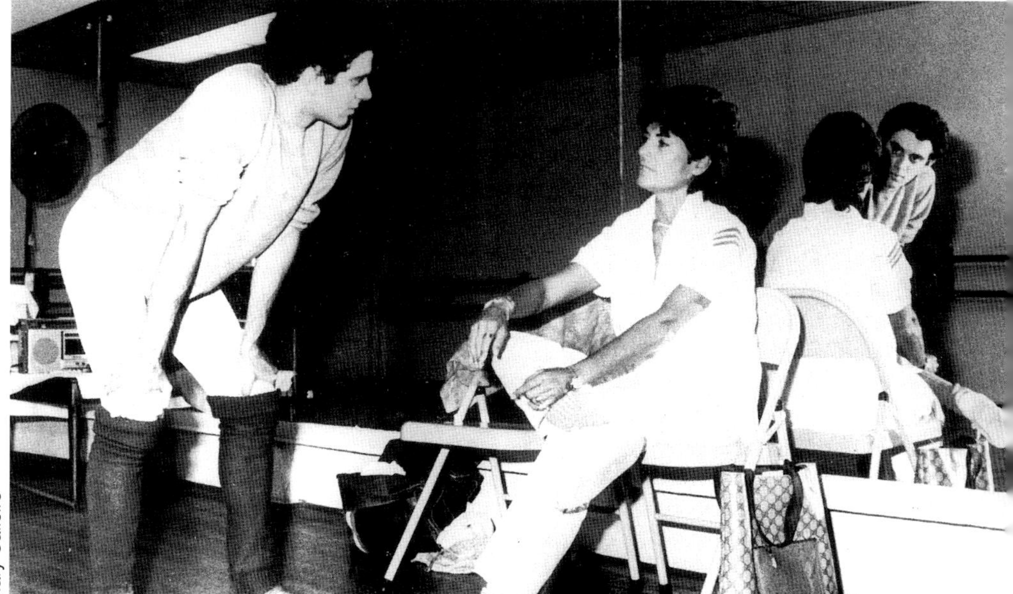

Mary Calleiro

The never ending one-on-one coaching with Zeida.

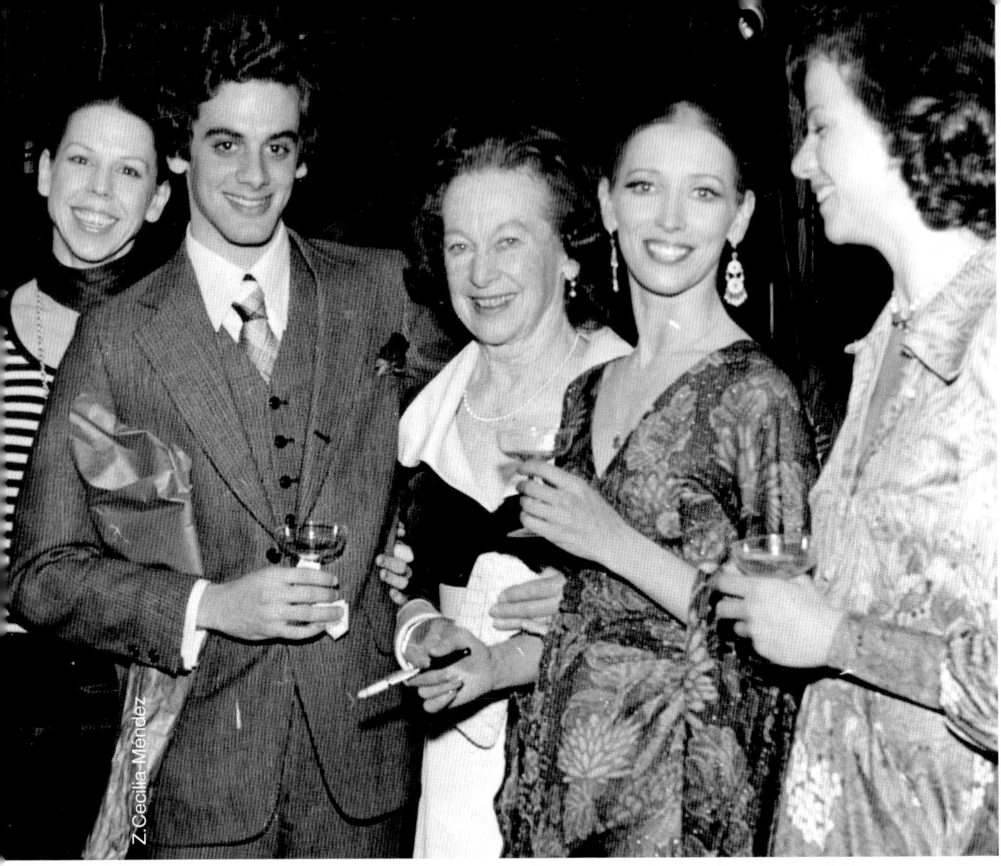
Z.Cecilia-Méndez

With Lucia Chase and ABT stars Sallie Wilson, Natasha Makarova and Martine Van Hammel at the company's party after the New York City Met season.

Z.Cecilia-Méndez

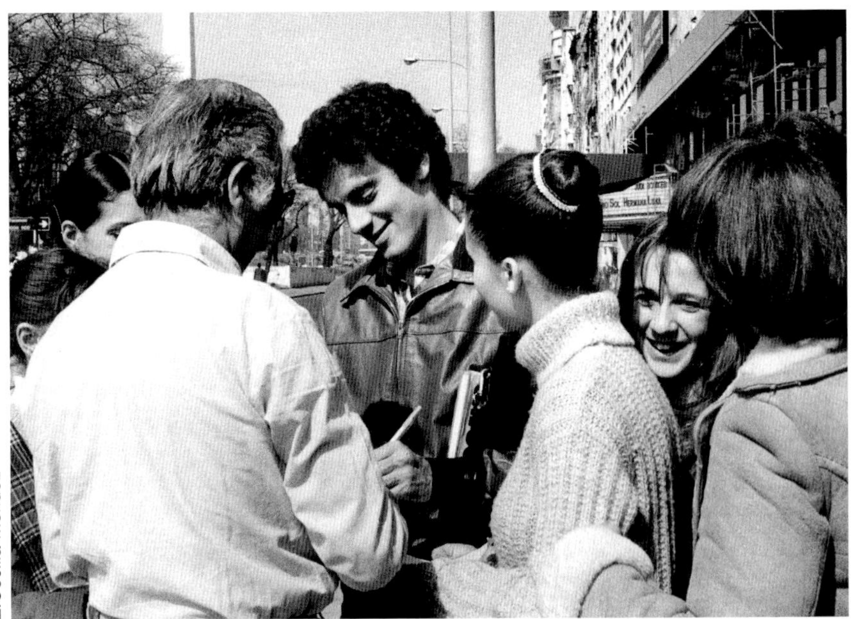

Signing autographs for young fans.

Atsushi Iijima

**Varna, Bulgaria 1974 International Ballet Competitions.** Candidate #78 in the first variation of the competition from "La Fille Mal Gardee."

Z.Cecilia-Méndez

Rehearsing the variation from "Le Corsair" at the open air amphitheater.

Z.Cecilia-Méndez

Z.Cecilia-Méndez

Taking open class in Varna.

Z.Cecilia-Méndez

Anton Dolin coaches me in his "Variations for Four."

Mary Calleiro

Going over details with Zeida.

Z.Cecilia-Méndez

Yoko Morishita, me, Zeida and Tetsu Shimitzu, in the front row, with Anton Dolin and the rest of the Japanese team.

CHAPTER 9

# *Talk About Timing*

The last week of July, 1974, I was back in America. I was feeling inspired, energized, and eager to rejoin my company, which still had two more weeks of performances at the New York State Theater.

I went to Varna to compete, not only representing my company, but also my country. Lucia Chase had actively supported and encouraged my trip, as well as so many others had put their faith in me. All this support made me terribly aware and proud in fact, I could contribute something important to dance in America through this honor.

While I was dancing in Varna, something unexpected happened that took America by storm. This was the height of the cold war. Tension and competition between the United States and the Soviet Union was at its peak. Suddenly the dance world was aroused by the news Mikhail Baryshnikov, one of the principal dancers of the Kirov Ballet had defected in Canada. The rumors of his defection had reached us while we were still in Bulgaria.

ABT wasted no time in making immediate arrangements for him to perform with the company's Russian ballerina Natalia Makarova, who in 1970 had also defected from the Soviet Union. So as I returned to New York, ABT's main interest was focused on the upcoming appearances of the latest Russian defector. Not since Nureyev's defection in 1961 had another Russian male dancer escaped, so this was big news. Besides, Nureyev had chosen to join the roster of the Royal Ballet and not ABT and Lucia had never been able to sign him up.

Baryshnikov's defection made headlines beyond the dance world. ABT wanted to capitalize from the free publicity and all of a sudden nothing else mattered. Lucia was so consumed with the New York season we never had the opportunity to talk about Varna. I wondered if she ever understood what it really meant to me.

In 1974 people in America were not as familiar with ballet competitions as they are today. Winning at Varna was a prestigious accomplishment, one that could bring fame and recognition to a dancer and I did start receiving invitations to perform with some European companies. But suddenly at ABT, there were other priorities. All my expectations were shattered.

On the plane coming back from Varna, Zeida and I agreed we would go directly from Kennedy Airport to the New York State Theater to see Baryshnikov's debut performance with ABT in "Giselle." Zeida and I had a great admiration for Nureyev, and we knew by heart his version of "Giselle," so we were very curious to see Baryshnikov. For a whole month in Varna, we had seen many Russian, Hungarian, Bulgarian, Czeckoslovaks and other very impressive male dancers... When Baryshnikov made his first entrance on stage, we were both surprised by how small he was!

During the performance, I was impressed with Baryshnikov's dancing, but Zeida was less impressed. On our way out of the theater, she said to me *"Listen, there is nothing he has as a dancer you do not have; the difference is in your bodies. You are taller, elegant, with classical proportions and better legs... remember, you are a danseur noble, like Bruhn, Anthony Dowell, Royes Fernandez... Technically, you are as good as he, if not better...you are an example of the impeccable American technique... he is a typical Russian, a bit too casual, a bit too short, demi-charactere.... He has a talented body that can do technique. So do you, but yours is a beautiful body, a very fine-tuned instrument that will serve you well. Do not worry about him."*

I came back eager to perform some of the exciting programs with which I had won the gold medal and trained so hard for. Instead I found myself cast in "Undertow" a ballet which downplays virtuoso technique in favor of the intense psychological drama. Although I was highly appreciative of Tudor and enjoyed performing his works, I had hoped to appear in a more exciting way. I was brokenhearted. Tudor, understanding my emotions, went to Lucia to request I be given an additional bravura pas de deux. Instead Lucia added the "Flower Festival" Pas de Deux to the second and last week, to dance with Cynthia Gregory.

A few days after Baryshnikov's debut with ABT, I went to check the rehearsal board and saw my name had been taken off an already scheduled performance for which I had been rehearsing. I had been cast as "Solor" in The Kingdom of the Shades from "La Bayadere." This was my favorite ballet ever since I saw Nureyev perform it and I had been looking forward to my debut in this role. Now my name had been taken off.

I went to Lucia's assistant, Enrique Martinez who was responsible for casting and rehearsals. I couldn't believe my ears when he told me *"The reason we have taken this performance away was because the company would like to offer Baryshnikov an extra performance during the season."* That's fine the company wants to give him an extra performance, but why at the expense of taking it away from me? Enrique couldn't answer me. I got furious and I yelled at him: *"If Baryshnikov is now scheduled to dance in my Bayadere performance, then I want to perform another similar work on that same evening! My name is already printed in the newspaper ads for that day and I have family and friends that have bought tickets to see me dance."* Lucia had to reconsider and I was allowed to choose the pas de deux I wanted to dance. I chose "Diana and Acteon," with Eleanor D'Antuono.

The much debated performance day arrived and it would begin with Baryhnikov and Makarova in "The Kingdom of the Shades" from La Bayadere followed by Eleanor and I in the "Diana and Acteon" Pas de Deux. In those days to see an ABT performance was to see ballet at its best, but many times there was high drama behind the scenes. The entire company was by now aware of the conflict between Baryshnikov and myself... actually between Lucia's choice in casting, favoring him over me most of the time. In the men's corps de ballets dressing room, which I still shared with the rest of the boys, talk about a possible future rivalry was commonplace, but most of the dancers were on my side and I felt grateful for their support.

The curtain went up at the Met for "La Bayadere" with ABT's corp de ballet in top form, receiving a well-deserved ovation. Baryshnikov and Makarova, as expected, received a thunderous ovation, too. Now Eleanor and I had to follow the two Russian stars. I thought to myself, it takes guts to follow a highly publicized Baryshnikov/Makarova performance in New York, but I hadn't won that Gold Medal in Varna for nothing. I was all of nineteen years old and the way I saw it was on this ballet arena, I was the under-dog with nothing to lose and maybe something to gain. The real competition of my career was about to begin.

Earlier that day, in rehearsal, I told Eleanor I was going to incorporate a couple of new steps in the variation and coda. I would start from inside the wings with a jump called *revoltade* which had impressed the judges in Varna. This jump had never been done before in the west, and I figured I could take the audience by surprise. It worked! By the end of our pas de deux we had the audience at the Met screaming.

The next day, August 8, 1974, **Anna Kisselgoff,** Dance Critic of the **New York Times** wrote in her review:

> ***"In program substitutions and cast changes that left unsuspecting ticket-holders in delirious disbelief Tuesday night at the State Theater, American Ballet Theater presented Mikhail Baryshnikov and Natalia Makarova in "La Bayadere," repeating the roles they had danced Monday. Fernando Bujones originally scheduled to partner Miss Makarova in the ballet, appeared instead with Eleanor D'Antuono in the season's first "Diana and Acteon" pas de deux, which was added to the program...Mr. Bujones was spectacular, going so far as to pull off a series of five double assemble turns in the air in the coda, and soaring about with breathtaking elevation in his variation."***

A few days later I appeared in another New York debut. Balanchine's "Theme and Variations." Once again Eleanor was my ballerina; she knew the work inside out. It was here I became aware what an extraordinary partner she was. She took the time to show me nuances in partnering I was still not familiar with. Part of the beauty of "Themes" is the intricate partnering of the main couple and she was so generous and patient with me. I loved this Balanchine masterpiece. On August 12, 1974, **Clive Barnes** wrote in **The New York Times**:

> ***"On Saturday afternoon Fernando Bujones, our own local hope and the new gold-medal winner from this year's Varna Competition put in his own 10 cents. And he was very fine. It was excellent that Mr. Bujones, the first major United States competitor at the prestigious Varna competition, won his gold medal, but it was also interesting that he was particularly singled out by the judges for his technical excellence.***
>
> ***One of the judges, Anton Dolin, wrote me a letter simply saying: "Bujones is even as good as you said he was." And***

***I am sure he must have been. Mr. Bujones was making his debut in George Balanchine's "Theme and Variations" in a role created for the great Igor Youskevitch. He danced so well, and so modestly. In this he was really like Mr. Youskevitch, who was always brilliantly cool. At times Mr. Youskevitch seemed to dance in a shower of talcum powder, and Mr. Bujones has something of this same reserved, essentially couth-like quality. There is a perfection here that inspires its own awe."***

*Eleanor D'Antuono Remembers:*

*"After Varna Fernando had gotten even stronger and we were getting paired in other roles. Together we danced "Etudes" and "Flower Festival" Pas de Deux. Technically, we had no problems, for we were very well matched. He was spectacular in "Don Quixote" and remarkable in "Diana & Acteon," but he was fantastic in "Theme & Variations." He was beautiful, just a beautiful dancer. "Theme" is the most difficult partnering I've ever done but especially, the partnering for the male dancer is so difficult because the girl at that point is so tired... But we accomplished it and had a big success with it. Both of us loved to dance it. I loved it and he loved it."*

ABT's 1974 summer season came to an end and I was promoted to principal dancer, making me at age nineteen, one of the youngest principals in the world. In two years I had gone from corps de ballet to principal dancer status with ABT. The January, 1975, issue of **Dance Magazine** featured an article by **Olga Maynard** where she wrote:

***"Fernando Bujones: America's pride!***

***"Bujones aplomb is altogether remarkable. Although a tyro (he joined ABT two years ago, straight out of the School of American Ballet) he is being featured with veteran dancers, some of them international stars ... It may be that he is in a class beyond that reached in American ballet now, as the rarest of performers: the true danseur noble."***

Things were now starting to look up. I was assigned my own dressing room, a major boost to my morale, which made life at the theater much easier. They also provided my own make-up artist and I no longer had to do my own make-up, something I had never really mastered, ending up with too much make-up on my face. And best of all, I no longer had to sew the elastics on my ballet shoes! They now came ready for me to wear. From then on, I got as many shoes as I needed. I used different pairs for class and rehearsals, where the shoes got really beat up. The shoe department knew I loved my shoes soft. While other dancers used two and three different pairs in one performance, I would use one performance pair for two and even three different performances. Our shoe attendant was always ready with the white-out liquid to make my worn-out shoes look like new again. Those were some of the fringe benefits of being promoted to principal.

But one thing was coming to me loud and clear... life at ABT was one of intense competition. The company was getting ready to go on its yearly national tour and I could see by the casting there were lots of politics going on. Whenever Baryshnikov and I performed on the same night most of the audiences and critics were thrilled because we certainly gave them a performance to remember! But what they never saw was our faces behind the curtain! I felt the company's publicity department was not properly handling this rivalry, which was getting intense.

Trying to please Baryshnikov, ABT hired Gelsey Kirkland, the fantastic dancer from New York City Ballet. She had already been dancing with Baryshnikov in some of his outside guesting engagements, and they were attempting to establish a special partnership. Gelsey was the right size for Misha and she indeed raised the bar for him whenever they were together on stage. She was such an extraordinary artist and technician, and whenever I saw her perform I never failed to experience a very special thrill.

By now, the company once known for having a magnificent roster of great dancers and choreographers was starting to change. Even the repertory started to change and revolve around what Baryshnikov wanted to dance. Choreographers were brought in to specifically produce works for him and no one else. All the other principal and soloist dancers in the company became secondary players and the company's morale started to plummet. Lucia and the ABT's Board of Directors were going all out to please Baryshnikov.

Lucia was now constantly casting Baryshnikov and me to dance on the same nights. ABT's performances were double whammys but the casting decisions were making most of the company principals uncomfortable. The New York Times, smelling blood, sent one of their writers to do a story on me. At one point, the interviewer asked me what did I think of Baryshnikov, to which I promptly replied: **"Baryshnikov has the publicity, but I have the talent."** Well, that was it! Next day, on the Arts section of the New York Times, the huge headline read: **Fernando Bujones, The Bad Boy of American Ballet**! All of a sudden the press was very interested in talking to me. My interview had Lucia and the company's public relations department blowing smoke and for sure it didn't win me any votes with them, but it won me a lot of press.

Since Baryshnikov's defection and his joining ABT coincided with my return from Varna as a Gold Medal winner, the company's public relations department had to make a decision as to what special event they were going to promote. All their efforts went to promoting Baryshnikov. I decided to hire a press agent.

This worked. Now the press was keeping up-to-date with me too, but ABT's publicity department trembled every time I gave an interview. In 1975 I turned twenty and started my fourth year with the company. It was one of my most productive years since I joined ABT three years earlier. It was also the year I began to perform regularly the leading roles of those full-length ballets as a student I dreamt about. Franz in "Coppelia," Fritz in "La Fille mal Gardee," and James in "La Sylphide," a true favorite and the first full-length ballet that I danced with Cynthia Gregory...

*Cynthia Gregory Remembers:*

*"La Sylphide was one of my favorite ballets to dance and although I wasn't much of a jumper, somehow I could jump in the Bournonville works, because all the steps had that musical quality so I felt that I could sort of hold my own with Fernando, who had this fabulous jump.. At that time Fernando hadn't really... well, he was starting to become a better partner, but his partnering still needed some work, and so this, our first full-length together, was perfect because I was tall and he didn't really*

*have to lift me or partner me a lot, but yet we could get to know each other on stage, get to know how the other worked, how we felt the music together, how we felt the characters together, so it was a wonderful first ballet for us to do ..."*

I was also finally cast as the Slave in my first Pas de Deux from "Le Corsair," partnering Natasha Makarova....

The rehearsal for Le Corsair with Natasha the day before the performance had been a difficult one. For some unknown reason Natasha was having a bad rehearsal. She had a fit and started crying. Enrique Martinez, who was also in the rehearsal and I looked at each other and decided to leave her alone. She was mumbling something about cancelling the performance. For about a minute there was complete silence in the studio. When Natasha realized this was her own decision to make, she got herself together and we continued the rehearsal. The next day the two of us received an ovation in front of the curtain at the Met that lasted longer than the pas deux itself. And **Clive Barnes'** review of the performance in **The New York Times** read:

> ***"Also special, very special, were Miss Makarova and Fernando Bujones in his New York debut in this role dancing in "Le Corsair" Pas de Deux. Miss Makarova was all melting grace and Mr. Bujones danced magnificently. One should use the word phenomenal rarely-otherwise dictionaries would complain, but Mr. Bujones was indeed phenomenal."***

That spring, I was invited to perform in Japan with the Matsuyama Ballet Company partnering ballerina, Yoko Morishita, who had been the women's Gold Medal Winner when I won the men's. This was a wonderful opportunity to travel to the far east and get to know a new culture, new people, and in May, 1975, right after ABT's season ended, my mother, Zeida and I were on a plane to Tokyo.

This was a fascinating country. Arriving in Tokyo we were welcomed by Mr. and Mrs. Shmizu, the directors of the company, with the entire staff and all the dancers of the Matsuyama ballet company! They made me feel so privileged and special. Tokyo seemed an even bigger city than

New York. There was a huge anticipation in Tokyo to see the two Gold Medal winners performing together. The Japanese audiences responded with a heart-warming and endless ovation. The people's hospitality and their work ethic was extraordinary. This would be the first of my many visits to Japan.

On my return to America, I was pleasantly surprised After more than a decade, Rudolf Nureyev was invited to work with ABT again. He came to stage his full-length "Raymonda" and dance in it, too. There would be different casts for the leading role of Jean de Brienne, and I was one of them! Working with him personally for the first time and dancing in his exciting production will always be one of the fondest memories in my career. Rudi, as we called him, had quite a temperament. He was demanding, intimidating, hilarious, but above all, if he was on your side, he was a very inspiring presence. He was, at least, for me.

I will forever remember the day when he was taking the full company rehearsal of Raymonda. I am ready to do the semi-circle of four double front cabrioles and can sense his eyes focusing on me. I take a deep breath and start the jumps. I am trying to outdo myself and put everything I have into the steps. As I leap past Rudi, I hear him say: *"You monster!"* In mid air I lose it and start laughing. After the rehearsal he comes to me grinning... *"If you jump like that in front of me again, I won't let you dance in my ballet."* I felt great! Rudi knew he was a role model for me but I knew he admired me, too.

By far my most cherished performance that year was the one I had been waiting for. My New York debut as Solor in "La Bayadere," opposite Natasha Makarova in The Kingdom of the Shades. My memories of when I first saw this ballet with Nureyev in the leading role were still fresh in my mind and now the day had arrived when I too would be performing it. As those first magic music chords filled the air and the "*bayaderes*" in their white tutus began to come down the ramp, only one thought came to my mind, *"This is it... this is my life, this is what I love doing, this is what I've been working and waiting for... this ballet that I truly love..."* On July 7, 1975, **Clive Barnes** of **The New York Times** had the following words:

***"For one dancer in particular Saturday night like the Friday night performance proceeding it, was a signal triumph. This was Fernando Bujones, Ballet Theater's youngest premier danseur, who was making his New York debut as Solor in "La Bayadere" on Saturday and as the hero in "Raymonda" on Friday. For Mr. Bujones it was a busy but presumably happy weekend.***

***Nowadays this young man trained largely at the School of American Ballet is one of the most spectacular performers to be found anywhere in the world. Partnering Miss Makarova, and partnering her superbly in "La Bayadere" he was impeccable and his solo dancing had a brio and freedom that had the audience on the edge of its seats. Mr. Bujones was not merely exhibiting tricks- although he has plenty of them in his technical armory- but dancing with heroic grace. His line remains classically perfect even in motion, his musical phrasing is begining to be interesting (note the way he holds a pose) and his whole style at present has a mixture of boyishness and virility that is most engaging."***

Performing "La Bayadere" confirmed to me why dance was the most glorious way to express myself. And with that, ABT's 1975 New York State Theater season came to an end.

By January, 1976, the company was getting ready for its two-week January season at New York's Uris Theater and when the casting notices went up, I got my first surprise. There were several mixed repertory programs, and I was cast in just two performances throughout the entire two weeks. The two performances were as "The Jungle Boy" in Antony Tudor's ballet "Shadowplay," a ballet based on the idea of a jungle boy who learns to adapt to his surroundings and eventually finds spiritual enlightenment.

While I didn't mind finding spiritual enlightenment in "Shadowplay," I did mind not having any other role to dance in two weeks. I felt the management was purposely downplaying me as a principal dancer. At home we all agreed a confrontation between Lucia and me should be avoided, and Zeida, now acting as my manager, called Lucia. She expressed my disappointment at dancing only in "Shadowplay" and requested that if possible I be given one more role to dance during the two weeks. Lucia was her regular stubborn self and refused to consider it. Zeida hung up the phone on her. A few minutes later Lucia called back and said: *"I think I found a solution, I have a third performance of Shadowplay for Fernando."* Was Lucia serious? I decided to skip the entire two-week season in New York. When Zeida told Lucia I would not be available for those two weeks, she said, as if nothing had happened, "I'll see him in two weeks time then."

I got on a plane and flew down to South Florida and made it a point to relax and enjoy other things in life. There, my good friend, ballerina Lydia Diaz Cruz got me a ticket and together with her daughter I saw my first live Super Bowl game at Miami's Orange Bowl! The superb Pittsburgh Steelers were playing against the Dallas Cowboys. I had always loved the game of football and Super Bowl X on January 18, 1976, left an impression in my mind like nothing I had ever seen before. It was such a thrill to see athletes like Terry Bradshaw and Lynn Swan, who looked like a perfect ballet dancer to me, leaping through the air to make his legendary catch.

During the two weeks in Miami, I took class with my friend and excellent ballet teacher Martha Mahr in her Coral Gables studio to stay in shape. Then I went back to New York and ABT. The company was ready to start rehearsals for the upcoming national tour. I guess standing up for myself paid off and got some results, for I was cast in the leading roles of various full-length classical ballets, including the lead in the new production of Rudolph Nureyev's "Raymonda."

The tour started in February, in Los Angeles. Nureyev would be joining us as a guest artist, but he arrived with a nasty cold. He was scheduled to dance the opening night performance of his own Raymonda production, but everybody was very worried about his health. On the day of the performance there was much anticipation because backstage Nureyev was fighting a high fever and a chronic cough. The company called a doctor and asked me to stand by in the wings with my costume on, in case Rudy would not be able to finish the performance. I knew Rudolf too well and I was sure he would rather die on stage than be replaced. I was right! When he finished the performance he walked towards me and with a grin on his face he said, *"You didn't think I was going to let you go out there, did you?" "I would have been very surprised if I had to,"* I replied.

Unfortunately, his effort came at a high cost for him, because the following day he wound up in the hospital with pneumonia. The next day, while taking the morning class and getting ready for my own scheduled matinee performance of "Raymonda," I was told I would need to step in for Rudi for the evening performance, since he was too ill to dance. Somehow, I survived two back-to-back full-length "Raymondas!" The next day it felt like I was the one that needed to go into the hospital.

From Los Angeles, the company went on to Santa Barbara. While there, I got a phone call from Zeida that the San Francisco Ballet was asking for me because of an emergency situation. Their guest artists, Kirov Ballet stars Galina and Valery Panov, were scheduled to dance in the "Don Quixote" and the "Le Corsaire" Pas de Deux, but Valery had suffered an injury during rehearsals!

The morning after my scheduled performance in Santa Barbara, a car was waiting to take me to the Los Angeles airport; and off I went to Sacramento to join the San Francisco Ballet. I went immediately to the theater and met Galina Panova for the first time. We rehearsed for about three hours until late afternoon. Everything was happening so quickly that by the time the curtain went up that night, I had no more nerves. My adrenalin took over as the curtain opened!

At the end of the performance, Galina and I looked at each other with relief. We pulled it off! It was nerve-wracking and very hard work, but it paid off when we saw the audience on its feet. Valery Panov walked on stage during the final bows, handed me a rose and said: "You're the best..." and signaled to the audience to give me an extra round of applause.

We were still in the month of February and I was back on tour with ABT... and I received a second call from Zeida. This time due to an injury, Mihail Baryshnikov could not appear in his scheduled performances of Erik Bruhn's production of "La Sylphide" with the National Ballet of Canada in Toronto, and the company director, Erik, was requesting me to replace Baryshnikov. I had some time off between my ABT performances, so I packed my bag and ballet shoes and was off to Canada. I had three full days of rehearsals, but this was "La Sylphide," a ballet I was very familiar with.

My debut with the National Ballet of Canada was as good as they come. I was very happy to dance two performances with one of their most beautiful ballerinas, Veronica Tennant, who was an absolute darling. The performances went extremely well. The National Ballet of Canada and their dancers have remained very close to my heart. On February 26, 1976 **Lawrence O'Toole** in the **Toronto Globe and Mail** wrote:

> ***"Forget Baryshnikov... Bujones is just as great"***
>
> ***From the moment he shot up from the corner like a jet of human flesh... Fernando Bujones was mercilessly spellbinding.. Bujones, a last minute National Ballet guest artist filling in for an ailing Mikhail Baryshnikov with whom he works at American Ballet Theater, is, as some reports suggested, every bit as dynamic and breathtaking as the Russian superstar. Quite possibly- and we're talking in terms of millimeters here- his elevation is higher and the distances he covers in leaps stretch even farther. The way Bujones moves has a furious push and he's quick, so the effect is startling. There's hardly anything as exhilarating as a body like Bujones soaring skyward, riding on the music, coming down to earth again as if the flight had been planned ... It's forceful, gut-gripping dancing, yet everything is tempered with a kind of delicacy that comes from the way he adorns the push and shove of his movements with his long, slender arms and legs... There's nothing of the showoff in this performance, though there is a great deal of authority and hardly any effort... the poetry is in his dancing."***

Baryshnikov and I were totally different dancers. But we were both exciting dancers to watch, and since we ended up performing the same roles in the same companies, we could not avoid the feeling of competition, even if we never talked about it. February, 1976, had been an exciting month for me. I had been called to replace the three most famous Russian dancers now performing in the west.

As a result, this opened wonderful new guesting opportunities for me. By June I was back in New York with ABT at the Met and the company was getting ready to perform Mary Skeaping's new full-length production of "The Sleeping Beauty." I was cast on the opening night to perform the "Bluebird" Pas de Deux with Yoko Morishita, who was guesting with ABT that season. She was also cast to dance the leading role as Aurora.

Baryshnikov was to dance the role of the Prince on opening night and in two more performances with Makarova as his Aurora. I was down only to do the Bluebird! I went to Lucia. This was now becoming standard procedure. I asked her why was I down to dance the Bluebird Pas de Deux, but not Prince Florimund? She answered there were not enough performances. I got angry with Lucia and decided to skip the "Bluebird" stage rehearsal. I was serious. Lucia sent me a telegram that read: "If you miss another rehearsal, there will be serious consequences." She was even more serious, and I thought to myself I better reconsider, so I showed up and waited for future events to unfold. I didn't have to wait long.

During his first performance, Baryshnikov injured one of his hands and had to cancel the other two. All of a sudden, here is Lucia with a smile wider than the Mississippi offering me not one, but two performances dancing the role of Prince Florimund with Makarova as my Aurora! The audiences loved us and the performances were not only critical successes, but box office sellouts as well. But deep in my heart, I knew then I needed to find my own better opportunities. There was pressure inside ABT's Board to push and promote Baryshnikov, if need be, at my expense.

At this point I was at the peak of my dancing. I was being invited to perform in all major roles with the top dance companies and ballerinas around the world, but at home, things could be better. Everywhere I went, I felt very much appreciated; and it became a pleasure for me to appear as a guest principal with other companies, while my performances with ABT were loaded with tension. All of a sudden, I was having to fight in order to get this or the other role...

The one thing that kept me going were the audiences. Whether in New York at the Met, or Los Angeles, San Francisco, Chicago, Tokyo or Toronto and simply everywhere ABT went, the public responded to my dancing in such a way all the pre-performance aggravations would melt away the minute I got on stage. These were people that bought tickets to see me dance and their support kept me going. I was also partnering the most wonderful ballerinas, but I needed to find a different way to deal with ABT.

CHAPTER 10

# *Brazil*

By the summer of 1976, I could feel that my relationship with ABT was not getting any better. In July, I received an invitation to perform in Brazil. It came in the form of a letter from a lady named Dalal Achcar, who owned a ballet school in Rio de Janeiro and was the organizer of the International Winter Dance Festival in Rio. The contract was co-signed by another lady named Marcia Kubitschek, the Associate Executive Director of the Dance Festival. I had been recommended by Dame Margot Fonteyn, a good friend of both ladies.

The festival would include four guest artists and they were to be Natalia Makarova, partnered by Anthony Dowell, the Royal Ballet's principal dancer, and Merle Park, principal ballerina with Royal Ballet with Danish partner Peter Schaufuss. At the last minute Peter Schaufuss could not make it, and Margot had suggested me as Merle Park's new partner.

At the airport in Rio, we were met by an assistant to Ms. Kubitschek. She drove us to the ballet school where Ms. Dalal Achcar and her associate and close friend, Marcia Kubitschek were waiting.

After a good night's rest, it was time to get down to business. Through my hotel's window, we stared at the glorious Sugar Loaf peak in all its glory. I could have stayed there for hours, but I needed to get ready for class and my first scheduled rehearsal with Merle Park. Meeting for the first time, I found Merle to be quite witty, with a great sense of humor. Throughout the class and during my rehearsal, I kept seeing Ms. Kubitschek standing at the second-floor window staring at me with curiosity. Every once in a while I would look up and smile at her.

By the end of the day I had found out some surprising facts about the beautiful lady who kept looking down at me. Marcia's family roots came from Czechoslovakia; she was the daughter of the former and famed Brazilian President, Juscelino Kubitschek, who had been president of

Brazil from 1955 to 1961 and whose presidency had done much for the development of the country and the industrialization in Brazil.

The most well-known accomplishment of his legacy was when he accepted the challenge of changing Brazil's capital city to the country's hinterland, where he eventually founded Brasilia, the new capital city of Brazil. He was also the President who in 1958 at the Presidential palace received the first Brazilian World Cup soccer champion team, when a seventeen-year-old rising star by the name of Pele scored two goals and sealed the championship victory for the Brazilians in Sweden. On our second day in Rio, all the guest artists were invited to a dinner reception at Dalal Achcar's home.

A few minutes after we arrived, Marcia Kubitschek made her entrance; and from that moment on, my eyes never left her again. In all fairness, when I first met her at the ballet studio, I thought she was a nice lady but I was not overly impressed. Now she was strikingly elegant in a beautiful long dress, her hair soft and flowing and she was simply gorgeous! While I kept talking to various people somehow my eyes kept focusing on her. By the end of the evening Marcia walked over towards where I was sitting, sat next to me and in the most disarming manner remarked, *"... tell me Mr. Bujones how is the city and the people of Brazil treating you?" "They couldn't be better, they are treating me just fine..."* I answered. We continued talking to each other as if there was no one else in the room. That night while I laid in bed with my eyes wide open, the only thoughts I had were about the woman I could have continued talking to all night long.

My first week in Brazil just flew by. Our first performance was to be at the Manchete Theater, owned by the Manchete Magazine conglomerate. After the performance there was a reception, and I met Marcia's family. Her father, former President Kubitschek was not in Rio, but her mother, former first lady of Brazil, Doña Sarah Kubitschek was there. She was an elegant woman with a commanding personality. Also there I met Marcia's oldest daughter, Anna Christina.

Saturday evening and Sunday Matinee performances would be at the Maracanazinho, an open-air smaller soccer stadium, next to the gigantic Maracanã regarded as the world's biggest open-air soccer stadium. I quickly realized soccer is a serious matter in Brazil. When Brazil plays its scheduled games during the world cup, many businesses and banks all close.

Maracana's stadium holds up to 200,000 fans when completely full and many of those fans, known as "o povo" or "*the people*" that had come to see the soccer matches on Saturday and Sunday would also be coming to see our ballet performances. On Saturday evening I danced the "Don Quixote Pas de Deux" with Merle Park, and Natasha Makarova danced the "Black Swan Pas de Deux " with Anthony Dowell.

The Sunday Matinee was unforgettable. Our show was scheduled to start at 4:30 p.m. but a soccer match had already started much earlier at the Maracana next door. Around 5:00 p.m., the soccer match finally finished as I was getting ready to perform "Le Corsaire Pas de Deux" with Merle. The "povo" or *the people* at the stadium next door were coming over to see our performance. All of a sudden our audience of around 5,000 people tripled to 15,000. When I started my variation from "Le Corsaire" I maximized my leaps all around the huge stage; as I finished my solo, the audience let go with tremendous applause, screams and whistles and started chanting "bis! bis!

They would not stop, so I ran to center stage and took my fifth bow. As I returned to the backstage area, I asked what were they shouting? And they told me the people are asking for a repeat of my variation. I gasped because I was totally out of breath! Not only did I have to dance the solo again, but Merle and I ended up repeating the coda as well. Wow! What a sensational response from an audience, I thought! The kind one dreams about but never expects will really happen. This experience made me love Brazil and its people in a way I never suspected, and it became one-of-a-kind in my career.

After the performance I was totally exhausted. I was lying down limp on a bench outside my dressing room when I saw mom, Marcia and her family all coming towards me. I hardly had the energy to move from where I was. I looked at them and said, *"...Is there an ambulance nearby?"* It would not be the last time an audience would request a repeat performance from me, but that was the first time, and I never forgot it.

Capitalizing on the success of my performances, I decided to try my luck on a more personal terrain. I could not get Marcia out of my mind. Next evening when all of us went out for dinner and dancing, I asked her to dance with me and began to flirt with her. *"You know you are a nice woman to touch,"* I said. She hardly looked at me and replied

*"... Dear, look, but don't touch!"* Her reaction was to be expected. She was ten years older than I, with lots more experience. She probably thought *"This is another young guy wanting to have a good time."* But I already knew she was separated from her husband and was starting a new life. The last thing Marcia was looking for was a serious romantic involvement. However she did not know much about me. Soon she would find out how persistent I could be.

By the time we started the tour in the city of Curitiba, my mother had gone back to New York. We had enjoyed and experienced so many new countries, so many new cultures together... but now I was glad to have some time by myself.

Marcia and I had the opportunity to get better acquainted. We shared some special moments together and by the time we got to Porto Alegre, we were romantically involved. I was attracted by her beautiful looks and radiant smile, by her knowledge and sophistication, by her culture and personality. When I met Marcia she was an experienced world traveler and spoke several languages fluently.

She was an avid reader and a lover of history and an incredible romantic. The wedding to her first husband had taken place in Portugal, after the military coup in 1964 which sent her father into exile there. The reception she and her family received from the Portuguese people was truly astounding. Years later I asked Marcia what did she ever see in me? And she replied, *"A young man with a passion, with an intensity to live and love."* There was also a certain melancholy mood to her I could not explain. But we both began to live a beautiful romance in Brazil. Then, while we were still in Porto Alegre, close to the border with Argentina, fate struck!

Anthony Dowell and I were in our dressing rooms getting ready for our next performance when Merle Park came in and said, "Have you heard the news? It seems that President Kubitschek has been in a car accident as he was traveling from Sao Paulo to Rio de Janeiro..." My first thought was of Marcia, and I felt like someone had punched me in the stomach. Totally stunned I ran out of the dressing room to look for her, but it was too late.

I was told that Marcia, accompanied by Dalal's husband, had already taken a plane and the two of them were on their way to Rio de Janeiro. Rodrigo would later tell us in the Porto Alegre airport Marcia kept calling back home, but the line was always busy. That is when she had a premonition that her father was dead. He also told me during the hours of flight, Marcia just looked out the window staring into darkness and never said a word. When she arrived in Rio, her worst fears were realized.

On August 22, 1976, former Brazilian President Juscelino Kubitschek's life ended in that fatal car accident. Brazil had lost a political giant, a man truly loved by his people. When his coffin was paraded through Brasilia, practically everyone in the Capital city he had founded, as well as other surroundings cities, walked alongside all the way to the cemetery. It was an overwhelming image to see, as it was televised over and over again by all of Brazil's television media.

This tragedy stirred very deep emotions inside of me and brought me even closer to Marcia. She had a very close relationship with her father, and I could see through the television images she was falling into a profound sadness. I felt for her and longed to see her again, but didn't know if we would even meet once more before I would have to travel back to America.

Even though I was hardly in the mood to continue performing, we had to honor our commitments and continued our touring obligations. From Porto Alegre we traveled to one of the most important cities in Brazil, the industrial powerhouse city of Sao Paulo. This was to be the last stop on our touring schedule and the entire company was anxious to finish the tour on a high note. We were all making an effort to get into the right mood, for the death of Juscelino Kubistchek had affected not only our small group but the entire country of Brazil.

I was standing in the wings, getting ready to perform "Le Corsaire" when all of a sudden I felt a warm embrace from someone behind me. I turned around and there was Marcia in a black dress, with swollen eyes and a light smile. Not a word was said, just her tight embrace said it all. Last minute encouragement from close friends and maybe some matters of the heart convinced her to see the last performance of the festival. After all, she was the co-chair of the ballet festival and the main fundraiser. Her prestige and reputation practically guaranteed the success of any event in which she participated. Marcia's presence there suddenly gave me a much needed boost in excitement level and I know for her sake, I danced that last performance in Brazil with an energy that came deep from my heart.

The next day we were all back in Rio, and Marcia invited me for lunch at her beautiful colonial house in Gloria. After lunch we sat and talked for hours about how we felt for each other. Marcia confessed she was very fearful to let the relationship grow any further. I told her love was a feeling that came upon you suddenly, even if you are not expecting it, and if it was meant to grow, there wasn't anything that could stop it and all I wanted was the opportunity for us to remain in touch and see what the future would bring. She listened and handed me an envelope, and with a tender kiss told me *"Have a good flight; we'll be in touch and hopefully we will soon see each other again."*

On my way back to America, I kept looking at her smiling picture, the one in the envelope she had given to me. On the picture were the words, *"The smile of love, Marcia."* That nine-hour flight to New York provided me with much time to think. I had precious moments to remember, but I was exhausted from the range of emotions I had lived in those short two weeks. I thought about Marcia, and somehow on that plane I knew my life was going to take a new direction. Cupid had struck my heart in Brazil.

CHAPTER 11

# *Life Beyond Dance*

I returned to New York and ABT, a different person from the one who traveled to Rio a few weeks before. Dancing in Brazil in front of huge audiences and meeting Marcia were two new fascinating experiences. Up to then, my life had revolved exclusively around ballet. Before meeting Marcia, I had dated a couple of girls, both dancers. Suddenly there was Marcia, and she was opening a whole new world for me which I had not seen before. It wasn't long before mom and Zeida sensed something out of the ordinary was happening.

Suddenly, I got a phone call. It was Marcia on the phone, and she said, *"Hello, where are you? Aren't you going to visit me?" "What do you mean?"* I asked. *"Well I'm calling you from the St. Moritz Hotel, on 59th Street by Central Park. I had to settle some legal issues in New York concerning my father's estate, and I certainly didn't mind having to come here...."*

But the real surprise was my mother's reaction when I told her I would not be sleeping at home because I would be staying with Marcia in her hotel for a whole week. Mom was not prepared for this. Whatever her reasons were, we had a serious confrontation. Despite her tears during that afternoon, I packed a small bag and left our apartment. A taxi took me immediately to where Marcia was waiting.

The next morning Zeida called me at the hotel to see how things were going and suggested we meet for lunch. We had a very good conversation. She supported my decision, but also helped me understand mom's overreaction. Zeida had also had a lengthy conversation with mom the night before. I was able to understand this and that same afternoon I went back home to meet with mom. She was still full of emotions, but by the end of the day she also understood my feelings. She wisely decided to make the most of it and welcomed Marcia into our tight family group.

During that week we spent together in late October, 1976, Marcia and I were able to share some real quality time, getting to know each other more; and by doing so, we realized even though there was an age difference between us, we were solidly attracted to each other, intellectually and physically. One evening after dinner back at the hotel Marcia told me: *"Fernando, even though you are still very young, your capacity to love and live life to the fullest is so compelling. Darling, don't ever let anyone take that away from you."* I told her, *"Marcia, the moment I met you, a whole new world opened up for me. Life has a whole new meaning; all of a sudden dance is not the only thing in my life, because love is now the motivating force behind everything I do."* Those were the feelings that allowed us to break the barriers of a long distance romance and come together in a lasting relationship others did not believe would last any longer than a year.

From that moment on, Marcia and I constantly looked for and found opportunities to see each other. After her surprise trip to New York, she returned to the United States and saw my debut performance as Count Albrecht in "Giselle" with the San Antonio Ballet in Texas partnering Eleanor D'Antuono. I had worked very hard with Zeida and Eleanor in my interpretation of Count Albrecht. Like Albrecht, I too was a man in love. This was going to be my very first time at this difficult role and the performance in Texas went well for us. From there we flew to New York and Marcia returned to Brazil. However, by January, 1977, she joined Zeida and mom for my debut in the same role with ABT for the New York City Center season, again with Eleanor.

Lucia was giving me the opportunity to perform "Giselle," but at twenty-one years of age, I guess my Count Albrecht was still a work in progress. The New York reviews came out saying there was still room for improvement and were rather critical of me. Eleanor kept reminding me this was my first try at this complex role. I had put all my heart into it, but maybe I was still not coming through.

*Eleanor D'Antuono Remembers:*

*"Finally Lucia gave him his first "Giselle." This role was very familiar to me and I had had the most wonderful examples to follow in Alicia Alonso and Igor Youskevitch, who were to become one of the best known interpreters of that ballet, and of course, Rudolf and Margot. The last two personally coached me and worked with me in that role and by now I was very comfortable with my interpretation.. Technically I had no problems and neither did Fernando. He could dance anything. I was thrilled to be dancing it with him, because by now we were creating something special together... "*

After the January season in City Center, Marcia went back to Brazil and stayed there for a couple of months, but agreed to return and join me in March for the ABT winter tour in Los Angeles and San Francisco. It was Marcia's first trip to San Francisco and she fell in love with the city, just as I did four years earlier on my first ABT tour.

San Francisco became our favorite city in the United States and our time together there was wonderful. In Los Angeles Marcia saw me rehearse "The Kingdom of the Shades from La Bayadere" (my favorite ballet) for the first time. After the rehearsal she could not hold back her excitement. *"Listen to me darling... You know that I love ballet. For many seasons I have seen the best of what the Royal Ballet has to offer, most of what the Paris Opera has to offer, and most of what the Russian dancers have to offer. But what I have just seen has taken my breath away. Your dancing belongs to the world and no one has the right to stop you from dancing everywhere you can. I just don't know if I'll be able to follow you."* For the first time she was analyzing the possibility of our future together and she was seriously concerned for it. She understood my passion and devotion to dance and valued it too much to think of us in a selfish manner. After Los Angeles, Marcia went home to Brazil. We wouldn't see each other again until July, 1977, when I would be performing at the Metropolitan Opera House in New York City.

After March, it was time to get ready for my upcoming trip, which would take me to Italy for the first time. I had been invited to dance six performances of the full-length Sleeping Beauty at the Rome Opera house with the popular ballerina, Galina Samsova. Her husband Andre Prokovsky, a former principal dancer with the New York City Ballet was the company's artistic director and choreographer of the production. With invitations like these, I was able to further my development as a dancer and as a partner, exploring new choreographies, new interpretations, dancing with world-class ballerinas.

Two days after my arrival in Italy, on the way to the Rome Opera house for my first dress rehearsal, I noticed a commotion outside the theater. Aldo Moro, a high-profile politician had been kidnapped! The company's staff was trying to decide what to do. The day's work was cancelled in support for Aldo Moro, protesting this act of terrorism. I wasn't sure if this cancellation was going to make any difference in the fate of Aldo Moro, but the loss of my one and only dress rehearsal was surely going to make a big difference for me!

Thanks to the professionalism of Galina Samsova and the entire company, the performances went really well and by the end of the week the Italian dancers were taking me to the local trattorias, and offering me car rides around the city. It didn't take long for me to love Rome. In Rome, you are walking in living history; and the ruins are so overwhelming. You can easily visualize how the ancient Romans must have looked and lived during the glorious days of their empire.

A month earlier I had traveled to Vienna to rehearse with ABT for what was to be the beginning of their European tour. I did not stay with the company in Vienna during their performances, because I had been invited by the Berlin Opera Ballet in West Germany to partner Merle Park, dancing the role of Franz in "Coppelia" and the pas de deux from "Le Corsaire." Those performances provided a wonderful opportunity to dance again with Merle.

The Berlin Opera House was an impressive theater and I had some time to explore that great city. There I saw Maurice Bejart's "Bolero" for the first time, with his all-male ensemble, which I adored. At the time I visited the city, the infamous wall built in the early 60's was still up, dividing East Berlin from the West.

In the meantime, Gerhard Brunner, General Director of the Vienna State Opera and Carlos Gacio, a Cuban dancer now exiled from the Alonso's

National Ballet de Cuba company and currently the State Opera's Chief Ballet Master, extended an invitation for me to return in the fall of 1977 to perform with the Vienna State Opera Ballet in Nureyev's full-length "Don Quixote" dancing the role of Basilio!

Carlos Gacio and I were extremely surprised to see each other in Vienna, because the last time we had been together, I was nine years old and he was the Giant through whose legs I escaped as the smallest of the seven dwarfs in the Cuban National Ballet's version of "The Sleeping Beauty!"

From Berlin I traveled to Athens, Greece to join ABT. The company was to perform at the Herodus Atticus, an ancient Greek theater that could seat over five thousand people. Standing on stage, if you looked up, you could see beyond the last row, the magnificent spectacle of the glorious Parthenon all lit up. My performances there became some of the extraordinary pleasures which my life as a dancer offered me. I shall never forget the roles I danced there. Solor in "La Bayadere," Count Albrecht in "Giselle" and Basilio in the "Don Quixote" Pas de Deux. It felt as if the Greek Gods inspired me. During my times off I was able to visit some of their incredible museums and learn even more about my favorite historical hero, Alexander the Great.

From Athens, ABT went on to Rumania and Italy while I continued to Toronto to start rehearsals with the National Ballet of Canada partnering Vanessa Harwood in their new production of Sir Frederick Ashton's "Fille mal Gardee," to be performed in New York at the Met. Ashton's production was a jewel although technically and artistically challenging as I needed to perform with various different props. The most difficult was the pas de deux with the ribbons, where Vanessa and I had to weave in and out of a pattern with the ribbons and ultimately create the English flag, but in every rehearsal I kept messing up. The company then traveled to New York, for our scheduled performances at The Met. It was only in the actual performances that I finally got it right and the ribbons showed off the beautiful flag.

Marcia returned to New York and joined mom and Zeida in the audience for my performances. During the first intermission of the second night, all the lights backstage went out and everything became pitch black. How weird I thought, and I asked the stage manager if he could bring the lights up a bit, so I could continue my warm up. Then somebody with a flashlight appeared and said that all the lights in the theater, including the ones out in the audience, were out! But it wasn't only the Met without lights. The entire city of New York was without power! A sudden and complete blackout! Everybody, including the audience, waited to be told what to do.

During the next three hours everyone in the audience was escorted out of the Opera House; Marcia, mom, and Zeida made their way backstage and joined me in my dressing room. The dancers were told to get out of their costumes and go home. From a window in my dressing room, I could see a human flood of bodies on the run crossing the street behind the theater, towards Broadway, in a frenzy of looting! All over the city, the same was happening, and it was impossible to stop it! We felt it was too dangerous to leave the theater and waited for another full hour before attempting to go outside. Fortunately, we were able to flag down a taxi!

New York City would be without power for the rest of the night and it wasn't until late the next morning the lights started to come back. The incident (July, 1977) made everyone think New York City was far more vulnerable than anyone expected. Twenty-four years later on September 11, 2001, that thought became the most horrible reality when the twin towers of The World Trade Center in downtown Manhattan were blown to pieces by a terrorist attack.

Right after my performances with the Canadian company I joined ABT for the second part of their European tour with London and Paris waiting for us! ABT hadn't been there in quite a few years. Marcia had arranged to travel with me. We enjoyed a fantastic time together. I had just learned to drive before this trip and while in Europe decided to rent a car and do some traveling. I ended up being a terribly poor driver and so was Marcia, and some of the incidents that we got ourselves into are better forgotten; we would invariably end up on the wrong side of the street, in all the wrong places; but regardless, we had lots of fun.

In London Marcia and I stayed at the Grosvenor House and through her friends I was able to meet most of the dancers and personnel from the Royal Ballet. Many of them came to see ABT's opening night at the London Coliseum. We were opening with a very strong program consisting of "The Kingdom of the Shades from La Bayadere" led by Makarova and

Baryshnikov; "The Leaves are Fading" danced by Gelsey Kirkland and Ivan Nagy, "Grand Pas Classique Pas de Deux" with Cynthia Gregory and myself and "Push comes to Shove" with Baryshnikov, Martine van Hamel and Marianna Tcherkassky. The company had a great success and the London audiences were terrific.

The morning after our opening performance I met with Peter Darrell, the Scottish Ballet Artistic Director, who had invited Makarova and me to dance in a month's time with his company at the prestigious Edinburgh Festival in Scotland. When he saw me that morning, his first words were: *"Young man, have you seen the London Times?" "No, I just woke up."* I replied. *"Well if I were you I'd buy two dozen copies of it,"* and as he spoke he handed me the newspaper. **John Percival**, of **The London Times** wrote:

> ***"...How clever to cap that, after the interval, with another virtuoso display, revealing that the company has a younger male dancer who, for sheer classical bravura can outshine Baryshnikov...The Grand Pas Classique which Bujones danced with Cynthia Gregory bears only a vestigial resemblance to Victor Gsovsky's choreography as previously shown here... But as a display of scintillating technique, punchy attack and exuberant personality it was a triumph for both dancers, showing Bujones as a unique phenomenon..."***

The company moved on to France. During August, 1977, the weather in Paris was obnoxious. Our scheduled opening night performance was to take place outdoors, at the courtyards of the Louvre museum. For three days in a row it was cancelled due to heavy thunderstorms. Marcia had invited me to stay at the magnificent Ritz Hotel in Place Vendome where she used to stay, and we were enjoying the most luxurious surroundings! Every day we visited some of Paris' spectacular sights. I loved the Louvre, and went crazy seeing all the Greek art and collections; the Palace at Versailles and Malmaison, the precious summer home where Napoleon and Josephine lived their happiest and most peaceful times. We took the barge on the Seine

River, and had our portraits painted by the street artists. Hand in hand, we walked all over Montparnasse and visited Notre Dame and Sacre Coeur.

Finally the skies cleared, and we began our Paris season. We were there for three weeks, and I was able to dance in more ballets than in London. Paris was where ABT's European tour came to an end; everyone was exhausted but happy, for our tour had been a success.

Now it was time for some fun. And Paris seemed like the perfect place to start a vacation. After a few days in Paris, Marcia and I decided to go to one of the most beautiful regions in the world. We took a train and headed south to the Cote d'Azur in the south of France. After a few days in St. Tropez, we drummed up enough courage to rent another car. Neither Marcia, nor I, felt comfortable behind a wheel. But this was a special opportunity and again we decided to risk it and we drove to Cannes, Nice and Monte Carlo.

It was time to head back to Paris and from there we flew to Brazil. A whole year had already gone by since I first performed in that country and so much had happened in my life. Anna Christina, Marcia's oldest girl, was by now a sharp teenager, aware of everything, and cute baby Julia, whose sweet disposition, reddish hair and freckled face I loved, made me feel like she was my own.

By late August, I had to pack my bags and get ready for the next flight that would take me to Scotland, to perform with Natasha Makarova and the Scottish Ballet at the Edinburgh Music Festival dancing the role of James in "La Sylphide," one of my favorite ballets. I had already heard about the breathtaking beauty of the Scottish highlands with its vivid valleys and lakes, but seeing them in person, you get to feel that mysterious, haunting quality about them and even wonder if real Sylphides may actually be hiding there.

Arriving in Edinburgh I could see that Natasha's pregnancy was starting to show. She was already close to four months, and still performing! She was incredibly light and swift, and I didn't have any problems partnering her in "La Sylphide." Things did become more challenging with the lifts of the "Don Quixote Pas de Deux." *"Don't you think I have enough responsibility to partner the great Makarova, but now instead of a pas de deux, it will be a pas de trois,"* I kidded her. But the performances went well for both of us, or maybe I should say for the three of us!

Especially satisfying were the reviews, since after all, we were an American and a Russian dancer interpreting probably the best of the best of the Scottish classical ballets! On August 31, 1977, **Clement Crisp** wrote in the **London Financial Times**:

> ***"I know of no better production of La Sylphide than that staged by Hans Brenaa for the Scottish Ballet... and very fine too, Fernando Bujones as James. We might suppose that he would glory in the dances. Bounding through them with his impeccable legs and feet, he catches exactly that quality which Bournonville declared to be his ideal: a manly joy. Temperamentally, the role suits the youthful Bujones: the vivid response to every dramatic nuance, his alert, charming manner, makes James credible and appealing. Kneeling to salute the Sylph, he is the incarnation of romantic devotion; pursuing her, he is all ardour..."***

After my performances in Edinburgh, I decided to treat myself and booked a flight on the supersonic French Concorde from Paris back to Rio! They were wonderful airplanes, those Concordes, and I felt sadness when they were retired. I was fortunate to fly twice on this marvel of a plane!

Back in New York City, ABT was now involved in the making of the movie "The Turning Point" directed by Herb Ross. Leslie Brown, one of our young dancers had recently been promoted to principal, and she was selected to play a leading role opposite Baryshnikov, after Gelsey Kirkland refused the part. Shirley McLaine and Anne Bancroft were the leading characters and the entire corps of ABT appeared throughout the film in several sequences. Some of the other principal couples from ABT and other companies were also seen. I was to be partnering Lucette Aldous, principal dancer from the Australian Ballet in the Don Quixote "pas de deux."

My mom thought that my hair would look better in film if it was lighter and without thinking twice about it, I agreed that she give me a rinse to lighten my hair. Well, it did not exactly work out the way she had planned, and my hair turned out orange. This was the night before the filming of my scene! As much as we tried rinsing if off, orange it remained. I was furious at mom, but it was too late to do anything about it. So to everyone's surprise, I appeared at the theater with flaming orange hair. Herb was kind enough not to say anything about it, and the filming went on as scheduled.

CHAPTER 12

# *Moving On*

January, 1978, and Marcia and I had been talking about the possibility of living together in New York. For almost two years now our relationship had been mainly via long distance, but we decided life was too short to live it without those we cared about. We found and bought a great apartment on East 58th Street, by the East River; and together with Anna Christina, baby Julia and a Brazilian nanny named Maria, we became one big happy family. Sharing Marcia's political background meant being around other people outside the dance world. It was the starting point of another life style from the one I was used to and one that broadened my outlook.

At ABT there was turmoil. The Met season this year started in April and the company was getting ready to start rehearsals and assign the different casts. Rumors were flying in every direction that Baryshnikov was leaving ABT to join Balanchine and the New York City Ballet. He had been absent from the company for his own reasons many other times and the dancers did not totally trust him. Nobody knew what to think. When the casting was posted, I found myself dancing only one bravura pas de deux. I could dance "Etudes" or "Theme and Variations," or any of the Tudor roles, but I was left out of the full-length classics. If ABT was not going to use me in their big productions, other companies were ready to fill the void.

I received a call from the Vienna State Opera finalizing the details for my three performances as Basilio in Nureyev's full-length "Don Quixote." The Stuttgart Ballet wanted me for two performances of John Cranko's extraordinary version of "Romeo and Juliet" partnering the legendary Marcia Haydee. These engagements kept my spirit and excitement going, despite ABT's woes.

And then it happened. Misha left to join City Ballet. ABT's season at the Met was about to begin and there was casting chaos. Suddenly ABT's directors began to notice the success I was enjoying elsewhere, and Lucia decided to use me as Prince Siegfried in the company's full-length production of Swan Lake. I would be partnering Eleanor D'Antuono as Odile-Odette and we began rehearsals in earnest.

*Eleanor D'Antuono Remembers:*

*"Emotionally and artistically "Swan Lake" is one of the great roles of the classical repertoire and it sets a mark in the career of a dancer. And this was to be Fernando's very first Swan. He had been studying the role and working on it with his coach, watching films, and was very well prepared. Also the high level of technique he brought to the role made it extra special. He was so elegant by nature and fit the character very well. Just the partnering was huge, huge– but by then, he was far more polished. In the Third Act Black Swan pas de deux, he was simply phenomenal. I think Fernando was the first male American dancer that had just about everything that a premier danseur should have. Definitely, he brought to dance the expectations of what a great male dancer should look like. Up to then, we had not had a dancer with his elegance, extraordinary facility, training, and desire. I think he brought male classical dancing to a whole different level."*

I was also cast as James in "La Sylphide" opposite Natasha Makarova; as the Prince in "Sleeping Beauty;" again as prince Sigfried this time with Yoko Morishita, and as Basilio in the full-length "Don Quixote" with Natasha. In April, 1978, **Anna Kisselgoff** of **The New York Times** wrote:

> ***"Swan Lake" is now one of the great ballets of all time and New York is fortunate that American Ballet Theater once decided that the full-length four act version could endure in***

> ***an American company's repertory. On Friday night at the Metropolitan Opera House, the company presented its first "Swan Lake" of the season in an exciting performance led by Yoko Morishita and Fernando Bujones...It is at heart a dramatic tale and the virtue of Mr. Bujones' Siegfried and Ms. Morishita's Odette-Odile was their ability to build up the narrative tension. They are in addition fabulous technicians, able to turn in a virtuoso performance with no effort. Mr. Bujones, not long ago the boy wonder of American Ballet, has matured most impressively in his approach to Siegfried. The first act gave him more of a showcase for pure dance in the brief solos he executed with polish and perfect finishes. But the second lakeside act showed him a considerable partner whose attentiveness was obviously stressed as part of the characterization."***

In May I danced James in "La Sylphide" with Makarova as my partner and **Ms. Kisselgoff** wrote:

> ***"...Much of the drama in "La Sylphide" comes through in mime but it can also be visible in the dancing. This was true in Mr. Bujones' case. The hot blooded hero who wept at the end was also the magnificent dancer whose solo in Act I and two variations in Act II soared incredibly into space... Both in his acting and dancing, Mr. Bujones delivered an exciting performance... The clues were in the details."***

More good notices continued and on Monday, May 29, 1978, **Clive Barnes** of **The New York Post** wrote of my Sleeping Beauty performance:

> ***"...This young man is rapidly improving these days - not so much in the matter of his dancing for there was scarcely any room for improvement there, but in his whole manner and approach. He acts with real authority now and commands the stage with his presence."***

The 1978 Met season was a turning point for me; not only when Baryshnikov decided to join City Ballet and was no longer a part of ABT, but also when we lost Ivan Nagy, a wonderful principal dancer and special mentor and friend of mine. He was leaving and looking forward to becoming the Artistic Director of the Ballet Nacional de Chile. As a result, I was being cast in those wonderful roles. **Frances Herridge**, dance critic for **The New York Post**, writing on June 8, 1978, said:

> ***"Don Quixote is back in the American Ballet Theater repertory and this time Natalia Makarova has him. She and Fernando Bujones made their debut in Baryshnikov's all dancing, all festive version of the Russian classic. They made a superb team. ... The role gives him plenty of opportunity to display his elegant technique which he does to perfection... He is taking over the Baryshnikov role in more ways than one. With Barybnikov gone, Bujones is without doubt the male star of the company."***

The truth was now out in the open. With Misha gone, ABT had no problem casting me in those roles, and I got the chance to show the ABT public what the rest of the world was already seeing. But it was a shame ABT could not have dealt properly with having two major principal dancers sharing the top roles, when they had the opportunity.

At the end of that wonderful season **Anna Kisselgoff** wrote :

***Bujones Joins The Top Rank...***

> ***" Beyond the obvious fact that Baryshnikov's name must now be added to this group in the west, it is also time to include another name - that of Fernando Bujones. There will always be those who say that, as a child prodigy, Bujones should have been taken earlier into this class. Yet Bujones is only 23 years old, and while his exceptional gifts were already evident when he was a 15 year-old at the School of American Ballet, it is only fair to say that greatness had very***

> ***naturally –at his age– still eluded him in succeeding years. This season with American Ballet Theater, however, this still young dancer has made an astonishing breakthrough. Interestingly, it is a change sensed and almost willed by Bujones himself. The virtuosity that Bujones brings to his classical solos is very special. For years he has been fond of saying that he sought to dance with the power of Nureyev and the pure classic line of Erik Bruhn... The final result is neither Nureyev nor Bruhn but Bujones. Bujones' dancing is too reserved to suggest Nureyev's animal tension, but it is too meteoric to be identified with Bruhn's innate nobility. Bujones offers something else. Brilliance! It is a quality rarely found in male dancers. Too often it is mistaken for mere bravura. But bravura can be raw while Bujones makes bravura diamond-sharp.***

The moment the Met season finished, Marcia and I were on a plane looking forward to a summer filled with wonderful new experiences and travel to exotic locations… and we landed in Australia! I had accepted an invitation to become part of an elite eighteen-member troupe known as "The Stars of World Ballet." The troupe was led by Dame Margot Fonteyn and was going on a six-week tour. Marcia and I were staying only three weeks, but they were the greatest three weeks! Maris Liepa, David Wall, Peter Breuer, Australia's own Danilo Radojevic, Merle Park, Birgit Keil, Yoko Morishita and Cynthia Gregory were some of the dancers that made this tournee so exciting and so much fun. My partner would be Cynthia Gregory and our repertoire consisted of the "Don Quixote" Pas de Deux, "Le Corsaire" Pas de Deux, "Black Swan" Pas de Deux, "Grand Pas Classique," the "Gopak" solo and "The Sleeping Beauty" Pas de Deux!

*Cynthia Gregory Remembers:*

*"This was one of the several outside tours Fernando and I did together, which were such fun for us to do. We were getting very comfortable dancing*

*with each other and also becoming very good friends. In Melbourne, we talked about ABT's staging a new production of "Sleeping Beauty" for the next season and we thought, why not include the Third Act Pas de Deux as part of our rep here, and in case ABT would ask us to dance in the new production, at least we would already have the pas de deux under our belt... so we started to work on it during the tour.*

*"But here we had Margot Fonteyn watching us, and Maris Liepa and Marina Kondratieva watching us, and the three of them were at odds... because Margot was showing us the British version and Maris and Marina were insisting on the Russian version ... I was used to the British version myself and they were telling us things that were typical of each one and Fernando and I would say "what are we going to do...?" Then Fernando said, "Let's be ourselves, because we can't please everybody..." but we were so nervous, that first performance, because Margot was in one wing and Maris and Kondratieva were in the other wing watching every move we made..."*

At the top of their respective careers, each a superstar in their own right, this group had a depth of talent, respect and knowledge of dance difficult to match. It was a pleasure to be among such professionals, each of us offering something unique and different to the audiences. In a group at this level, there is no jealousy, no mistrust; everyone was self-motivated to be at their best and a real camaraderie developed among us. As physically tiring as these three weeks were, being in such company indeed lifted my spirits. The last performance was a riot, for everyone dressed up in someone else's costume and exchanged partners, much to the delight of the screaming audience. Some of the boys ended up with tutus and toe shoes, and the women had to "partner" their new "ballerinas." I was horrendous. Wearing toe shoes and a tutu with no tights, (you could see my hairy legs) I performed a segment of the "Rose Adagio" with Cynthia as my "cavalier." You can imagine what that was like!

The highlight of this Australian tour for me was I had the opportunity to partner Dame Margot, even if it was just for a few minutes in the finale of "Birthday Offering!"

*Cynthia Gregory Remembers:*

*"One of the funniest moments came during Fernando's last performance. We were all to dance in the finale of "Birthday Offering" and that night Margot decided to let her hair down; when she did her sequence of pirouettes with Fernando, her hair went "zip, zip, zip" across his face, which he had not expected, so he just closed his eyes and hoped for the best. He then had a small solo of jumps and beats, and in the middle of it, Peter Breuer came from behind and lifted him; Fernando did not know he was going to be lifted, and there he was in the air, arms and legs all over the place, hanging on to Peter for dear life.. We danced like crazy, but we also had fun.."*

On July 6, 1978, *The Sun News* from Melbourne said of "Stars of World Ballet" that we were "*The greatest show of virtuoso dancing ever seen in Australia."*

Between rehearsals and during days off, Marcia and I found ways to get acquainted with the beauty and peaceful nature of the great Australian continent.

From Sydney we returned to Melbourne, headquarters of the Australian Ballet, where I had the pleasure to meet ballerina Lucette Aldous again, who had been my partner in "The Turning Point." Thank God I had committed to just three weeks of touring. We had performed five days a week for three weeks and my legs kept reminding me this Australian tour followed an intense eight-week season at the Met. By now, my body desperately needed a vacation. So, on our way back to New York, we stopped in one of the most beautiful and astonishing places in the world, the French Polynesian Islands of the South Pacific.

We spent one day in Papeete, the capital of Tahiti. From there we took a small plane that made three local stops in the islands of Moorea, Raiatea and finally we arrived at the tiny, but spectacular island of Bora Bora. These islands are the true treasures of the South Pacific with their translucent blue-green water, tranquil lagoons and mountain peaks disgorged by the sea centuries ago and sculpted by mighty volcanic explosions.

We were ferried across to a small meeting center in Bora Bora and from there a World War II Red Cross bus awaited to transport us to the hotel. What an odyssey to get to our hotel. But when we finally got there we had one reaction, "It was worth it!" Our room was a private bamboo bungalow on stilts! There was a floor hatch door that opened to a small staircase which lead directly down to the lagoon beneath us. We had our own private beach and one could wake up and just step down and out of the bungalow to go swimming, canoeing or snorkeling.

Of all the trips Marcia and I took, this was clearly the most memorable. This was life at its loveliest, no stress, no need to hurry, just open your eyes and enjoy the beauty around you. There were signs everywhere that read: "No need to hurry," or "There are no reasons for you to get upset." I could easily understand why the great impressionist painter, Paul Gauguin, found such an inspiration and heaven in this part of the world.

We stayed there for a few days, and hated when the time came to leave this paradise, where telephones, televisions, traffic or stress didn't exist. Too soon we were back home to a more realistic world, but happy to be together with Christina and Julia and anxious to tell mom and Zeida the incredible experiences we had shared in Australia and in the South Pacific.

Now much more rested, I rejoined "Stars" for a Gala potpourri program at the Royal Festival Hall in London, the first week in August, with Dame Margot, Natasha Makarova, Yoko Morishita, Lynn Seymour and Ivan Nagy. On August 8, 1978, in **The London Observer**, **Alexander Bland** wrote:

***"...To many, the appearance of Fernando Bujones (also from ABT) must have seemed almost like a London debut,***

> ***since he was hardly given the chance to show his talent in his company's short season here last year. The rumors of his prowess have been well founded. Still only 23, he is already a strong partner in spite of his slim build and has a virtuoso technique which is unsurpassed anywhere. To this he adds an elegant line and a pure classical style which he managed to maintain even in the fireworks of Le Corsaire and Don Quixote."***

*Zeida Remembers:*

*"By now ABT was well aware that Fernando was one of the company's top box office draws, and they needed him. He was seldom seriously injured, could replace anybody at any time in a split second; he knew the entire ABT repertory and if he had to learn something new, he would learn it in record time.*

*"I had also learned how to get the best terms and conditions when negotiating contracts with other companies that were calling Fernando to guest with them. His fees as a principal dancer zoomed up tremendously and, they were being accepted. His dressing room would always be stocked with nice snacks and drinks without him having to ask for them. He was receiving a wonderful star treatment everywhere, and as his manager and coach I was making sure this became standard. I kept his international guesting schedules, and when the time came to negotiate the yearly contract with ABT for the upcoming season, we were ready. When ABT gave me Fernando's new contract for the coming season, we reworked it and presented them with our new version. It was accepted!"*

From now on I would appear with ABT on a per performance basis for a minimum and maximum amount of performances. These performances, as well as my partners, were to be discussed and approved by Zeida and me in advance, and I would be paid per performance like the rest of the top roster of principals. My fees at ABT were raised accordingly; I was granted my own dressing room, my own dresser, makeup and hair persons not only at the Met, but wherever the company performed. When Zeida came home with the contract approved and signed, much to our delight, we went out to celebrate!

CHAPTER 13

# *Around the World in Ballet Shoes*

In November, 1978, I flew to Vienna to fulfill my engagement with the State Opera Ballet in Nureyev's full-length production of "Don Quixote" with ballerina Gisella Czech, and Marcia again came with me.

I had arrived six days before my opening performance and when I discovered the role of Basilio had four variations, plus additional codas and bits of dancing throughout the ballet, I knew I had to get to work! A massive production full of dancing for the male lead was the stamp of all Nureyev productions. I asked him *"Why he felt he had to perform so much throughout the evening?"* and he answered, *"I don't like sitting down or waiting around too long to dance; it makes me nervous."* This may have worked for him, but it wasn't easy for other dancers to perform his highly demanding and draining productions. I had loved performing his version of "Raymonda" for ABT, but once the performance ended I was physically numb.

The experience of working with Rudi in "Raymonda" at ABT had given me much insight about his choreographic style. Now, learning his version of "Don Q," I found myself drained from dealing with so many new steps in the intense daily rehearsals. Still fresh in my mind was Baryshnikov's ABT full-length version of the same ballet, which I had recently performed with Makarova and my mind kept mixing up details from the two totally different productions.

After the day's work, I would return to the hotel with Marcia and collapse in the room. Still suffering from some jet lag, I'd wake up around 3:00 in the morning and go over the sequences in my mind. One night Marcia woke up and saw me dancing in the dark room: *"What are you doing?... Are you crazy?" "No! But I am going nuts with so many different steps that I need to remember!"* and kept on dancing in the dark.

Two days before opening night I got a fever. My body and mind had collapsed, and I was feeling very weak. I'm sure it was from nerves. Marcia found a doctor who gave me a multiple vitamin shot and that helped. I was so fired up that opening night! Nureyev was in the audience, watching, and he came backstage immediately after the first act to find me. "*Dancing is very strong and pantomime is good.*" His compliment got my spirits up tremendously.

When the performance finished, the audience was on its feet and Gisella Czech and I had innumerable curtain calls, more times than I can remember. Minutes later backstage, Nureyev again came to me but this time there was a strange look on his face and pointing a finger at me he said: *"If you want to remain friends, don't make any changes to my choreography and dance my production as it is."* I was stunned!

True, at the last minute I had made two minor changes to my variation in the Grand Pas de Deux of the third act. I had seen Rudi himself do the same thing many times in different productions, so I never thought twice about it... I never thought this would upset him the way it did. He started to walk out on me. I ran after him to explain about the changes. Suddenly I felt a hand on my shoulder that stopped me. It was Dr. Gerhard Brunner, the Director of the Vienna State Opera, who said, *"Rudolf has identified your success with his when he danced for the first time his own Don Quixote in this same Opera house twenty years earlier. Since then, no one had ever matched him. The two of you have won the biggest ovations from our ballet audiences at the Vienna State Opera House and your performance must have brought back memories...surely you can understand..."* But Nureyev knew how much I admired him and how much I embraced his productions, because I told him so every time I could. Regardless, I left Vienna with an invitation to return in Nureyev's full-length productions of "Swan Lake" and "Raymonda" with Rudolph's approval. So after all, his being mad at me lasted less than two days.

By December, we were back in New York, ready for ABT's season at the Kennedy Center. During that season, Makarova and I were scheduled to dance the full-length Don Quixote on opening night.

The Kennedy Center opening was not our best performance and the next day one local reviewer let us have it. I was upset but Makarova was even more. The following week we were scheduled to dance the same ballet, but four days prior to the performance, Natasha sent a message with Lucia's personal secretary she was feeling sick and did not know if she would be able to perform. I was still scheduled to perform and needed a ballerina to rehearse with. I was eventually given a young soloist named Yoko Ichino to rehearse with. After three days of rehearsal with Yoko and one day before the performance, Natasha sent word she might be able to perform. But still there were no Makarova/Bujones rehearsals scheduled.

At this point I sent a message to Natasha "*that I needed to know if she was going to perform and when could we rehearse, otherwise I would perform with Ichino.*" My message didn't sit very well with a ballerina still upset with the opening night review, and now with me. Natasha did not perform. She sent word to Lucia Chase that she would not perform in any of the other Don Quixotes that were already scheduled for the company's upcoming West Coast tour unless she could dance them with Anthony Dowell, then a guest with ABT from The Royal Ballet. I was hurt by Natasha's action. When Lucia told me I was to be replaced from the various performances already scheduled because of Natasha's wish to change partners, I had another encounter with Lucia. "It is not right. *Lucia, you are breaking our signed contract. I am to perform in all those "Don Quixotes" you are now taking away from me. I have no problem performing with Natasha, but if she has a problem with me, then you should remove her not me.*" Lucia replied, *"I am sorry dear, but I cannot do that"*... I left her office fuming and saw some of my performances vanish.

Zeida, acting as my agent, informed ABT's management that I would be canceling my performances on the West Coast, and I sat out the Los Angeles engagement. After some hurried negotiations between Zeida and Lucia, I rejoined ABT right after Los Angeles and continued on with the tour.

In the meantime, Makarova and I would not speak nor dance with each other for almost a whole year. I finally broke the ice as I went to congratulate her after an incredible performance of the "Manon" Pas de Deux she danced with Anthony Dowell at an ABT gala. A short time later she invited me to perform with her "Makarova and Company" at the Uris Theater in New York City, and we were friends again.

That December, Marcia, Christina, Julia and I spent our first holiday season together in the United States and it was magical! Fifth Avenue and the Rockefeller Center with its enormous Christmas tree were beautifully lit, the department stores were buzzing. And on this first Christmas in New York, my mother, Zeida and Doña Sarah, Marcia's mother, were also to be with us, and we all enjoyed a very special holiday season. Life was good.

1979, a new year! Early January, I received an extraordinary invitation. The Stuttgart Ballet, one of the world's most prestigious ensembles, had been founded by legendary choreographer, John Cranko. After Cranko's death, the company was currently led by one of the most distinguished ballerinas of the 20th century, Marcia Haydee, who had been Cranko's muse and inspiration and lead ballerina for most of his works. The company was filled with incredible dancers and artists... one of the best, her notable partner Richard Cragun; the sensational Egon Madsen, whose acting was supreme; and, the exquisite Birgit Keil blessed with the ideal ballerina's body. It was with Birgit that I was invited to perform in John Cranko's full-length version of "Swan Lake."

The depth of the Stuttgart artists, of their repertoire, made the company a unique repository of talent and it was a privilege to be with them in classes and rehearsals. Add to that a wonderful Opera House, a jewel in the heart of a city. From the beginning I loved Cranko's version and the ballerina I was dancing with. The chemistry Birgit and I developed allowed us to go into the performance with a confidence that made the night unforgettable. The two of us took countless curtain calls, and the audience was quite pleased.

On this particular night the Opera House was holding its highly popular "Opernball," or huge party. In a split second the entire theater becomes decorated with flowers and balloons everywhere. Musicians appear in the balconies, food kiosks fill the theater and the audience, having just seen the end of a ballet performance, suddenly participates in an elegant and colorful fund-raising Gala. The party begins and everyone has a great time.

Then one of the corps dancers came to me with an unusual request: *"Would I share a dance with his girlfriend, a young dancer from the school who happened to be a big fan of mine?... her name was Maria."* He had made a bet with her he could get me to meet her, since she was embarrassed to do it herself. And I ended my stay in Stuttgart dancing with a girl named Maria. The following day **Heinz-Ludwig Schneiders** of **The Stuttgarter Nachrichten** wrote:

***"A Superstar ... Bujones is one of the best technicians in the world ... every step, every pose and every jump is executed with the same value that won him a "Gold Medal" in Varna, Bulgaria in 1974 ... He earned an enthusiastic response from his colleagues as well as the public ... and to sum it all up Bujones conquered Stuttgart by storm."***

As usual, I returned to ABT to perform with my regular partners. It is not easy to find a good partner. So many things have to come together just right, and so many things can go wrong while dancing with a partner. It can make or break your performance! But from the very beginning, from my very early first steps in Cuba, I was taught in order to be a good partner, you also need to make your ballerina shine. By now I had seen some legendary partnerships -- Melissa Hayden and Jacques D'Amboise, Lupe Serrano and Royes Fernandez, Eleanor D'Antuono and Ted Kivitt, Carla Fracci and Erik Bruhn, Marcia Haydee and Richard Cragun, and Margot and Rudolf. This was magic of the highest order!

By April, 1979, ABT was getting ready for the Kennedy Center season in Washington. I was scheduled for my first full- length ballet of the season and it was to be "Swan Lake" with Cynthia Gregory! They were going to try me with Cynthia in Washington to see if it works. If it doesn't, I wouldn't get to do it during our summer season at the Met in New York City.

Cynthia already had great reviews for her "Swan Lake"; so now it was up to me to see if I could partner her. Everybody had their doubts, even Cynthia. I confess that it took me a little while to gain enough confidence to dance with Cynthia in "Swan Lake." But I got so excited, I knew I could do this. Her technique and her style are very similar to mine. However, with her incredible technique and her magnificent balances, she was much easier to partner than so many others! She was already being acclaimed as one of the great Odile-Odettes of our times and had her interpretation all worked out. So I just went along and let myself follow her every move, match her beautiful lines, react to all her actions. If she got excited, I got excited; if she got tender, I got tender. I kept my concentration totally focused on her at all times, on her range of emotions. Technically, the choreography suited us both marvelously, so it was a matter of projecting our feelings through the dance.

*Cynthia Gregory Remembers:*

*"Our first Swan Lake together at Kennedy Center was going to be a test for Fernando to see if we really could be paired. I remember thinking then we were very well matched... I felt a bit tall but I felt I was strong enough and felt he was strong enough. By then his partnering had gotten so much better, and he was determined, you know, really determined to do it. He had a confidence about him that permeated all our rehearsals. Again, we worked things out together and it was... I remember, it was good; it was not extraordinary, but it had potential... that's what it had.."*

In a partnership, it is not the age, the height, the weight, or the look that can define the extraordinary rapport between two artists. In dance a partnership either clicks or it does not. As partners, Cynthia and I clicked! We had the right chemistry on stage. Our first Swan Lake together in Washington worked out, so we would get to dance it again together on tour, in San Francisco.

*Cynthia Gregory Remembers:*

*"By the time we got to San Francisco, we had gotten used to each other. There are two legendary performances, to me, that I did with Fernando -- they were both Swan Lakes. One was in San Francisco and the other was in New York at the Met. There were so many other fantastic performances, but I remember those two so well because the audiences went absolutely crazy in the middle of the performances. Usually they go crazy at the end, but to have them standing up and cheering in the middle, that was different!*

*There was something that happened that night... and it happened to us too, and it just... I can't explain it, but everything went with absolute perfection... more than just perfection, there was this electrifying chemistry that happened, with the music suddenly pulling us in; we started feeling the passion. We had the lines, we had the technique, but it wasn't just the technique... that we could do the myriad of difficult steps that make Swan Lake such a challenging role to dance. It was also the way we were reacting to each other on stage, the way we were telling the story... I became Odette / Odile and Fernando became my Prince and the drama of the story overtook us... We were both on the same emotional wave and whatever we were feeling, it connected with the audience in a tremendous way, and they lifted us... it was such an incredible feeling..."*

Cynthia and I were cast together again, this time in the full-length "Sleeping Beauty!" This performance was being taped for a "Live from Lincoln Center" broadcast and after it aired, the ballet world started talking about Gregory and Bujones together! We both loved to challenge each other on stage and tried to best one another! It was such fun and so exciting to dance with her.

*Cynthia Remembers:*

*"In the beginning, I used to hold back a bit with Fernando. For example, when I had to do an arabesque-penche, you know, I would do it, but I would not throw myself into it. But by now, I could. He had worked so hard, he knew me so well. It had to do a lot with musicality, which he and I felt the same about. He knew when I would do something, he felt it with me, so he was always there for me, he was always strong, so secure in his ability, in his talent, but always giving of himself. Such a generous partner, really, you know... he really was..."*

During ABT's season at the Met, I also got to dance "Themes and Variations" the "Diana & Acteon" pas de deux, "Fancy Free" and James in "La Sylphide." Then a fascinating new role came up for me. I was cast as Jean, the Butler, in "Miss Julie." As a student I had seen this ballet with Toni Lander and Bruce Marks and had heard of Erik Bruhn's terrific interpretation.

Lucia Wayne, a friend and faithful balletomane had an extensive collection of ballet films, (she used to sneak into the second balcony at Met with her tiny super 8 camera and film every performance of her favorite dancers) offered to lend me a copy of Bruhn's performance in Miss Julie. Every night, for an entire week, I'd play the film on my super 8mm projector against a white wall in my room until I knew Jean the Butler inside out. Kristine Elliott, another of ABT's principal dancers, beautiful ballerina and a wonderful friend, was to be my Miss Julie. The company rehearsals started and we learned the choreography.

Then Zeida, Kristine and I went to work. We discussed Strindberg's play thoroughly, analyzing the characters until we really understood every movement of Birgit Cullberg's choreography and how they related to the Strindberg's play. We worked on small details that would give our two characters definition. I did not want to be a Bruhn carbon copy, but wanted to create my own interpretation. We would rehearse first with Zeida all our sequences together, and then join the company for the group rehearsals. Kristine's Julie made it simple and very special for me. She was just so perfect for the role. On May 26, 1979, **Clive Barnes** of the **New York Post**, reviewing my New York debut in "Miss Julie," wrote:

> ***"...American Ballet Theater's Fernando Bujones is, together with Anthony Dowell, the company's peak of princes, its ideal of classicism. Yet last night at the Metropolitan Opera House, Bujones was jumping clear out of type-casting. He was quite extraordinary as Jean, the viciously intent Butler, in Birgit Cullberg's somewhat turgid, and even unnecessary, balleticisation - should that be a word of Strindberg's bitter psychodrama Miss Julie. It was Erik Bruhn who gave the role character - gave it the dimensions of a Strindberg sightseer at a Strindberg event. Bujones cool and rough, made this figure of fantasy and death, into a reality of arrogant machismo."***

Right after the Met season, I flew to London and joined the Scottish Ballet for their week at Sadler's Wells, dancing James in their production of "La Sylphide" with Scottish ballerina Elaine McDonald, whom the London critics called "...*Scottish Ballet's resident jewel...*" As always, I enjoyed that role enormously, and on August 31, **Clement Crisp**, of **The London Financial Times** wrote:

> ***"...whether taking to the air in light, expansive jumps–he looks as if he needs twice the stage space to do his style real justice – or extending his pure, taut line, or beating beautifully sharp entrechats, he is a danseur noble of the grandest abilities."***

In early January, 1980, I made my debut with the Tokyo Ballet partnering Noella Pontois, in the full-length "Sleeping Beauty." Aside from my regular ABT schedule, new, exciting guest engagements were increasing each year.

In March, Marcia and I traveled to Munich for three performances of Cranko's full-length "Swan Lake," partnering American ballerina, Joyce Cuoco. In Munich, Marcia and I befriended the nicest Germans who drove us around the Bavarian landscapes to show us some of the most beautiful lakes and castles of the region. King Ludwig of Bavaria had been good friends with composer Richard Wagner and was fascinated with castles. During his reign, three of the most exquisite Bavarian castles were built including Neuschwanstein, the one that Walt Disney used as a model to create his own castle at Disneyland's Magic Kingdom!

After Munich I performed "Giselle" in Caracas, Venezuela at the beautiful Teresa Carreño Theater with Zhandra Rodriguez, a friend and ABT principal dancer.

All these guesting engagements were sandwiched between my scheduled performances with ABT. Zeida kept my performing calendar and travel schedule, which was getting pretty full. These international guest appearances were having a positive effect on my dancing and also gave Zeida more leverage during her negotiations for my yearly contracts with ABT.

Then, much to my disbelief, some critics in America started writing that I was *"...sacrificing an exceptional artistic talent in favor of mere superstardom."*

But no matter how much they tried to criticize me, I never gave up. I never stopped believing in myself. I can only be so thankful I had the opportunity to dance with so many different ballerinas, with so many different and wonderful dance companies! Each and every one of those performances helped me grow artistically, as a dancer and as a man. I can never be grateful enough for having been able to share my dancing with so many different audiences, step on so many wonderful stages, in so many different roles!

I joined ABT again for their New York season at the Met, and this time I would be appearing in all of ABT's full-length productions of their traditional classics. The warm ovations from the audiences were my greatest motivation. On March 7, 1980, **Clive Barnes** from **The New York Post** wrote:

> ***"...Fernando Bujones is a star already risen. Despite his youth -- he is 25 -- Bujones is one of the great male dancers of the 20th century. His technique is possibly unmatched anywhere. His style is a growing awareness of the joy of dancing... On Monday night this eighth wonder of the ballet world danced in Balanchine's Glinka Pas de Trois. The man performed like a dancer's living dream."***

On May 15, **Anna Kisselgoff of The New York Times** reviewed my Don Quixote performance at The Met:

> ***"...Mr. Bujones has been dancing with extraordinary new power. It erupts into a dance image that bursts out with no reference to anything but its own dazzle... Mr. Bujones's jump is higher than ever and his various air turns simply caused pandemonium in the theater... It is always a sign of a dancer's value when the faces of other dancers light up when he comes on stage."***

And on May 26 she reviewed my performance of "La Bayadere":

> ***"...Mr. Bujones was absolutely peerless -- as he has been all season -- in the dancing. To see Mr. Bujones on stage is simply to see a dancer execute complicated steps and movements seen nowhere else in New York this season and to see them done with unmatched power and precision."***

For sure the most arduous artistic challenge for me during that Met season came when I was cast in "Le Spectre de la Rose," the greatest dancing role in the celebrated career of Vaslav Nijinsky. Actually I was asked if I wanted to dance in the revival, and I said yes. This role required technical strength and brutal stamina, but also an unusual softness in the upper body. Even Zeida, my own coach, was not totally convinced this ballet would suit me. Still, I began to question if this might not be a mistake?

The night of the performance, the curtain went up and I made my first entrance in the famous "grand jeté" through the window. There was total silence! I knew I had given the jump of my life, and yet there was no customary applause like an audience usually gives to acknowledge the artist's first entrance. I was concerned, but kept on going. The next day, June 16, 1980, **Barton Wimble**, in **The New York Daily News**, wrote:

***Spectre is a Splendor...***

> ***"...Fernando Bujones received the ovation of his career and probably a great deal of satisfaction when he danced his first Spectre de la Rose Friday during an all-Fokine evening at Ballet Theater. Spectre is an elusive work to bring off. Not only is it a non-stop challenge for even the most accomplished dancer, the essential quality of androgynous athleticism is the keystone to the success of the eight minute work. Of the three famous dancers New York has recently seen, only Bujones really fits the otherworldly quality demanded by Fokine. Nureyev is fussy and somehow very literal, and Baryshnikov, for all his enormous stage skill, is simply too healthy and solid."***

The most incredible Met season for me was coming to an end and the best was yet to come. The last performance was to be the full-length "Swan Lake" with Cynthia Gregory. We had already performed it, once in Washington and again on tour at the San Francisco Opera House and both the audience, as well as our ABT colleagues, called that performance "one in a lifetime" where some incredible spontaneous things happened. We both agreed there was no way we could match it. Still we wanted to give our New York audiences something to remember us by. This was New York City, our home town, home of our biggest fans, and we did manage to produce some very exciting moments. Euphoria is the word that comes to my mind as we finished the "Black Swan" Pas de Deux.

**Anna Kisselgoff's** review in **The New York Times** June 27, 1980, read as follows:

> ***"Cynthia Gregory and Fernando Bujones made their first appearance in American Ballet Theater's "Swan Lake" Wednesday night at the Metropolitan Opera House much to the delight of an audience that gave them one of the most exuberant standing ovations of the season. Ballet's version of pandemonium broke loose after their Black Swan Pas de Deux in the third act. Spectators of all ages leaped up, waved their programs and simply roared. It was a spontaneous reaction and obviously dancers that can excite a public that much, have a special line of communication to an audience."***

ABT's 1980 summer season was finishing on the highest note. Now it was time for Marcia and me. We had been a couple for 4 years and had lived together the last two, so it was time to make it official. I had already proposed to Marcia twice, and twice she put me off, saying that we were already as good as married. She was also concerned about her previous divorce and the fact she had two young daughters. I guess the third time was a charm, or she just got tired of me not taking no for an answer. She finally said "yes" and made me the happiest man in the world.

We were legally married on June 8, 1980. Zeida and Christina were our maids of honor and the late Joseph Rogosik, a longtime friend of the Kubitschek family, much loved by all of us, was our best man. We had a private ceremony at home and celebrated the occasion over dinner at a gourmet Brazilian restaurant owned by a family friend, with our closest family members and friends. Marcia's mother, Doña Sarah flew from Brazil, my father from Miami, and the three ballerinas I performed with the most at ABT, Cynthia Gregory, Natalia Makarova and Marianna Tcherkassky joined us with their husbands for the dinner celebration.

After dinner Marcia and I escaped from the rest of the family and that night we lived it up in one of New York's finest hotels. Because of my upcoming schedule, we agreed to delay our honeymoon.

At the end of June, following the end of the ABT season, Marcia, Christina, Julia and I headed south to Rio de Janeiro for some weeks of rest and recreation and to be together with the rest of the family in Brazil.

In August 1980, I returned alone to New York City, leaving Marcia in Brazil to handle some family matters. Shortly thereafter, I boarded a flight to the Philippines, where I had been invited to perform with Yoko Morishita in another full-length "Swan Lake" and invited my mother to join me. When we landed at the airport in Manila, Gladys Celeste, ABT's favorite and beloved pianist, herself from the Philippines, was there to receive us. It was she who had arranged our performances there! Gladys had become a special friend to me, and I was delighted and thankful to her for arranging the opportunity for me to dance there and get to know her beautiful country. The company's Board of Directors and all the dancers were there too with a huge banner that read:

***Welcome Yoko Morishita & Fernando Bujones: Mabuhay!***

This country, made up of more than three thousand islands, is a historically rich land. One of the most spectacular experiences in my life was the helicopter ride around the islands.

After an hour's ride, the pilot stopped the helicopter in mid air and we descended onto a large concrete platform. We walked down a few rocky steps towards the edge of the island's beach. There was a gorgeous open-style bamboo home, and I was told it belonged to the ballet company's President of the Board. It was on this private island that about five of us were invited to lunch. *"Wow!"* I thought, *"Not a bad place for lunch!"*

Next, I traveled to Verona, Italy to dance in a gala the Pas de Deux from "Le Corsaire" with ballerina Noella Pontois. The roster of ballet stars was impressive, with Vladimir Vassiliev, Ekaterina Maximova, Carla Fracci, Paolo Bortoluzzi and others.

Especially memorable that night at the Arena, when the last lights of the day start to fade, the thousands of people in the audience light up small candles. From backstage we could see this amazing moving wave of tiny lights flickering in the dark. Then, just as the music started, everyone simultaneously blew out their candles. Then the stage lights were turned on and the night belonged to the dancers. Noella and I were totally inspired by our surroundings! When we struck our last pose, the audience was in a total frenzy, and they would not let us go. They wanted us to do an encore! Fortunately a very slight drizzle began, and we moved on so other dancers could continue and we did not have to do the encore! From Verona I went to join my wife for a much-awaited honeymoon in one of the most romantic cities in the world, Venice.

CHAPTER 14

# *The End of an Era*

After only a year and a half, Mikhail Baryshnikov had not been as successful at the New York City Ballet as everyone thought he would be.

All through the summer the rumors were everywhere that a change in artistic direction at ABT was in the works; and though in front of the curtain the company continued to perform well, the turmoil behind the curtain was inescapable.

It was no secret after Baryshnikov defected and joined Ballet Theater, ABT's Board of Directors started to change. Some of the older, more faithful members began to leave, and gradually a new group took their places, steering the company down different paths. ABT was going to be "modernized!" This past season at the Met would be Lucia's last. The company got a new Executive Director as well. By September, 1980, ABT had a new Artistic Director, Mikhail Baryshnikov. Lucia Chase had been replaced!

Everyone knew ABT was Lucia's life. She had given everything of herself, her fortune and her family to develop and sustain a company that flourished and made history throughout the almost 40 years she was at the helm. We knew she would never quit on her own and wondered whether she was forced to step down or talked into retiring. Suddenly there was an honorary gala for the founding directors, Lucia Chase and Oliver Smith; shortly after, the change in artistic direction took place. ABT's Board of Directors named Mikhail Baryshnikov as the company's new artistic director and made Lucia resign. Not long after that, she suffered a paralysis that eventually led to her death. Lucia was truly one of a kind, and I shared with many others the grief of knowing she was no longer with us. We all believe she died of a broken heart.

*Cynthia Gregory Remembers:*

*"The night when the Board decided to get rid of Lucia Chase and put Misha in as director, Fernando and I were dancing the full-length Don Quixote. We got a message backstage from the Executive Director that he would like to come and talk to the two of us for a minute between the second and third act... As we were getting ready for the curtain to open, Herman Krawitz came backstage directly to us and said he didn't want us to read it in the paper the next morning, but he was telling us, now of all times, during a performance, that Lucia Chase was no longer the director, and Mikhail Baryshnikov was being appointed as the new director.*

*"He also knew quite well that decision was a very controversial and unpopular one among the dancers, yet he chose this moment to tell the two of us about it. It was the worse thing he could have done to us as dancers, to the entire company, disrupting our concentration, our emotions, ... That's how insensitive he was to what dancers felt, to their emotional well-being, but again, it was so typical of what was happening at ABT by then... Fernando and I finished the full-length Don Quixote like zombies that night... wondering what lay ahead..."*

Sometime later, writing in the ABT Program Book, Baryshnikov tried to justify the upheavals that followed his appointment: *"It is not without some anxious moments that I became ABT's artistic director in September, 1980. Ballet Theatre had flourished for 35 years under the guidance of Lucia Chase and Oliver Smith and I doubt there was ever a more accomplished act to follow. I found myself in the ironic position of having to direct the same dancers who only months before had treated me as a peer and wondered if one of their own would now be able to lead them into ABT's fifth and most challenging decade."*

First of all, he never treated us as his peers nor encouraged us to treat him as a peer. Secondly, he was anything but a leader and rarely inspired any following or devotion from the dancers. He had his own small group with their own separate agenda and now this group was at the helm of the company. They were almost a separate entity from the company, which they intended to use as a backdrop to promote Baryshnikov and their personal interests. What concerned the rest of the dancers most was the new direction the company was taking. Those were the thoughts on everyone's minds that September, 1980. Then at the dancers' requests, a meeting was held between the company's new Executive director, Herman Krawitz and a substantial number of company dancers. On the day of the meeting, I asked Cynthia Gregory if she was planning to come and she answered *"I don't know; I don't know if it is going to make any difference."*

That evening at the meeting, principal dancers Martine van Hamel, Cynthia Harvey and Kirk Petersen were present as were many others; Cynthia Gregory, then ABT's foremost ballerina who represented ABT's legacy at its best, did not attend. Herman Krawitz tried explaining why the Board of Directors had appointed Baryshnikov. One dancer asked if any other candidates had been considered? Mr. Krawitz said the Board felt Baryshnikov would be the best candidate for the job and others had been approached, but they had not expressed any interest. Then I asked Krawitz, *"What other candidates have been considered or approached? ... was Erik Bruhn, Lupe Serrano or Eleanor D'Antuono or any of the other former Ballet Theater principals asked if they were interested?... They are reputable artists that have a history with the company and a profound knowledge of ABT's tradition and style."* Without blinking an eye Mr. Kravitz said *"Yes! They were approached and were not interested."*

I went on... *"And what about Nurey....?* Before I could finish Mr. Krawitz interrupted me with his own sharp question, *"Mr. Bujones were you not along with other dancers in a luncheon the other day with the company's president, Mr. Kendall, at his home and did you not speak with him and have a good time?"* I replied, *"Yes, but what does that have to do with ..?"* and for the second time Mr. Krawitz stopped me short: *"Thank you very much! Next."* And that was the end of the matter.

The meeting failed to ease the tensions between the dancers and the new administration. We all wondered who was Herman Krawitz, what did he know about ballet and specifically about American Ballet Theater? As it turned out, he was a music promoter and was now associated with the production of two television specials titled: "Baryshnikov on Broadway" and "Baryshnikov in Hollywood" as well as Baryshnikov's other outside interests. During the meeting, Kirk Petersen, another principal dancer, specifically voiced his concern as to why Baryshnikov was not the best choice for Artistic Director. It did not take long for Kirk to be fired. By the end of the meeting, it was clear to the dancers the Board of Directors and the Executive Director had their own agenda. They had made their decision a while ago and nothing was going to stop them. Now they wanted to make ABT behave like the New York City Ballet, where only one star was allowed to shine and it was going to be Baryshnikov.

The traditional ABT classical repertory started gradually fading out, as well as the dancers that were most familiar with it. New choreographers were being invited to create works for Baryshnikov, mostly smaller, modern works. The dancers had to adapt to the new repertory or leave. And that is what many of them did.

Because of our supposed dance rivalry, there were people who thought the moment Baryshnikov came back to ABT I would be out of there. But that thought had never crossed my mind. I had been a member of ABT long before Baryshnikov joined, and now after eight years with the company, I knew more than ever that ABT was where I belonged.

But the changes didn't stop with Lucia's removal. Now Enrique Martinez, Lucia's Assistant Director, company regisseur and artistically the person closest to her, suddenly also left. His place was taken over by Charles France, who worked at the ABT office. After Baryshnikov's arrival, Charles became his personal assistant and was officially appointed as Assistant to the Artistic Director. Charles France also had his own private agenda. All of a sudden, he was in charge of the press, and in control of public relations for the company. He started participating in the casting meetings! The few full-length classics that remained, the staple of ABT's repertoire, the difference between City Ballet and ABT, and the reason for audiences to buy tickets to see us, ended up with casts of young newcomers and Misha's favorites, rapidly promoted with no real experience or preparation and far from ready for the major roles, much to the detriment of their future careers. With more arbitrary departures of some of ABT's best dancers, the company started going down a very different road.

So I took off again, and in November I traveled to Mexico City for my debut with the Mexican National Dance Company at their glorious Teatro Bellas Artes in the full-length "Coppelia" plus the "Don Quixote" Pas de Deux partnering their leading ballerina, a firecracker named Susana Benavides.

By the end of 1980, the company had gone through an incredible roster change. Gone were names like Ivan Nagy, Ted Kivitt, Eleanor D'Antuono, John Prinz, Nannette Glushak, Sallie Wilson, Christine Sarry, Zhandra Rodriguez, Karena Brock, Gayle Young, Dennis Nahat, Ernie Horvath, Rhodi Jorgenssen, Jonas Kage, John Meehan, Kirk Peterson, Yoko Ichino, Johan Renvall and so many, many others. These were not only excellent dancers in their own right, but they had the knowledge and depth of ABT's repertoire. They were artists who had contributed much to ABT's rich history and its reputation. These were dancers I looked up to when I joined ABT in 1972. They should have continued their association with ABT in one way or another. The company was gradually losing its identity, its repertoire and its core dancers. Time would tell what the future would bring, but for the moment I wasn't going to walk away from the company I wanted to continue being a part of.

Other Russian and East block defectors started coming in, thinking that once a fellow Russian was at the helm of this magnificent American company, they would also be welcomed. They joined as teachers and dancers, such as Sasha Goudonov and Alexander Minz, Elena Tchernicheva and Jurgen Schneider; but in less than two years, they too were gone.

January, 1981, and ABT is starting the year on tour in Miami. I will be dancing "Giselle" with Cynthia Gregory, and continue with the company to Los Angeles. But the top priority for that year was my debut with the Ballet of the Paris Opera in the full- length production of "La Sylphide" dancing with Noella Pontois at the Theatre des Champs Elysees. This was a very happy occasion for me.

Rudolf Nureyev was in town, too, since he was also guesting with the company and sharing the lead in the same ballet. It was nice to see him again in classes and rehearsals and the two of us enjoyed each other's company. I learned I was the first American male dancer to ever perform as a guest artist with the Paris Opera Ballet company and by coincidence I would be dancing with them during the week of my birthday. Partnering Noella was such a treat. She is the incarnation of the romantic French ballerina, like a small jewel case. Small but perfectly proportioned, extremely feminine, delicate in her gestures but with a strong clear technique, she was very easy to partner and very secure in her romantic style. She was also very considerate of me, knowing it was the first time I had to deal with such a huge production where I had to dance constantly and her help and encouragement were of great importance to me. I happen to love Paris, I love French history, French art, and had great respect and admiration for many of the legendary and contemporary French dancers. And now I was here myself. This was another childhood dream come true.

I danced four back-to-back performances of this very demanding version of "La Sylphide." This was the version choreographed and staged by the French choreographer, Pierre Lacotte. Rosella Hightower, the famed ballerina, and at the time the company's artistic director, had warned me I was in for a big surprise and she wasn't kidding. Nothing was the same! The choreography was different, the music was different! In any case, I managed to learn and perform the entire new work in a week's time and survive the marathon dancing of the gigantic production.

Right after the performance on March 9, my birthday, I was surprised with a huge cake and those wonderful French dancers sang happy birthday in French and made me feel right at home. I will always remember the nice rapport I developed with the French dancers. I celebrated my twenty-sixth birthday with an inspiring company and the French press gave me a gift of their own: Jacqueline Cartier of the France Soir newspaper wrote:

***"Fernando Bujones: un nouveau Noureev"***

Marcia, my mom, and Zeida were with me and I couldn't be happier. If I had to be compared to someone else, (though I have my reservations about comparisons) I was honored that my dancing was praised in Paris at the level of my long-time mentor and hero, Rudolf Nureyev, who was worshiped in France.

My career continued moving forward thanks to the many guesting invitations that kept coming in. I performed for the first time with the Ballet of La Scala in Milano, and the Ballet Estable of the Teatro Colon in Buenos Aires, Argentina. Now, more than ever, I was not about to refuse to perform the classical masterpieces, partnering outstanding ballerinas with top world-class dance companies. At ABT, this opportunity was moving further and further away.

From Paris, Marcia, mom and Zeida continued with me on our way to Stuttgart.. We took the train so we could see some of Europe's countryside, but it also gave me some time to relax. We loaded up with lots of food, books, and magazines. I had my tape player and listened to the Prokofiev score the entire time!

I was to dance the lead in John Cranko's production of "Romeo and Juliet," to perform with none other than Cranko's muse herself! Marcia Haydee was one of the great artists in the ballet world, already a legend in her own time. Her extraordinary interpretations in "Taming of the Shrew," "Onegin," "Tristan and Isolde" and other roles made her one of the most renowned dramatic ballerinas of our time. I had already danced "Romeo" in Anthony Tudor's version for ABT with Hilda Morales as my Juliet, with Tudor himself coaching me extensively in the role, so I had my own idea of what "Romeo" was all about. The Prokofiev music for Romeo and Juliet has been familiar to me since I was an 11 year old and saw for the first time the film with Nureyev and Fonteyn dancing the leading roles in the Kenneth McMillan version, which I knew by heart and adored.

We arrived in Stuttgart and Marcia and Richard Cragun came to pick us up at the train station and took us to our hotel. During rehearsals I mentioned to Marcia I was still not the most experienced partner when it came to the difficulty of Cranko ballets, which were full of beautiful but complex lifts. She put a hand on my shoulder and said, *"Oh don't worry, I'll help you lift me and I won't let you drop me, because if I see myself going down, I will hang on to any part of your body and you will fall first!"* Her coaching and especially her confidence in me were to be the essential factors in my ability to dance the role properly or not.

The company was, of course, thoroughly familiar with the work. All the main characters, as well as the corps, were superb in their roles. They functioned as one and once they were on stage they became one incredible dance ensemble. The feeling one gets in such an environment is very different from what was happening at ABT, which by now was a very disjointed and unhappy company, with new dancers thrown prematurely into roles with no real understanding of what they were doing. With the European companies I always got the feeling I became part of these already formed and mature ensembles and I could easily let myself go emotionally and just breathe in what they were giving and sharing with me. They made me feel totally secure and my dancing became so much easier because of it.

Finally opening night came, and I had adrenaline running through my veins. Mom, Zeida, and my Marcia were seated in the second box, first tier at the theater with the best view of the stage, close to the action.

The ballet is based on Shakespeare's tale of the Monteques and the Capulets, whose families are absolute enemies. As the curtain opens, I am on stage with my friends, looking for mischief. Pretty soon we decide to attend a party held by Juliet's family to which we have not been invited, and we create havoc! But when Juliet comes in for the first time, my attention is immediately diverted to her. I was secure in my dancing, and comfortable with the choreography. But I was not prepared for what happened next.

As Juliet makes her first entrance, I almost could not recognize Marcia Haydee. Standing in front of me was a very attractive woman, sensuous and somewhat shy but instantly attracted to me. I could feel her vibrations. As the scene develops, I remember reacting to her, more and more, until I was totally fascinated by her transformation. She was no longer Marcia Haydee, ballerina; she was Juliet and she was reaching for the deepest feelings inside of me. And without realizing it, I started responding to her. I could feel myself doing the steps as rehearsed, but I was being drawn by a current of emotions I had rarely felt before. Her touch, her body and all of herself became an ardent, passionate love. When I held her in my arms she made me truly believe I was Romeo, I was the man she wanted and from now on no external force could separate us. This woman wanted me, needed me and through her dancing, made me know it. And I just let myself go.

*Zeida Remembers:*

*"I had just bought a brand new Leica camera with a set of the best lenses available because I was planning to photograph the performance. I was ready with the camera on its tripod. When the performance started I managed to shoot a couple of pictures, but then Juliet appeared. Marcia Haydee was no longer the dancer I had seen during rehearsals, nor the funny person and raccounteur she was during our nights when she and Richard Cragun would take us to the different restaurants around the city. She had become someone else. She must have been at*

*least twenty years older than Fernando, who was then twenty six, but what started happening on stage between the two of them got to me in such a way that I ended up forgetting my camera and totally focusing on the performance.*

*"Here was an older woman in love with a younger man and she was inciting him, asking him to love her despite their differences, clawing at him, begging him to stay with her and not to let her go. This was not just your regular Romeo and Juliet story and it was fascinating to see the drama unfold on stage. Fernando's reactions to her were raw, natural and spontaneous. You could see the range of his feelings as he responded to her. This was not just dancing. Marcia Haydee's physical presence, her body going through the most incredible motions during those beautiful Cranko's lifts was magic and Fernando's reactions and partnering reached a level where he had not been before. This was terrific theater taking place that night. I got so emotional that sometimes I could feel tears choking my throat. I finally turned off my camera and just sat there, taking in the most memorable performance I ever saw Fernando dance."*

The next day **Eberhard Layer**, dance critic for **The Stuttgarter Zeitung** wrote:

> ***"Fernando Bujones took up the artistic challenge presented by the Stuttgart ballerina and reacted in his own way. Taking advantage of his solo part in the second act, he demonstrated his breathtaking elevation and, with his perfect arabesques, revealed his status as one of the leading classical dancers of our time, also proving himself as a reliable partner to Haydee. His dancing was masterful, impeccable – at the same time, he did not forget, however, to develop the character of his part in a logical and consequent way. At first a more reserved, rather juvenile, very sensitive Romeo, he then convincingly turned, as the story progressed, into a passionate and eventually tragic lover."***

To be on stage with Marcia Haydee was one of the most enlightening experiences of my career. And having the company's brilliant dancer-actor

Egon Madsen as Mercutio was the icing on the cake! In Europe, dance is not separated from theater. The Europeans use their sets, costumes and lights to create atmosphere, and for me that is very important.

During our second scheduled performance an unexpected incident made the performance unforgettable for me. I had rehearsed the dueling scene with Thybalt to exhaustion. Thanks to Egon Madsen's remarkable coaching, I was becoming a rather good swordsman and my fencing with Thybalt felt and looked quite right. However, towards the end of the duel, as I'm getting ready to kill him, my sword broke off leaving only a small piece in my hand. The audience gasped! I still remember Thybalt's face when he looked at me trying to hide a smile, and my uncontrollable desire to laugh; but without losing a music count, I looked at my broken sword for a split second, pretended that my weapon was a knife and I lunged at him as ferociously as I could! Thybalt jumped off to one side, and throwing his own sword aside, jumped to grab my hand with the knife, at which time, I thrust it under his arm and "killed him" in the most unceremonious way! Believe it or not, at that point, the audience erupted in applause! They all approved of the way we had covered up the problem with the faulty sword.

I returned a second time to the Vienna State Opera, dancing the full-length "Don Quixote" and "Swan Lake"; went on to The Munich Opera House, to the Ballet Nacional de Mexico at Bellas Artes in Mexico City, and to the Municipal Theater in Rio de Janeiro, Brazil. Add ABT to this performing calendar, and I had one very busy performing schedule

By spring of 1981, I was back with ABT for the New York Met season. I would be dancing a new version of "Raymonda" with Cynthia, a full "Swan Lake" again with her, a full-length "La Bayadere" with Natasha and a "Giselle" again with my extraordinary partner, Cynthia Gregory. Here was a role that in the past had presented me with some artistic challenges, but now I felt I was finding a technical and artistic balance in my interpretation. That performance won me one of the best reviews ever when **Anna Kisselgoff** of **The New York Times** on Sunday, May 3, 1981 wrote:

> ***"Bujones reaches New Heights: There are times when technical prowess in a dancer is so astounding and unprecedented that even artistry must momentarily take second place. Fernando Bujones provided this kind of brief but unforgettable, even unbelievable, moment within the current***

***"Giselle" marathon the American Ballet Theater is presenting at the Metropolitan Opera House. The clue that something extraordinary was in the works came in his main solo as Albrecht in Act II... This added excitement paled, however, by the series of leg beats, or entrechats, he introduced into the coda. Could any dancer ever have jumped so high? Each time he reached higher and higher, until he seemed to hang more than four feet above the ground. This suspension and exceptional height allowed him to increase the number of leg beats--at least entrechat-huits. It is the kind of feat one reads about but never sees and one that has, one suspects, never really been seen before. The audience reacted with all-American enthusiasm, with individual yelps and a cry of "Go." It might be argued that such virtuosity would be out of line in "Giselle." Yet the point of Mr. Bujones' performance with Cynthia Gregory's Giselle on Thursday night was its artistic totality. This was the most mature and finished Albrecht he has shown."***

Thanks to all my international performances and the opportunities they gave me, I felt I was at a point in my career where technique and artistic maturity were getting closer; I was starting to feel more at ease with my characters. After that "Giselle" performance at The Met in 1981, even Artistic Director Baryshnikov came backstage to congratulate me.

After the 1981 Met season, Cynthia and I received an invitation to perform at the Teatro Colon, in Argentina. We chose to do "Grand Pas Classique" and the pas de deux from "Diane & Acteon" as well as two full-length performances of "Giselle." The audiences at Teatro Colón gave Cynthia and me some of the most incredible ovations I can remember. The Argentineans are great music connoisseurs, opera and ballet lovers with a huge tradition of bringing the best artists to their country and we were happy to receive their warm and enthusiastic reception.

In October, I rejoined ABT for their smaller late autumn tour; and then, by the end of November, I was again in Mexico City and Teatro Bellas Artes with Susana Benavides. On the early morning of the dress rehearsal I discovered the stage at Bellas Artes has a raked floor. It was freezing, and the altitude of Mexico City was making me a bit more tired than usual. I started my variation, but the moment I landed from the first cabriole, I knew something was wrong. I felt a sharp pain in my left foot, as if someone had hammered a nail into the side of my left ankle.

By the time I got to the dressing room the ankle was the size of a lemon. I iced the swollen ankle the rest of that day and night. The next morning the swelling was down some and I could even put the foot down, so I thought maybe I could dance! I began to shift all my big jumps to the opposite side, so I could land on my healthy leg and changed the choreography with other jumps and turns.

I still was able to do all my variations, but to the weaker side. Some of the steps were not as strong as I was used to; still I was able to do all four performances and no one noticed anything wrong! At the end of the four shows, we had a grand dinner to celebrate, and I was even convinced to try my first and only ever shot of tequila!

The success of my previous performances in Paris at the Theater of the Champs Elysees brought a second invitation, again with Noella Pontois in Nureyev's full-length "Don Quixote." This time the performances were to take place at the magnificent Theatre de L'Opera, best known as Palais de Garnier, or the Paris Opera. And so December found us back in Paris with Marcia, Christina, Julia, Zeida and mom; traveling with my harem, as I jokingly called my family, performing for the first time in that grandest of all theaters, the grand dame of the world's opera houses, the most beautiful in the world, especially at night. That was as special as it could ever get for anyone.

We had decided to stay in Paris until New Year's Eve. That night Marcia suggested we all go to a small Russian nightclub, which had been very fashionable in the early 1950's. By now the place was not as glamorous as it had been, but we still piled into a taxicab to see a middle-aged Russian singer, with excessive make-up and a worn-out costume held with safety pins on her back, singing sad Russian songs, while we had blinis and caviar! Celebrating Christmas in Paris with my family made that particular holiday season one of my most cherished memories. After midnight, we took a taxi back to our hotel, and found out that Marcia's wallet, with all her money, was missing! We flagged down another taxi and rushed right back to the little nightclub in search of the wallet. And we found it, still on the floor under the table by the chair where Marcia had been sitting! All in all, it was a great way to finish 1981 and celebrate the coming of the New Year.

## CHAPTER 15

# *Injuries!*

A dancer's worst nightmare! As in any athletic career where our bodies are the instrument we depend on, a serious injury can become a giant psychological hurdle. From 1962 when I first began my ballet training in Cuba, up to 1981, nineteen years had gone by, and in all that time I had been fortunate to suffer only minor injuries; a twisted ankle from jumping when tired, and aggravating the same area years later. Perhaps the main reason why I had been so injury free was because I was always very careful in my work, warming up well prior to my rehearsals and performances. My body and long flexible muscles also helped. Still, an injury is unpredictable. Body fatigue or a streak of bad luck can result in an injury that can physically and mentally bring you down.

I met my bit of bad luck during the "Giselle" stage rehearsal at the raked, freezing Bellas Artes theatre in Mexico City. Even though at that time I did not cancel any shows and was able to dance all the performances in Mexico and Puerto Rico, the repercussions of having to dance with a sore ankle came later on.

By January, 1982, I was back rehearsing with ABT. Whether it was due to fatigue or because I was still recuperating from the weak left ankle, I landed awkwardly from one of the jumps during class and felt a sharp pain in the back of my right ankle. That bad landing irritated the slight case of tendonitis I had developed at the end of the Met season, and now all of a sudden I had two ankles that needed extra care.

I spoke to Nureyev, who at the time was in New York taking class with the company, and told him I got a cortisone shot in the foot. His reaction was frightening. He hated injections and he said *"Don't ever put a cortisone injection anywhere...it's very bad for you. Avoid it at all costs... work it out in some way or another, maybe getting massages, icing your foot, but avoid injections"* ... I followed his advice.

At the time, the best remedy would have been total rest. But I could not stop, or maybe I should say I did not want to stop. This was the busy winter season when I had some wonderful performances lined up in Europe and a most important guest engagement was coming up in a month's time. I was looking forward to my debut in February with the Ballet of La Scala di Milano. I couldn't wait to step on that legendary stage, dancing the role of Prince Sigfried in the full-length "Swan Lake" with ballerina Anna Razzi.

Marcia and I flew to Italy for the special occasion but I was worried with the many hours of flight. When we arrived in Milano both of my ankles were quite swollen. I knew I was not in the best condition to perform, because just to walk, hurt! The pain I was feeling from my shoe rubbing against the back of my right foot, just below the Achilles tendon was like an excruciating burn, and I knew this injury was not one to be taken lightly. I knew the risks of a serious tendonitis, but I didn't even want to think of canceling. This was my debut in La Scala and that's all I kept thinking, and the opening night performance was in five days.

Marcia was being very supportive, but I was going up the wall, so I called mom and Zeida and told them about the pain and discomfort I was experiencing. They told me to call my masseur, Armando, in New York. Armando, understanding clearly my situation, told me to find a masseur in Italy so that the injured ankle wouldn't continue to stiffen up, and said, "*If you need me, I will fly to Milano,*" and I knew he meant it! Armando was not only a great masseur, he was an even better friend!

Right after talking to Armando, I tracked down Luigi, Nureyev's own private masseur, who also happened to be in Milano at the time. He told me: *"I am going out of town tonight, but I will tell you Rudi's secret. Just ice your foot for about twenty minutes around the clock during the day and night and pour some Vodka on the towel that the ice is wrapped in. The effect of the ice with vodka will be much stronger... like dry ice."* The way I felt, I was ready to drink the whole bottle of Vodka if it was going to make a difference. Luigi had to travel and could not see me, so he recommended another masseusse friend of his in the suburbs of Milano. That afternoon with Marcia's help I limped my way to see the lady. When I told her who I was, about my injury and when I was scheduled to perform, she raised her eyebrows and said: "Let's see what can be done."

She put some medication on my foot and before going to work said: *"What I have to do will hurt, but it needs to be done, if there is any chance for you to perform."* She worked all around the ankle and then went right to the source. When she pressed on the back of the ankle, right where it hurt the most, I screamed! She ignored me and continued to massage the injured area until I was practically ripping the towel. I'd look at Marcia in despair, and she would comfort me by holding my hand. When it was all over, I took my first steps, and it felt worse than when I arrived. I knew I could not stand that kind of pain one more day.

Back in the hotel my morale was sinking rapidly. So far I had been to two company rehearsals and had to walk through both of them in street clothes, using them only as a means to learn the new version of "Swan Lake." Time was running out and one of the company's principal dancers was already on standby. There was nothing else I could do except what Rudi's masseur, Luigi had recommended. So I went to bed, raised my foot higher than my body, wrapped it in ice, and poured the vodka all around the towel. In twenty minutes my ankle was totally numbed. I would take the ice off, wait a while and repeat the whole procedure over and over again. It was getting late, but I was scheduled for a dress rehearsal the next day. I prayed and without realizing it, fell asleep with the ice on my foot.

The next morning was a Sunday and I woke up to the sound of church bells. My first thought when I saw the towel on the floor was I forgot to take the ice off my foot before falling asleep. I wondered if I had a foot, as it felt slightly numbed, but without pain. I walked my first steps and I was in disbelief. The excruciating pain was gone! The ankle was still stiff, but the pain was gone. Oh my God... this is a miracle! I tried to plie! I put the full weight of my body on that ankle and it didn't hurt! Marcia kept asking me, *"Are you sure the pain is gone?" "Yes!...yes!"*

From the start Anna Razzi and I got along really well. We hardly had a chance to rehearse together but she knew what I was going through and was very supportive and encouraged me to hang in there. She was very secure in her role and interpretation and I started relaxing a bit. By the second act I felt my foot getting stronger and by the third act it responded when I needed it the most! Anna and I didn't hold back, and we delivered the fireworks! The audience already knew their ballerina, but they were getting to see me dance for the very first time. They responded with great enthusiasm.

I returned home with a sense of relief, satisfied I had overcome a challenging situation. But just when I thought the worst was over... there was still more ahead. While rehearsing with ABT, my other foot, the left ankle which I had injured in Mexico City began to act up again. It started to throb and kept swelling up. And this was happening just before the company's annual west coast tour.

I should have rested for a while to give the foot some time to heal, but I took my chances and went on tour with the company. However my performances in Los Angeles put a heavy burden on that left foot. By the time I got to San Francisco, the foot was extremely swollen and I was only able to dance for the opening night performance, which happened to be "Swan Lake" with Natalia Makarova. The audience's anticipation for that performance was high, and I wish I would have been healthier, but I did what I could.

I then left the tour and returned to New York and immediately went to see one of the finest orthopedic doctors, highly experienced in treating dancers. Dr. William Hamilton was a very pleasant man and in his easy manner he asked me, *"What's a dancer like you doing in a place like this?"* I showed him the problem foot and after X-rays were taken of my left ankle, he explained that I had developed some calcifications, or small bone spurs, probably from the first sprained ankle injury I had suffered years ago. Dr. Hamilton explained bone spurs were a common thing with dancers and they could be removed through surgery, but the worse part was the psychological fear caused by the pain.

I asked him if he thought it was necessary for me to go through surgery, and he replied with a question of his own, *"Well let me ask you something; is the pain so unbearable that it doesn't allow you to sleep or walk?" "No, the ankle throbs, but it doesn't stop me from sleeping or moving around... what I cannot do is dance,"* I replied. Dr. Hamilton looked at me... and said: *"Then I don't want to operate on you... I don't want to have to cut you, unless you come into my office crawling on your knees and totally unable to walk. As long as you are able to move around and do exercises that will strengthen your muscles and ligaments around the area that is injured, then I don't see any reason why you need surgery."*

Dr. Hamilton's words were a huge beam of hope, and I will always be thankful to him. He knew the importance of avoiding surgery if at all possible. I trusted him fully. He bandaged my foot, recommended I use crutches for about a week until the swelling was gone, and as soon as I could, start working with a strengthening program called "Pilates" which at the time was just starting to be known, but was an excellent therapy to strengthen the muscles, tendons and ligaments in the body.

After a week of rest and a week of "Pilates" exercises mom, Zeida, Marcia, the girls and I decided to head down to our own version of paradise, our beach home in Anna Maria Island on the west coast of Florida. Every morning Zeida and I would go to the beach, and under her supervision I would do strengthening exercises in the water and in the sand. After ten days of a disciplined schedule of rest and work, I managed to strengthen my foot enough to be able to dance again and not have to cancel my next guest appearance. In April I would be dancing for the first time with the Ballet of the Teatro Municipal in Santiago, Chile in celebration of the 125$^{th}$ anniversary performance of their fantastic theater.

Back in New York, I joined ABT at the Met and on May 1 danced my first "Swan Lake" of the season with Natasha. My foot was getting stronger. On May 3, I was to be honored with the prestigious Dance Magazine Award. Bill Como, Editor in Chief, announced in front of the whole company I would be one of the 1982 Dance Magazine honorees, and the youngest recipient in the magazine's history to receive the award.

After much thinking, Zeida suggested Lucia Chase would be the best person to present me with such an award, especially since she was by now withdrawn from the dance scene. Even though there were times she had been really difficult to deal with, Lucia was still one of America's foremost dance icons. She had been a big part of our lives. Despite their frequent clashes regarding my ABT contracts and appearances, Zeida admired Lucia tremendously and was hoping to produce a film about her life. Asking her to be my presenter was something I believed would honor her and make her happy. She gladly accepted the invitation. At the ceremony, when it was time for Lucia to introduce me, she put on her glasses and read:

> ***"Fernando Bujones, American trained premier danseur whose exuberance and technical excellence in roles ranging from classical to contemporary have stimulated audiences around the world to deeper insights into the beauty and joy of dance."***

My family was there to watch. As I listened to Lucia's words, the thing that stood out the most in my mind was "exuberance," because dancing to me was about energy, exuberance and total joy. Not long after that day, Lucia Chase passed away into dance history. I was glad the last time we saw each other at the Dance Magazine Awards was a happy occasion for all of us.

Years later, in 1999, I was invited as a guest choreographer and lecturer to the North Carolina School of the Arts, and they, along with Lucia's son, Chancellor Alex Ewing of NCSA, honored me with the "Lucia Chase Fellowship Award." I received that distinction with great pride, knowing that now, my name, too, would form part of Lucia's legacy in the history of American dance.

1982 had been a roller coaster time filled with injuries and success, but my body was in serious need of rest. Though I had received numerous invitations to perform during that summer, I opted for a vacation instead, and flew with my family to Brazil. It was the year of the world cup and where better to enjoy it than in the country regarded as home to the world's soccer champions?

For an entire month I didn't think about dance at all. I literally watched every world cup match that was televised. Unfortunately, the Brazilian team, with players such as Zico, Junior, Falcao, and Socrates would not win the world cup. That ultimate victory would belong to the Italians, led by Paolo Rozzi. But in Brazil, life was a wonderful and a beautiful thing to enjoy; Marcia and I took the time to visit some of the most gorgeous and romantic places in that country, with the most blessed consequences... Marcia got pregnant!

Upon our return to New York, I continued with the Pilates strengthening exercises, as well as numerous visits to Armando Zetina, to get in the best shape possible.

*Armando Remembers:*

*"You know, I first saw Fernando when he was still a student dancing with the Andre Eglevsky group... you could not help but notice him... he was like a little shining star lighting up the stage and I thought to myself, "Who is this kid?" And after several workshops at the School of American Ballet, everyone started paying attention.*

*"The next time I saw him was the first time he came into the office. By then he had joined ABT, was enjoying a very rewarding first year, but had twisted an ankle. It was not a serious injury for he had a very forgiving and strong physique, with long, pliable muscles, tendons and ligaments, and was very careful in his way of working, so with some therapy and disciplined rehab, he was back dancing in no time. We hit it off immediately and from that day on I became his masseur, but better yet, his friend. Throughout all his dancing years he never failed to visit regularly and after that, we always kept in touch…*

*"What I remember the most was what an absolutely complete marvelous dancer he was. On stage he not just danced… he created, projected an image, a complete experience that to my eyes, no one else yet, to this day, has been able to create. There is still today, no one like him. His line is unsurpassed; his legs and feet, his arms and torso were like a superb musical instrument, tuned to perfection. And then, there was his technique. What couldn't Fernando do? I told him: "Fernando you are not just a dancer, you are a poet of dance." Because of his sensibility, his elegance, his taste in executing the movement to convey the essence of the character he was portraying, he was so sensitive… when he turned, it was not a simple turn, it was an image he would create, whether en l'air or in the ground…*

*"Today, when I go to the theater, I still end up comparing everyone to him.,. and I find myself nixing this one and the other one, for they do not compare to Fernando's quality, no one comes up to his standards. At my office, I also treated such dancers as Rudi Nureyev and Natasha Makarova. These were very temperamental Russians, divas in their own right, but one day Natasha turned to me and said: "Fernando is perfect." And those words were from the great Makarova. "He is perfect." What more can you say, coming from such a person?*

*"It was a privilege to work with him and above all, to be his friend. He trusted me completely, for I did know his body and how to get results when needed. He was so special, so gifted; he knew how to work in a very smart way, that's why he had relatively few injuries throughout his career. He knew how much to push and when to hold back. And to this day, I can tell you, he remains unsurpassed. Other dancers have the tricks, the jumps, the turns, but no one has everything combined in one perfect package like he had."*

I also tried again to take a class at SAB with my teacher Stanley Williams, but quickly found out I was still on the blacklist. Mr. Balanchine's decision was something I could not comprehend, but I didn't let it affect me. I know Stanley was equally disappointed. It would not be until after Mr. B passed away that I was given permission to return to SAB.

By then I was twenty-seven years old, and had lived my share of ups and downs, but overall life had been extremely good to me. Now Marcia and I were also expectant parents. For two years Marcia and I had been talking about having our own child. Marcia was thirty-eight years old and taking into account her past health history, both of us knew we were running out of time. Marcia would have to be closely monitored, making sure throughout her pregnancy her health, particularly her back problems, would not be severely affected. We knew she would need to have a caesarian section, as Julia's birth had been, but we were looking forward to the next few months when life was about to surprise us with a most remarkable gift that would bring me unmatchable joy.

CHAPTER 16

# *Alejandra*

During the last week of January, 1983, ABT started its winter tour again in Miami, with a splashy gala evening consisting of a somewhat crazy mixed program, reflecting the "new modernized ABT." The program opened with a revival of Balanchine's "Symphonie Concertante" (seldom in ABT's repertoire), followed by John McFall's funky duet "Follow the Feet" especially created for Baryshnikov and his latest protégé Robert La Fosse; Marianna and I danced "Le Corsaire" pas de deux, and the night ended with the full company dancing "Great Galloping Gottschalk" another modern, light piece commissioned a year ago from choreographer Lynne-Taylor Corbett.

Erik Bruhn had just restaged his magnificent new version of "La Sylphide" and it was to be the company's big full-length featured production on tour this year. I was scheduled to dance the opening night "James" with Marianna Tcherkassky on February 4, and the performance went very well for both of us. While the company went to Chicago for the rest of its run, I flew to Caracas, Venezuela for four very special performances.

ABT's Ex-Balletmaster Enrique Martinez had staged his wonderful version of the full-length "Coppelia" for the ballet company of the Fundacion Teresa Carreño. Two dear friends, ballerinas Zhandra Rodriguez and Ana Botafogo from Brazil, shared the top roles of Swanilda. Enrique himself danced Doctor Coppelius in two performances. We had an excellent live orchestra, conducted by Alan Barker, also from ABT. I was totally among friends, dancing a production I loved. The entire experience was a breath of fresh air for me.

On February 23, I flew to Oklahoma and the Tulsa Ballet Theater to partner their principal dancer and wonderful ballerina Melissa Hale in their excellent production of "Giselle" at the Chapman Music Hall, with the Tulsa Philharmonic, under the direction of Akira Endo, another ABT expatriate. From **The Tulsa Tribune, Lili C. Livingston** wrote:

> ***"...Bujones deserves his title of the American superman of ballet."***

And from **David McKenzie** of the **Tulsa World Sunday**:

> ***"...Melissa Hayle and Bujones illuminated the stage like lightning. Fittingly, the audience roared its approval like thunder!"***

From Tulsa, I went back to New York for a week to be with Marcia who was getting very close to her delivery date of our baby girl. I was to join ABT in Los Angeles and was not too happy about leaving at this particular time. Marcia's mother had arrived from Brazil to be with her, as well as her sister Maristela; and Anna Christina, Marcia's oldest daughter, by now a very responsible teenager, would make sure things would remain under control. So after the doctor guaranteed me the baby would not come until the end of the month, I went. I had already arranged with ABT that my last performance with them would be a week before the scheduled C-section.

March 17 was my last scheduled performance with ABT in Los Angeles. Immediately after the show, I would return to New York, so I could be by Marcia's side as quickly as possible and be there a few days before the delivery date. But on the morning of the seventeenth I got a phone call from Marcia. She had started to feel some labor pains, and as a precaution she had decided to check into the hospital. Hours passed as she waited to be moved to a private room, and by the afternoon she was exhausted. Still the C-section was not scheduled for at least three more days and by that time I would be by her side.

On March 17 at 8:30 p.m., west coast time, I performed "Le Corsaire Pas de Deux" in Los Angeles. Right after, I jumped into a taxi, rushed to the airport, and got on the plane. It was a good thing I decided not to phone Marcia at that hour knowing that because of the time zone difference, it was already very late on the east coast and everyone should be sleeping. I landed in New York City at about 6 a.m. and got to our apartment at 7 a.m. I found a sleepy Anna Christina in her room, who said to me, "Hi Fernando, Alejandra was born last night."

"WHAT! ... WHAT HAPPENED?... WHAT TIME?" I dropped my bags on the spot, ran down, hailed another taxi and rushed to the New York hospital. When I got there, the first thing I did was look for my newborn daughter. I was guided to the nursery and shown my beautiful daughter. There were many babies in the nursery, but my eyes were fixed on her. I was speechless, and as I kept looking at her through the large glass window, I was completely captivated by her tiny reactions. I could have stayed there all day long, but after a while I realized I needed to look for Marcia and the rest of the family.

Alejandra Patricia Kubitschek Bujones had been born on March 17, 1983, at 11:33 p.m. New York time. She was a healthy baby, weighing six pounds, eight ounces; and as my eyes fixed on her, looking so tiny and adorable, all I could think was how wonderful the miracle of life was and how at twenty-eight years of age I felt a happiness I had not ever felt before! I was the father of this baby girl! I was spellbound, staring at her and thinking, *"Is it real what I am seeing? My own baby girl."* And she had been born on the same day as my mentor Rudolf Nureyev. To everyone's surprise, the awaited delivery occurred earlier than anticipated and Marcia's own obstetrician was probably the one most surprised by the events that led to it.

I finally found some familiar faces, our good friend Joseph Rogosik, and my mother-in-law, Doña Sarah, who were walking back and forth in a corridor outside the emergency area, where Marcia was being cared for. Both of them seemed quite anxious and upset, and that was the first time I felt something was wrong. My mother-in-law looked relieved to see me and explained Marcia had gone through an emergency procedure because late the previous night, her blood pressure had risen drastically, and the doctors fearing for her health and the baby's, had to act prematurely.

What upset Doña Sarah even more was Marcia's obstetrician was nowhere to be found. He had been monitoring Marcia's pregnancy for months, had seen her the previous day when she checked into the hospital, but when the moment of truth arrived, he was nowhere to be found. He was convinced before March 19, nothing was going to happen, and left a female medical assistant, Dr. Schrotenboer in charge. But on that evening, when her blood pressure began to climb sky high, Dr. Schrotenboer had to rush Marcia into surgery.

Thank God for Dr. Schrotenboer! The success of the operation and all my gratitude belonged to her and if not for her quick thinking and her skills, who knows what could have happened. I was convinced she saved my wife and my daughter's lives! Finally I was guided to Marcia's room. When she recognized me, she smiled, then with a weak and concerned tone she asked, "*Is the baby all right?"* I comforted her by saying, *"You did it, darling, the baby is in good health and she is beautiful!... but now you must rest.*" With those words she fell asleep again. Events had happened so quickly no one had yet notified my mother and Zeida. When I called and told them what had happened, they were as astonished as they were delighted with the birth of Alejandra. They also jumped into a taxi and came to the hospital to meet the new baby!

Alejandra remained a few more days in the hospital, but as soon as we could we took her home, while Marcia remained a few days longer to recuperate. I took the next two weeks off and stayed with my newly expanded family. Anna Christina and Julia were having a ball with their newest tiny sister. When it became Dad's turn to change the baby's diapers things became less funny. Eventually my diaper changing technique started to improve.

A week later Marcia came home fully recuperated. She was stronger and looking rested, and said to all of us over dinner, *"Well I am ready for another one!"* The birth of Alejandra brought the family even closer together and all of us who shared those intense moments were thankful the birth didn't turn into a tragedy.

**"Bujones jumps for joy over baby girl!"** said The New York Post on March 21, 1983. And for sure I had a lot to be thankful for! The moment Alejandra was born my life began to change. The birth of your own child is a spiritual and loving experience that is indescribable, but it is profound and very real!

After Alejandra's birth I had to go back to work and joined the rehearsal period for ABT's big season at the Met. Gradually the traditional ABT repertoire was starting to change; more Balanchine works were being brought over, new choreographers were experimenting with new works and finally a new first for me, as Billy, in "Billy The Kid."

I had seen and loved Scott Douglas and Terry Orr perform this ballet years back, and had liked Eugene Loring's choreography. I was always asking for any new work to be created for me, and since this was not happening, I asked to do "Billy." Technically, all the work is in your legs and thighs, into the ground, not up in l'air as in the classics; even the jumps are turned in. At first, my back and my thighs hurt so much I was so nervous, it was intense. But the role needed that intense quality. This was a new experience for me.

I loved portraying different characters, exploring their lives, and for a brief moment, becoming them. Zeida and I researched the life of Billy, and I started to incorporate some of his motivations in my dancing. Billy becomes an outlaw killer only after someone kills his mother. I could totally relate to that and brought that same feeling of outrage to my dancing. Those types of roles gave me tremendous satisfaction. The day after my debut, **Jack Anderson** from **The New York Times**, wrote:

> ***"Fernando Bujones made a promising debut in Eugene Loring's Billy the Kid. He was believably boyish at the start. But after the brutal accidental killing of his mother, one could see his entire body go tense, and that tension never***

***left him. Carefree Billy then and there became a wily, suspicious outlaw.***

And **Clive Barnes** of **The New York Post** wrote:

> ***"Fernando Bujones made an unexpected but terrific debut in Billy the Kid. Eugene Loring's outlaw killer, the cold-blooded scourge of the West, is not the first role you might associate with such an immaculate and ardent ballet Prince as Mr. Bujones. But the new passion to be found in his acting, as well as the strength of his dancing, made him chillingly effective and authentic."***

By then, my interpretation of the roles was catching up with my dancing. I myself could feel the difference, with my acting more convincing, stronger. The body begins to mold itself with time, you find the shapes, nuances and colors, and that's what my body and my soul, were beginning to feel. My other roles were also well received by the audiences at the Met. **Anna Kisselgoff** of **The New York Times** wrote:

> ***"There is still no one among those who choose to dance the role who can match Mr. Bujones' "Solor." The stupendous virtuosity and classical discipline he has always brought to the dancing, especially the solos, never fail to astound. Now it is the impassioned range of his acting that is amazing.."***

I could feel my dancing was acquiring a certain sensitivity that perhaps had not been there in the past. I was still in a perpetual search of my self and how to project this self into my characters. I guess you could say I have a Baroque personality, and I find in America there is a preference for "the boy next door" and I did not see myself like that. So I fit in very

Martha Swope

Third year with ABT promoted to Principal, 19 years old, dancing the lead, as Franz, in "Coppelia."

Leslie E. Spatt

and Colas in "La Fille Mal Gardee."

Martha Swope

The fabulous roles at ABT.

As Prince Albrecht in "Giselle" with Eleanor D'Antuono

Martha Swope

Martha Swope

"Spectre de la Rose" with Marianna Tcherkassky

Jaye Phillips

The Butler in "Miss Julie"

Dina Makarova

Don Jose in "Carmen" with Natalia Makarova .

"Le Corsair" Pas de Deux with ballerina Yoko Morishita.

Atsushi Iijima

Nina Alovert

Martha Swope

Nina Alovert

As Basilio, with Natalia Makarova in the full length "Don Quixote."

Martha Swope

Variations from
Don Quixote and
Diana & Acteon

Dina Makarova

Jack Mitchel

Z.Cecilia-Méndez

Leslie E. Spatt

Left, "Swan Lake" with Cynthia Gregory.

With Cynthia as Odile/Odette.

Z.Cecilia-Méndez

Z.Cecilia-Méndez

Rehearsing "Beauty" with Cynthia Gregory

Z.Cecilia-Méndez

Martha Swope

“Sleeping Beauty” with Cynthia Gregory.

Barry Gray

As James , in the Bournonville version of "La Sylphide" at the O'Keefe Center with the National Ballet of Canada in Toronto, Canada.

Z.Cecilia-Méndez

Daniel Cande

"La Sylphide" with Noella Pontois at the Paris Opera in the version by Pierre Lacotte.

Z.Cecilia-Méndez

Outside the Paris Opera with Noella, Marcia and Noella's friend.

David Simmonds

A wild and fun-loving Musketeer in "Three Musketeers" with the Australian Ballet.

Martha Swope

Billy, in "Billy The Kid."

Atsushi Iijima

Marcia and I in our wedding day, with her daughters, little Julia and Anna Christina.

Mom, Marcia and I at the party after our wedding.

With Marcia in Tokyo.

With new baby daughter, Alejandra.

well in European productions. At home, people seemed to perceive me differently. But that is who I was.

My work continued with an intense performing schedule, both with ABT and as a guest artist with other companies abroad, yet nothing matched the exhilarating feeling of coming back home to witness the constant new changes of my youngest daughter. With a brand new baby girl at home waiting for me, I couldn't wait to get there!

But I already had other commitments, and as soon as the Met season ended on June 20, I flew to Milano, Italy for three performances of "Sleeping Beauty" with Anna Razzi at the Nervi Ballet Festival and the ballet from La Scala. The Italian public and the press loved "Razzi and Bujones." All five Italian publications had us in their headlines and I became "**il Divo Americano!," "Specttacolosi!" "La famosa stella internazionale!" and "Uno splendido Bujones**!" I returned to New York feeling like a conqueror!

My next engagement with ABT would not start until October 1 with a five-week rehearsal period in New York City. So, I took off the rest of the month of July and all of August and September as the first, really relaxing and much needed longest vacation of my life. We enjoyed great quality time with the family and our new daughter. I also enjoyed watching football games and organizing my dance books, videos and music collections.

I started making my very first album of Alejandra. I loved watching how she was developing, her new little gestures; she was becoming very specific about her likes and dislikes, on food and music. I jotted down every person who came to see her, the gifts she received, her first few little trips to the park with the rest of us, her first teeth, her first haircut! I was having lots of fun with my baby girl.

The year was coming to an end, but I still had other performances in Chile and Nice-Monaco, for a Soiree de Gala hosted by the Royal Family of Monaco at the Salle Garnier, dancing with Joyce Cuoco. We were part of an incredible conglomeration of dancers: from Paris, Jean-Charles Gil, Florence Faure and the corps of the Ballet Nationale du Marseille de Roland Petit. Also, there were Pascale Doye and Denys Ganyo, and Jorge

Donn. I was just very glad to be a part of it. A week later I rejoined ABT in Washington for our December Kennedy Center season.

I got back home just in time to celebrate Thanksgiving with my family. This had been an amazing, incredible year for me. I really had a lot to be thankful for.

CHAPTER 17

# *Highs and Lows*

January, 1984, and I was back to my performing schedule. That month, during some time off from ABT between Miami and Boston, Alejandra, now almost a year old, together with her sisters Anna Christina and Julia, her grandmother Doña Sarah and her aunt Maristela, traveled to Rio de Janeiro while Marcia, mom, and Zeida traveled with me to Spain for my debut at the Teatro de la Zarzuela in Madrid. I had been invited to appear in two performances with Cynthia Gregory, who was also bringing her parents with her. Cynthia was without question ABT's principal prima ballerina. In the last two years the two of us had really developed a very special rapport on stage and our partnership was getting lots of attention at home and abroad. Our visit to Spain was especially memorable because we were able to have our families with us. We arrived with some days ahead of the performance and were able to visit some wonderful sights.

The audiences at the Zarzuela were ready for us. The minute the curtain opened and we appeared on stage in our Don Quixote costumes, they exploded in applause. From then on, loud cheers and bravos erupted after every important step or combination. "Olés" and clapping followed our solos and variations, with an enthusiasm and loudness that was more typical of a bullfight than of a ballet performance. We ended up having to repeat the coda as an encore for they just would not let us go!

My mother's family originally came from Spain, but suddenly here was a group she had never met before. We never knew this part of the family even existed. Some of them had migrated to Cuba many years before, and my maternal Grandmother was born there. But the rest of the family remained in the northern part of Spain known as La Coruña. It was a thrill for all of us to get to know each other. Mom had learned of their existence by accident and when they found out I was performing at the Zarzuela, fourteen of them drove down to Madrid to meet their American relatives and see me dance. Spain was a wonderful experience, leaving us with the desire to return for more.

We all flew back to America, and I rejoined ABT in Boston and stayed with them all the way back to the Met. But my performances were few and far between. One "Julie" in Boston, one "Swan" in Chicago, one "Paquita" and one "Swan" in San Francisco," and one pas de deux in Detroit. However, there were multiple works by Twyla Tharp, Balanchine, Paul Taylor, Jerry Robbins, but I was not in them. The repertoire was being changed, and I had fewer opportunities to dance.

Then I got a callback from Spain! I was invited to return, to partner a prodigious fifteen-year-old Spanish ballerina named Trinidad Sevillano at the famed Music Festival in Granada, which takes place every year at the open air amphitheater and the gardens of the "Generalife" at the Palace of the Alhambra, built by the Moors during their conquest of Spain. This is possibly one of the most beautiful and magical places one could dream about to dance in. The only other place in the world that could match this setting would be the Herodus Atticus in Greece with the Parthenon in the background. And I have been fortunate enough to dance in both!

Only 16 years old then, Trinidad Sevillano was a fresh jewel of a dancer, and it was a pleasure to dance with such a promising talent. In the open-air theater, with the Moorish arches for a background, the dark green pines and cypress trees surrounding the stage, those glorious gardens with their cascading water fountains gurgling all around me and an incredible moon shining above all of us, I felt like the perfect slave in love with the princess. The location was unbelievable, one that these eyes will never forget!

Again, about seventeen of my newly found Spanish family drove all the way from Galicia and Madrid, south to Granada to see me dance. After the performance, at about one o'clock in the morning, cousin Manolo suggested we all go into town to one of the top restaurants in the area whose owner was a friend. He asked for a table for about 50 people. The restaurant actually closed the entire street and arranged for tables and chairs to be set up in the street, right in front of their shop. My cousin had also invited a bunch of his friends from Granada, who joined the rest of us. We were still there when the sun came up on one of the most glorious mornings in Granada, at the foot of the incredible gardens of The Generalife! After stuffing ourselves with a magnificent banquet of fresh fish, meats, and a huge "paella" in a non-stop night of eating, now they began to serve us breakfast! I replenished all the energy I had spent dancing the night before.

After the incredible breakfast, we were all taken to our hotels to rest until mid-afternoon. Then, cousin Manolo, his wife and kids came to give us a tour of Granada as only the natives can. We saw the famous gypsy caves in the mountains surrounding the city, the historic places in Granada, and visited the house where Manuel de Falla, the legendary Spanish composer, lived. That night we went to a "tablao" where some of its most famous and respected dancers, singers and musicians were performing. And what a show that was! These flamenco dancers are all fire, blood and heart. I was very glad I got to see such passion and skill on display that night.

My cousin had alerted the owner I would be a guest there that night. To my surprise, the dancers on stage made a special salute to me, and some had actually seen me dance at the Generalife. I stood up to acknowledge their gesture, and felt a deep emotion, as if I were a part of them, part of that special community of dancers who give themselves to others through music, dance, and passion.

With our second trip to Spain now almost over, it was time to return home to New York City. Marcia and I also missed our girls, and we were all anxious to be back together. It was always lots of fun to see them grow. Alejandra was now learning to talk in English and in Portuguese, and she loved to give orders to her older sister, Julia, which made all of us crack up.

Back home more unexpected changes were taking place at ABT. We had been hearing the rumors, and here it was again. Baryshnikov, by now the company's Artistic Director, announced that he had presented his resignation to ABT's Board of Directors because he needed to fulfill other personal commitments! ABT's Board did not accept his resignation and somehow it was worked out he would remain with the company. We then learned he would be allowed to pursue other interests, limiting his role as a director with the company. ABT's Board was simply happy to keep his name associated with the company. But that meant now the company was more or less adrift, with no clear direction of its own.

Perhaps the lack of an Artistic Director at the helm was felt the most by the company when in October of 1984, ABT was invited to tour Japan. Baryshnikov was not with us throughout the whole tour, because he was in Finland filming a movie titled "White Nights." His assistant, Charles France, became acting director by default and the company was hardly pleased. For most of the ABT members, this would be their first time to the Far East, but it was my fifth visit to Japan. I had performed with the Matsuyama Ballet, the Tokyo Ballet and in two World Ballet Festivals. By now I had a strong following in Japan. For years I had been receiving gifts and letters from Japanese fans who had seen me perform and continued to follow my career. This trip would mark my first visit there with the full company.

Mr. Sasaki, the Japanese impresario who arranged the tour, had requested that I appear on all the opening night full-length ballets in each city, but I knew the chances for this were slim. However, I was fortunate enough that Mr. Sasaki insisted I was cast for the first opening night shows of "La Sylphide." During the opening night Gala, my partner Marianna Tcherkassky and I received a most stunning ovation from the public after our pas de deux from "Le Corsaire." During the intermission, Mr. Hirowatari, Mr. Sasaki's assistant, rushed to Marianna and I: *"I have a surprise! Please remain in your costumes and come quickly with me."*

We followed him to a VIP room where the Prince and Princess of Japan were waiting! They wanted to meet and congratulate us personally on our performance! Marianna's mother is Japanese, and she became a favorite dancer there.

Meanwhile, at ABT the trials and tribulations continued. The Board was fluid, with members divided and no clear direction. With the blink of an eye, there would be a new administrator, or a new company manager, or a new executive director, even a new artistic director. Quite a few came and went in a short period of time. The company Lucia Chase had famously held together through good and bad times, was breaking at the seams and showing the strain. I felt especially disenfranchised.

For the December season at the Kennedy Center with ABT, I only danced one "Donizetti Variations." Thanks to the faithful following of the ballet audiences, who never once failed to show me their support, my performances with ABT still brought me much joy those fewer times when I stepped on stage. I took off completely during Christmas. The year ended for me with somewhat mixed results. My international engagements were the ones giving me the most satisfaction. Life at ABT continued to be a very different story. My roles continued to diminish.

For the upcoming season at the Met, England's Royal Ballet Sir Kenneth McMillan's "Romeo and Juliet" was to have its New York premiere. During our December season at the Kennedy Center in Washington, D.C., Sir Kenneth, now ABT's latest Associate Artistic Director in lieu of the absent Baryshnikov, told me: *"Fernando, I'm sorry to tell you that you won't be dancing the opening night performance of "Romeo and Juliet" at the Met, because I just don't feel you're quite ready, and I would like to work with you some more."*

I remember I looked at him straight in his eyes, *"I'm not ready? What do you mean? May I ask you who will dance the opening night at The Met?" "Robert La Fosse and Leslie Browne,"* replied McMillan. Robert La Fosse was at the time the latest Charles France's protégé! Robert was a recently promoted young principal dancer with ABT, who had never performed the role of Romeo. I had already performed Tudor's Romeo and Juliet with ABT, John Cranko's Romeo and Juliet with the Munich Opera Ballet, and in Stuttgart, with Marcia Haydee, one of the finest Juliets of our times. I had enough experience in the role and a proven record, but here was McMillan telling me I was not ready! I looked at him and thought to myself, "*What a sorry excuse.*"

It could not have been his decision and he was probably having to do as he was told. McMillan, sensing my feelings, continued: *"You are still scheduled for the Saturday evening performance at the Met, and next year when I stage another one of my classics, I will certainly consider you for the opening night."* I just let him ramble and when he finished I said, *"I do not know what is going to happen next year, as I take one year at a time."* Making my decision on the spot, I told him, *"By the way, I will not be available to perform Saturday evening your Romeo at the Kennedy Center, because I have another engagement on that date."*

Of course I could have worked it out to be with the company at the Met, but under the present conditions, I opted not to. Right after McMillan spoke to me, he also spoke with Kevin McKenzie, another of ABT's well-established principal dancers who was being paired with Natalia Makarova for their "Romeo" performance. They too would have been a better pair for opening night! God knows what reasons he gave Kevin, as to why he and Natasha were also being bypassed for opening night. Kevin later told me that he just simply stood there, listened, said "thank you" and walked away, plainly disgusted. ABT was no longer even remotely the wonderful company I joined in 1970. Life at home with Marcia and my girls kept me sane, and I thanked God that part of my life was free of conflict and disappointments.

On January 24, the company arrived in Miami to start their winter tour and they were about to present a new world premiere. It was a small work, but it was useful as a filler. By now, ABT had many of these smaller, simpler works which they could use in their repertory nights. I was excited, but even more nervous than the dancers who would be performing it. This was to be my very first choreographic effort! Because I had only one role to perform, ABT gave me the opportunity to choreograph a piece. The idea of creating a new ballet was something that had been a thought inside me for a long time, but I had never had the courage or the time to actually do it.

The day came and I found myself in a studio with fourteen ABT dancers, led by Marianna Tcherkassky and Danilo Radojevic, all looking at me and waiting. A few seconds after that initial eye-to-eye contact, I was on the way to creating my first original ballet to music by Adolphe Adam which I titled, "Grand Pas Romantique."

I was delighted the ballet would have its world premiere in my hometown. It was well received and praised by the audience and the press and continued to be performed on tour and at the Met in New York. The best thing for me was how much I learned from creating this small ballet, and it set in motion my desire to continue choreographing. I found that choreography, which is totally different from dancing, was intellectually fascinating and in certain ways, when one sees the creation taking shape, that experience can be just as exhilarating as when one performs on stage.

When we finally got back to New York, I did perform "Romeo" at the Met, and though I didn't dance the opening night, the controversy about my not being "ready" was put to rest when **Anna Kisselgoff** of **The New York Times** wrote on April 26, 1985 of my performance:

> ***"...Mr. Bujones and Ms. Tcherkassky - they were truly a Romeo and Juliet, the best matched pair among the casts so far. ... Mr. Bujones acting was splendid - the playboy he projected vanished in an instant when pure love so visibly took over. Together, they made for a romantic pair, ranging over a spectrum of emotion that was expressed through the dancing itself. And the quality of the dancing does make a difference. Mr. Bujones is one of the world's few great dancers and it was no surprise that the dynamism and power of his solos brought these passages to new life."***

It felt a lot better.

CHAPTER 18

# *Presidents and Princesses*

During that 1985 Met season, another dream came true for me. I received an invitation to perform at the White House on April 17, 1985, for the President of the United States, then President Ronald Reagan and First Lady Nancy Reagan as part of the welcome and celebration ceremonies in honor of the President of the Republic of Algeria!

I asked Marianna Tcherkassky to be my partner and we put together a three-part program. Marcia, mom and Zeida were invited to share that evening with us. Marianna's husband, ABT ballet master Terry Orr, accompanied her.

On the morning of the 17th of April, we all got to the White House and were given a private tour. We were shown the impressive State room with Abraham Lincoln's portrait, where official State dinners are given. We joined all the other guests, personalities and government officials for the official playing of Honors for the President and Visiting Dignitaries. We stood with all during the playing of the Ruffles and Flourishes by the Fife and Drums Corps in their stunning uniforms, the 21-Gun Salute and Troop Review. We all got goosebumps.

Then Marianna and I were escorted to the elegant East room. Placed at the far end was a small wooden platform, right below a low hanging chandelier. Everyone who has performed at the White House is familiar with this set up. This would be our stage. Though the space was tight, I knew we could deal with it, but I immediately realized I would have to be careful with my leaps. I didn't want to make a fool of myself by hitting that chandelier during my jumps! I would have to concentrate and aim all my leaps either to the left or to the right of it.

We were instructed at the back corners of the platform there would be two curtains acting as our dressing rooms, so we could quickly change costumes. We would have less than two minutes to change between each piece, since we could not make our special public wait too long. Marianna and I realized this was a different kind of performance after all. At the end, both of us would join the President, the First Lady and all the honored guests for a formal State dinner. After rehearsing our numbers, getting everything set up and ready, we all went to our hotel to rest.

At 6:00 p.m. Marianna, myself and our families were back at the White House beautiful reception room with all its chandeliers lit and glowing, mixing up with the rest of the guests, waiting for President Reagan and the First Lady to make their entrance. When they did appear, my immediate thought was how tall our President was. He radiated a natural elegance and charisma! The national anthem was played with the guards holding flags all around us, and then we were escorted to another VIP room that soon filled with special guests, government officials, personalities and members of the Cabinet and Congress. Soap opera star Joan Collins and sports icon Joe Namath were there too. We were all lined up and introduced to and greeted by the President, the First Lady and Vice President George Bush. Soon afterwards, Marianna and I left, and we began to get ready for what would be a performance to remember.

As soon as the President, the First Lady and the honored guests took their seats in the private auditorium, our music started, and Marianna and I began to perform the first piece from Alvin Ailey's "River." The audience received us with strong applause and each one of us went quickly behind our curtains to change. In less than two minutes Marianna and I were back on stage, dancing the balcony Pas de Deux from "Romeo and Juliet." Again, the audience reacted with an even bigger applause, and we began to feel like everything was under control. Or so we thought.

We dashed to our curtains to change and came right back to dance our last piece, the Pas de Deux from "Don Quixote." We finished the first section of the duet, and Marianna and I took our customary bows. Marianna left the stage, and I turned and walked towards the back corner to start my solo variation. That's when from the corner of my eye I saw that President Reagan had stood up and was climbing the steps to the stage where I was ready to start my variation. He walked up to me, and I felt I had to turn and face him. The man cueing the music, seeing this, did not dare to start the tape recorder while the President was on stage! President Reagan looked at me, then at the audience and he began clapping, as if encouraging everyone to give me a round of applause. I instantly realized the President thought we had finished!

Should I just let the President shake my hand? Or should I dare say something? All of these thoughts went through my mind as quickly as lightning strikes, and before one more step was taken by the President, I saw my own hand reach out signaling him to stop! And with a smile on my face, I heard myself say, *"Excuse me, Mr. President, but I am not finished yet."* President Reagan stared at me with a confused look, then at the audience! Then he chuckled and repeated, *"Oh, he is not finished yet."* The audience broke out in laughter. Then, in his own unique way, President Reagan performed a funny dance step and with a sweeping hand gesture announced: *"Well, so then, the show must go on!"* which made everyone crack up, including myself, and he returned to his seat. The music quickly started and I resumed my variation.

As I danced, my thoughts were going a mile a minute, and when I finished with a double tour to the knee to loud applause, I still couldn't look at the President. I was just now realizing what had transpired and was terribly embarrassed, but at the same time glad to have had the nerve to deal with such a tricky situation. Marianna came out and danced her variation, we did the final coda and the entertainment for the evening was over! Phiuuu! Now, the first Lady, holding the President by the hand, led the walk up the platform to congratulate us. Once both of them were on stage, he turned to the crowd and said: *"Now, how many of you were excited with the dancing from these two? I certainly was and that is why I wanted to be a part of it."* Again, he had the audience in his pocket. Wonderful President Reagan.

Marianna and I went to change into our formal outfits and joined everybody else at the State room for the dinner that followed. I was seated next to the First Lady and her warmth and sincere praise of my dancing made my day!

When dinner was finished, the whole family had the chance to take some pictures with the President and the First Lady, and as we said our good-byes, the President turned to me and with a wink in his eyes and a hush in his voice, said: *"Young man I am sure this is an evening you will never forget."* I shook his hand, thanked him and replied, *"Mr. President you can say that again!"* And for years to come Marcia and Zeida never let me forget the words that jumped out of my mouth that night before my brain could stop them: *"Excuse me, Mr. President, but I'm not finished yet!"*... and we would roll on the floor laughing!

What could top such an experience? It was hard to imagine that anything could even match it. And yet such a thing was indeed waiting to happen. My debut with The Royal Ballet at The Royal Opera House Covent Garden in London, England, which happened on June 21, 1985.

The invitation came from the company's Artistic Director, Anthony Dowell, former Premier Danseur Noble and one of my role models. He had also danced numerous times with ABT, and we knew each other well. The ballet I was to perform was my very favorite, "The Kingdom of the Shades" from "La Bayadere," restaged by my mentor, Rudolf Nureyev himself.

This was another dream that came true at the right time in my career, and I took full advantage of the opportunity. For this most important debut, I again asked Marcia, mom and Zeida to join me in London, and I was doubly happy to have them with me. Watching my performance were some of the company's principal dancers, most of whom I already knew and admired.. Antoinette Sibley, Monica Mason, Merle Park, and others, and they all wished me the best.

As in Stuttgart, here was a company with some of the best professional dancers in the world, a company with a century of tradition behind them, yet there was no resentment toward a new young dancer coming from another country onto their stage to share their glory.

I felt as welcomed here as I did at the Paris Opera, and at Stuttgart, where tradition and the love of dance comes first; where you are made to feel you are now part of that special community of dancers, where you, too, are one of them. The company was beautifully rehearsed, and they were a pleasure to dance with. As I was warming up on stage behind those red and gold velvet curtains five minutes before the start, I had to pinch myself and think that here I was, performing in one of the most regal Opera Houses in the world!

After the show, Anthony Dowell and Princess Diana, who had also attended the performance, came backstage to congratulate me. It was such a thrill to meet her. The next morning on June 22, 1985, **John Percival** in **The London Times** wrote:

> ***"...But Bujones in La Bayadere was the star of the evening. His interpretation of Solor is distinctive and personal, but very much in the Nureyev tradition. Not since Nureyev in his prime have we seen such a combination of voluptuous movement with an absolute firm classical style. Another quality he shares with Nureyev is a strong masculine presence, so confident that he can dominate the stage with the quietest gesture."***

Awesome, I thought!

CHAPTER 19

# *Battle with ABT*

In the summer of 1985, I was invited to perform in Japan for my third World Ballet Festival, partnering the wonderful French ballerina, Noella Pontois. Also attending that festival was the Belgian Maurice Bejart, one of the most celebrated and respected contemporary choreographers, director of his own spectacular company, Bejart Ballets du XX Sigle, whose works I really liked. I had seen them during their New York City visits on a couple of occasions, and I had loved his "Bolero" and "Firebird."

During one of the rehearsals, I saw Michel Gascard, one of Bejart's principal dancers, practicing some of his solos from a work titled "Seven Greek Dances." I was blown away, to say the least. The music, by Mikis Theodorakis, struck such a chord in my brain that I became convinced I must have been a Greek dancer in a previous life. But watching Bejart's choreography, so beautifully danced, left me spellbound. It was then I realized I wanted to dance to that music, with those movements, that my body was craving to venture out and move in a way it had never experienced before. All my life I had performed the full-length classics, but Bejart was showing me something different. I asked to meet him. I mentioned the admiration I had for him and his work, and a luncheon was arranged for Maurice, Noella and me.

It was a delightful, funny and instructive lunch, since Bejart was such a well traveled, knowledgeable and fascinating person; but when we started talking about his latest works, I told him I was jealous he had created a ballet about Alexander the Great for a well-known Russian dancer named Alexander Godunov. (Remember that I am Alexander the Great's greatest fan!) Bejart instantly corrected me, *"No I never did the work for him, it just didn't work out"*... then he said *"... but if you like Alexander, I'll create it for you."* When I heard that, I really got excited! To be sure of what he had just said I asked him once again if he would really create the work for me and again he said: *"Yes, I'll do it for you with American Ballet Theatre."* That is all I needed to hear, and on my way back to the United States I felt like a rejuvenated dancer.

As soon as I got home, ABT management asked me to replace Baryshnikov, who had just gone through knee surgery, and had a scheduled performance at the Wolf Trap Outdoor Filene Center for the Performing Arts in Virginia. I did it in order to help the company. I decided to visit Baryshnikov in the hospital, thinking that my visit might minimize the tension between the two of us at work. I was hoping to talk to him about my conversations with Bejart and his offer of a new work for me. When I arrived around 11:00 in the morning, I was surprised to see there was nobody there with him. He looked rather unhappy, lonely and not in a good mood. I tried to cheer him up a bit by telling him he would soon be dancing with us again, but his reactions to my words were as if he hadn't really heard them. I decided not to mention Bejart. After a short visit, I wished him well and left.

I still danced "Giselle" replacing Baryshnikov in Wolf Trap with Marianna Tcherkassky. It was now the last week of August, and ABT was preparing for a two week run at the Met that would begin in mid September. Baryshnikov was still not ready to dance, and the company was counting on me for the season. However, I still didn't have my usual yearly contract with the company finalized. For years now, Zeida had negotiated my yearly contracts with ABT. These negotiations usually took place during the summer company break, and normally, everything was finalized before the new season started -- the number of performances, the opening nights, the repertoire, the partners, the cities, etc. This time, things were taking longer than normal.

Zeida was growing concerned. She felt that ABT was stalling with my contract. She had already been on the phone with Charles Dillingham several times, regarding the different aspects of the new season, plus the offer from Maurice Bejart to produce an original work for me with the company for the 86-87 season, a whole year away. This was a wonderful opportunity for me and she had written twice to Dillingham, first on July 13, again on August 12 regarding the new work from Bejart. On August 14, 1985, she wrote and faxed a third letter to Charles Dillingham, then ABT's Executive Director.

*Dear Charles,*

*As of this date, I haven't heard from you in regards to Fernando's possible schedule for the 1985-1986 season. As I stated in my letter to you of July 13, and then again in my second letter to you of August 12, the weeks and cities remain the same. The terms of the contract will be somewhat different.*

***Repertory:*** *Same as in letter of Aug.12*
***Grand Pas Romantique:*** *Same as in letter of Aug. 12*
***Added:*** *A new work created especially for Fernando by Maurice Bejart, should come into the repertory for September, 1986. Mr. Bejart has already agreed to do the work for Mr. Bujones and will be available to ABT since the summer of 1986. This has to be confirmed to Mr. Bejart no later than this coming November, so he can make his commitments for the rest of the year. Otherwise, we will lose his availability.*

*Please be aware that we have no contract with you still as of this date. Mr. Bujones will not be available to dance in September with American Ballet Theatre without a contract. I would appreciate your taking this letter into consideration as soon as possible and getting back to me so we can get on with the rest of our scheduling.*

*Regards,*

*Zeida Cecilia-Mendez*

As usual, before any contract was put in writing, Zeida would discuss candidly with Charles Dillingham over the phone the different possible options that would later become the basis for my final contract. Among other things, of course, she had spoken at length about the offer for the new work from Bejart. In her last letter to him dated August 14, she confirmed what she and Dillingham had been discussing verbally since July 13. ABT was also asking for me to accept the new contract without a salary increase and this point was also being debated back and forth, and we were using it as a bargaining point. At no time did Zeida's letters issue an "ultimatum" to ABT.

These were normal, hard negotiations. I would do without a salary raise, but we insisted on the one thing that meant a lot to me; the addition of the new work by Bejart. We were now two weeks away from the start of the season, and Charles Dillingham still could not come up with my contract. In all my years with ABT, I had never ever started a season without a signed contract by the company. By now we suspected that Dillingham really had no power to make company decisions, especially regarding my contract.

Finally, just one week before the season opener, Dillingham called Zeida and from their conversation it seemed everything would be resolved, so we were relieved. *"I see no major obstacles in trying to make the new Bejart ballet work for the next year"* he said to her. But the following day he called again! This time his normal tone of voice had a very different ring to it. He was curt and brief saying that my demands of a new work could not be met, *"because the company was not in a position to do this."* And that was their only explanation! He added that unless we accepted ABT's terms, there would be no contract. Zeida was not expecting that and she was shocked.

Zeida, mom, Marcia and I discussed the matter thoroughly. We weighed all the options as well as the worse possible scenario. It was left up to me to make the final decision. I felt it was time ABT did something extra for me, the Bejart ballet, especially since I was willing to go without a salary increase. By now, most of the dancers were aware of what was going on with my contract. Many of them were very fed up with "the new management." And I was not the only one being passed over in terms of new works. Every new choreographer, every new work or any type of new opportunity was accepted or not, only if it benefited Baryshnikov and his group.

I decided to hold out for my request. Mom, Zeida and Marcia were supportive of my decision. I thought even if I did not perform with ABT during the upcoming Met season, I would still remain open to future negotiations, as had happened before with other dancers when Lucia was around. This was not the first time a dancer would sit out a season.

Charles Dillingham, obeying orders from above, called me again at home, trying one last time to get me to accept ABT's terms with no new work from Bejart. I said to him, *"Charles I have nothing to talk to you about. Please talk to my agent." "Ok."* He replied and we both hung up.

The next thing I know, I received a call from Anna Kisselgoff from The New York Times! She told me she had received a press release from ABT that accused me of coercing the company with my demands for a new work, as a way of breaking a verbal agreement and walking out of the season! Why would I want to walk out of the season? This was crazy! I always wanted to dance! However, let it remain for the record that it was ABT's management who sent out their one-sided press release, and it was they who did not care about further negotiations for the future. They were openly trying to get rid of me.

On August 30, 1985, I received a telegram from Charles Dillingham that read:

> *This telegram will serve to confirm that your agent Zeida Cecilia-Mendez has informed us that you will not appear with American Ballet Theater for your scheduled performances at the Metropolitan Opera House in the next two weeks. We accept Ms. Mendez decision as final and regret that you will not comply with the agreement we had reached in July of this year regarding these performances. Your attempt at this time to increase your demands over the agreed terms with regard to future repertory constitutes in the eyes of this management a kind of coercion, which is unacceptable.*
>
> *Charles Dillingham, Executive Director*
> *American Ballet Theater*

We were very surprised, for we never expected this type of reply, much less, the accusation of "coercion." First of all, we had not reached any agreement with the company. We had not "increased our demands over agreed terms." No written agreement and no verbal agreement had yet been reached, as they were claiming! We had been exchanging letters, as we always did, including the different terms, requests and options in order to reach a final contract. Zeida's final letter to Dillingham clearly asks him: "*I would appreciate your taking this letter into consideration as soon as possible and getting back to me so we can get on with the rest of our scheduling.*" We were still waiting for a reply from ABT when Anna Kisselgoff from the NY Times called regarding ABT's press release.

Now, all of us were in shock. A reporter from the NY Times called my wife to get her reaction. "*The action from ABT was so surprising...*" Marcia said: "*It was such a quick decision from the company to issue that press release. We were all stunned and for a while we didn't believe it and still thought it would be resolved one way or another– that Fernando would be back with the company..*" but it did not happen. The Artistic Director and the Assistant to the Artistic Director did not want it to happen. Still, to have the internal contractual negotiations, arguments, and disagreements sent out to the press before informing us, was a very, very low blow.

On September 3, 1985 I replied to Mr. Dillingham's telegram:

> *To Charles Dillingham:*
>
> *This telegram will serve to confirm to you that my agent Zeida Cecilia-Mendez wrote you several letters in an attempt to start negotiations for a possible contract. A reply by phone did not arrive until August 28. ABT's management wasted precious time and acted inflexibly throughout the limited negotiations we had left. ABT proceeded in making their own final decision by sending a press release stating my absence from the Met. It is ABT that in my eyes has acted with a kind of coercion which was very surprising to me.*
>
> *Fernando Bujones*

The situation had regretfully escalated and immediately the press had a field day. The headlines started appearing:

Sept. 2, 1985, by **Jack Anderson**, **The New York Times**:
***"Bujones Canceled at Met"***

Sept. 2, 1985, by **Alan Kriegsman**, **Washington Post**:
***"ABT's Bujones Won't Perform at Met"***

Sept. 4, 1985, **New York Post**:
***"Battle of the Ballet Titans: Bujones' Story"***

Sept. 5, 1985, by **Clive Barnes, New York Post**:
***"Dear ABT-You Mustn't Lose Bujones"***

Sept. 25, 1985, **The Miami Herald**:
***"Bujones Up in the Air"***

Sept. 25, 1985, by **Lewis Segal, Los Angeles Times**:
***"Bujones Leaves ABT in Dispute Over Contract"***

Then I received a hand-written and hand-delivered letter from Baryshnikov to me personally at my home on the evening of September 3, 1985, the same day of ABT's opening night performance.

Mikhail Baryhnikov's letter dated September 3, 1985:

*Dear Fernando:*

*I have been told that you feel that your position has not been clearly or fairly represented in our current situation. I'm writing to you because I feel that my position has not been fairly represented. Fernando, our dispute is an inevitable conclusion to what at best could be called an unharmonious relationship. That you would make the kinds of demands on the company that you made in relationship to your Met performances is only yet another symptom of your unreasonable attitude and continuing rudeness towards both the company and me personally.*

*It is not critical whether these last demands were made four days ago (which did put the company in a terrible position with both the public and the press), or four months ago. The very manner in which these demands were made is distasteful and is not acceptable to me.*

*It seems to me that you do not and have not understood that American Ballet Theatre has changed in the last five years and that you have not shown any willingness to understand or accept these changes. At one time you may have thought my time here would be short and pass quickly, but I am still here and the policies I want the company to follow are still in effect. These policies have never meant to exclude you or diminish the image of the star you are. But what has changed is a policy which takes in the needs, as I see them, for the company as a whole and not for three or four individuals alone.*

*Furthermore, you have consistently voiced in the press your lack of understanding, and the way you have spoken about yourself, this company and the artistic direction is not only ill mannered but also detrimental to this organization.*

*Fernando, you always say that ABT is your home. My response to that is old Russian proverb: "don't spit in the well: for you never know when you may have to drink from it."*

*One day we may reach an understanding but for the moment John, Kenneth and I think we should let matters rest as they are. The gap is too great for us to bridge. For today goodbye,*

*Mikhail Baryshnikov*
*September 3, 1985*

His letter to me left no doubt in my mind I was no longer welcomed and this was indeed goodbye. ABT's publicity department, as directed by Charles France, rose to the occasion, making sure to give every newspaper their side of the story.

> ***"I was always ready to sit down with Fernando and discuss his future with ABT, but this could not take place without an apology for his actions" said Baryshnikov. (New York Times)***

***"...unacceptable demands at the last minute..." (New York Times)***

***"...breaching a firm verbal agreement..." (The Washington Post)***

***"...last minute attempts to coerce the company, irresponsible to his fellow dancers, the public and his fans. This incident is one of many that has severely damaged his relationship with ABT" (New York Post)***

***"...demanding that ABT commission a new work for him for the '86-'87 season as a pre-condition to his appearing at the Met this season" (New York Times)***

The above statements to the press were very misleading. We never gave ABT an ultimatum. We simply continued to uphold our request and waited for ABT to come up with a solution and a contract. Instead of communicating with us, in the end, they decided to send their press release to the NY Times. It was then we all learned that I was no longer a part of the company I had belonged to since the beginning of my career. I also never felt the need for an apology because I never did anything detrimental to ABT. On the contrary, the truth was that ABT's chaotic management continued making all kinds of accusations against me because they didn't want to have me back. My answer to their accusations was written in the same article:

***"If I must, let me clarify once again that my actions never meant to blackmail the company, a company to which I belonged for 14 years... Anyway one cannot blackmail a company. One can only defend one's rights. They know they do not have a legal case. They never gave me a contract. Secondly, I simply demanded a new work for myself like Mr. Baryshnikov has repeatedly done for himself in the past. I believe he has three new works for himself in this coming season. Unfortunately, Ballet Theater's management is not***

***as generous towards other artists needs.... I have nothing to apologize for.***

***My years with Ballet Theater have shown where my loyalties were. But I am truly sorry, sorry to see Ballet Theater now, because the Ballet Theater I grew up in was a company where I learned to admire and respect the management, its repertory, artistic tradition and stars that were the thrill and life of the company. I am sorry for them."***

Some of ABT's Board members acknowledged that no one had come out winning with my dismissal and I agreed. I received a confidential letter from one of them dated September 24, 1985 saying,

> ***"I have the greatest respect and admiration for you as an artist and as a person. I only hope that you and ABT can have a long relationship and that you will remain associated with us even when you are no longer dancing. Writing as a Trustee of ABT, it is difficult for me to say more. But please be assured that you have many friends among us. We all feel certain that this will be resolved so that we can have you back on stage with ABT where you belong."***

I waited a few days to cool off before replying to Misha's letter, and my letter to him September 13, 1985 said:

> *Dear Misha,*
>
> *I cannot permit your letter of September 3, 1985, to remain without reply. Your characterizations and assertions in no way are consistent with the facts which, on the contrary, mandate quite a different conclusion than that which your letter purports to draw.*

*In the first place, no one can say that ABT is not my home company, nor that ABT has not always enjoyed my entire respect and cooperation. To suggest that I have not fulfilled my commitments to ABT hardly withstands the test of scrutiny.*

*At one time you mentioned to me, that as an artistic director you could not force choreographers to choreograph for other artists. On this occasion, that provoked this whole incident. The choreographer Maurice Bejart wanted to choreograph a work for me and the company without being forced into the situation. If the problem to the matter was a financial one, I was ready to discuss the possibilities in helping to fund-raise the event.*

*However did you once discuss or even consider discussing the matter with me? Did you ever consider the possible benefits to ABT from this new work? Do you really see the simple discussion of a proposal other than your own, to be so unacceptable?*

*In your letter you try to discredit me, by attacking my credibility as a professional. You accuse me of continuing rudeness to the company, and to you personally and putting the company in a terrible position with the public and the press. Misha! Was your commitment as artistic director of American Ballet Theatre not relegated to a secondary position when you made your Hollywood films, your television specials and your personal Baryshnikov and Co. summer dancing tours? Surely, even an artistic director cannot operate in a self motivated way calculated to exclude the very artistic achievements for which he is engaged in the first place.*

*Misha, you cannot say that your commitment to ABT is more sincere or less rude than mine. And talking about rudeness, how can you say I have been rude to you, if the only time I have personally talked to you in the last couple of weeks was when I visited you at the hospital, and prior to my performance (filling in on an emergency basis for you) at Wolf Trap.*

*It is also very unfortunate that the situation has been treated with such prominence in the press. However it was American Ballet Theatre's management that called in the press, forcing me to make public my side in this issue.*

*No Misha, I do not consider my acts ill mannered nor detrimental to ABT. Let us be honest to ourselves. Let's mutually admit personal differences, but put them aside for the "good of the company." You left the Kirov, because of a lack of repertory and opportunity that cramped your skills, and limited your chances for advancement as an artist. I do not want to have to leave American Ballet Theatre for the same reasons. You talk about an approachable situation at a later date. I am at the peak of my career, and am well aware as you, that time passes by. I want to dance with American Ballet Theatre and put off fighting, if we must fight, until later.*

*Let us both give each other as well as the company, room to perform and grow. There is an international saying: "It is always easier to destroy than to build."*

*Sincerely,*

*Fernando Bujones*

After that, there was no more communication between us.

On September 5, 1985, **Clive Barnes** of **The New York Post** wrote:

> ***Dear ABT - You musn't lose Bujones! The brief season's first performance was to have been given by Fernando Bujones and Marianna Tcherkassky, but following the highly public inability of Ballet Theater and Bujones to reach a contractual agreement, Bujones withdrew and the leading roles were performed by Robert La Fosse and Leslie Browne. But the***

***absence of Bujones, obviously and audibly disappointing the audience, which indulged in a small pre-curtain demonstration, hung over the performance as palpably as might have been his presence. Ballet Theater depends on its stars for its particular luminosity, and although such stars cannot be permitted to dictate artistic policy, special care must be taken, and even special accommodation made. It is not as though Ballet Theater has created any works of any international importance since the days of Antony Tudor. You cannot behave as if you were a Balanchine-style company unless you have a Balanchine. Ballet Theater's destiny lies in its stars - and a clear-headed astronomer among the present team of astrologers might not come amiss.***

***Whether Bujones is right or wrong in his career demands, his absence from the company roster at best betokens a lack of managerial tact that seems symptomatic of managerial mismanagement. Bujones is the finest American male dancer we have so far produced. Now 30 years old, and at his international prime, he has been with the company for 13 years. During that entire period he has only had two duets by minor choreographers actually created for him. Mikhail Baryshnikov defected from Russia prompted by lack of artistic opportunity. But, in fairness, was he given such short shrift in Leningrad? Does he really wish Bujones to defect from Ballet Theater? Come let tact, reason and good sense prevail on both sides, as well as the realization that Ballet Theater has conceivably more to lose than Bujones from their parting. Certainly it would be a loss for the American dance public, and speaking as someone who has been a friend of the company for 39 years, I feel very concerned."***

I immediately called Maurice Bejart and explained what developed while trying to bring his new work to the company and how ABT's management and artistic director had reacted. He was naturally disappointed, but reacted very positively. He said, *"You know what I will do, I will invite you to dance the "Greek Dances" solos you loved with my company in our upcoming City Center season in New York, and later on I will create the new work for you with Bejart's Ballet XX Century and we'll have the world premiere in Paris!* I thought to myself, *"Ooh my!"*

Then a new fan appeared on the scene. I received a phone call at home, a female voice with a pronounced British accent who introduced herself as Lady Carmen Hall. She said she was an ardent fan of mine, had seen me dance many times and was offering her financial support for the new Bejart ballet I wanted with ABT! I thanked her with all my heart, but explained to her the decision was no longer mine to make. On November 1, 1985, Lady Carmen Hall wrote to ABT's Executive Director:

*Dear Mr. Dillingham;*

*I am writing to request that the American Ballet Theater company allows me to finance the Bejart Ballet that Mr. Fernando Bujones would like to perform. I believe there has been some problems with this idea and I can only assume they are mostly financial.*

*Sincerely.*

*Lady Carmen Hall*

With a sponsor offering to pay for the new work, things should have seemed feasible, but ABT's refusal in accepting a new work for me was now clearly revealing that the real issue behind my dismissal was not a matter of budget, as some wanted to insinuate.

The Executive Director wrote back to Lady Hall on November 14, 1985:

*Dear Lady Hall,*

*Thank you very much for your kind note of November 1st. Please excuse my delay in replying, but it did not arrive at our office until November 12. Mr. Baryhsnikov and his artistic associates have asked me to thank you for your generous offer, which is in the grand tradition of private patronage for the ballet.*

*However, they have not planned to present a work by Mr. Bejart at this time. We would very much appreciate an opportunity to meet with you and describe other projects which are planned and might appeal to your generosity. In the meantime, we thank you for your interest in American Ballet Theatre.*

*Yours sincerely,*

*Charles Dillingham*

Other friends, who at the time made a valiant effort to mend matters between ABT and myself, were Cynthia Gregory and her husband, Hilary B. Miller. Hilary managed to schedule a meeting between myself and John Taras, Baryshnikov's latest Associate Director. Hilary tried to restart a dialogue and new negotiations between ABT and myself, but we quickly realized that Mr. Taras had no real authority, and as he said, the only way he could forsee any future communications between us was if I wrote a letter of apology to Baryshnikov, which I refused. That meeting accomplished nothing. I could see Hilary's disappointment, for he had tried hard to help matters.

When ABT's leadership went from Lucia Chase to Mikhail Baryshnikov, a lot more changed than just the name of the Artistic Director. Dancers who had greatly contributed to ABT's success and tradition decided to move on when they saw the changes ahead. After five years under Baryhnikov's direction and seeing that the artistic director could care less about negotiating a new agreement with me, I too realized it was finally time to move on.

*Jane Herman Remembers:*

*"Fortunately for Fernando, he already was a renowned dancer with his own very special talent... and he went on to develop an extraordinary international career, dancing in all the major opera houses and theaters around the world. But Misha did not care. He had a different idea of what he wanted to do, and the casualties of those ideas, aside from the terrible toll on the company finances, which I could go into at length, were certain dancers... they did not fit in his overall plan, I guess, or were not what he envisioned... so he just got rid of them.*

*"There was a period at ABT when dancers grew up together, when there was a sense of family, sort of, under Lucia Chase... I mean, ballet companies are devoid of such things, people are so temperamental, but that kind of infrastructure is essential for the young dancers that show talent, to grow up and develop and then stay with their company... that is very heartwarming.*

*"Lucia always brought in different dancers because for many years they did not have their own ballet school, which they finally established until Baryshnikov dissolved it, but then she helped develop the young dancers with their partners, through the company's repertoire, with choreographers that were devoted to the company, like Tudor... look what Lucia did... starting with Jerome Robbins, Agnes de Mille, Eugene Loring, Glenn Tetley, Alvin Aley, Dennis Nahat, even up to the time of Eliott Feld, she kept looking for and finding people who developed the dancers and choreographed on them... like she did with Fernando, basically a true product of American Ballet Theater."*

During this difficult period, I received much support from many fans and friends who called me or wrote me letters and messages expressing their disappointment for what they called "ABT's mistake."

*"But then something very extraordinary happened,"* said Marcia Kubistchek, his wife. *"He started getting invitations to dance from all over*

*the world. The telephone at home was ringing like Grand Central Station. And it has been a challenge for Fernando. This helped him to pull up a strength he perhaps did not know he had, to face new ambiances and new people. It gave him a sort of self-assurance in his private life. It made him mature more as an artist. Every time he goes into a new company, he has to conquer himself, to prove himself, and that is stimulating for him."*

*"It was a shock,"* Tobias Leibovitz, a friend of the family said of his break with ABT. *"But really and truly he got quickly over the shock. It opened him up."*

Although this episode brought me new opportunities, it was still one I wished would have never happened. Peter Martins, by now the director of the New York City Ballet, called and offered me a permanent position with his company. However, I still had too many international commitments and could not accept Peter's offer.

In June, 1986, Kevin McKenzie, principal dancer and ABT colleague, said in a Dance Magazine article written by John Gruen, *"Of course Misha has made mistakes. I think it was a mistake to let Fernando Bujones go. I mean Ballet Theatre proclaimed him! That's what I don't understand."*

As sad as the situation was, my departure from ABT had many positive aspects. My guesting invitations tripled! What looked like a risk was turning into a reward. I began to dance with companies I had never performed with before.

Erik Bruhn immediately called and invited me to appear with his National Ballet of Canada, and his first words to me were "Welcome Home." Although I never joined NBC as a permanent member, it was the beginning of a wonderful and lasting relationship. Opportunities to appear in new ballets came my way and the experiences I had been searching for, new works created for me, emerged.

Soon enough I was back in New York City performing as a guest artist with Maurice Bejart's Ballets XX Century at The New York City Center, the solos from his "Seven Greek Dances." Bejart was coming through with his promise of inviting me to perform with his company, and he, along with his principal dancer, Michel Gascard, taught and coached me in the Greek solos for my debut with his remarkable company.

By the end of February, 1986, I was back in Europe for several engagements with The Royal Ballet and The Stuttgart Ballet.

I flew for the first time to Stockholm, Sweden to be part of a Bob Hope TV special and for my debut with the Royal Swedish Ballet, at the invitation of Egon Madsen, now the Artistic Director of the Swedish Ballet.

Many of these engagements were very rewarding, because I was discovering new places. They kept me motivated. Moreover, they served to prove my career was not limited, and there was life for me after ABT.

From Sweden, I returned to America. It was Sunday, March 9, 1986, and I was celebrating my 31st birthday. That day I got a call from Lady Carmen Hall who said, *"Welcome home...have you seen today's New York Times?" "No, I have not, why?"* I replied. *"Well get it, read it, and happy birthday!"* Generosity had no limits with Lady Carmen Hall and when she believed in something she just took her own actions. I opened the Arts and Leisure section of the **Sunday New York Times** and was totally flabbergasted. There was an almost full page article and photo of me. My first thought was how did this get here? The article, written by **Richard Mineards**, said:

***Fernando Bujones: American Superman of Dance.***

> ***"Fernando Bujones is a rare character in the world of ballet. Not only a living legend in his own time, but an American of universal ranking. ...Acclaimed the world over as the paragon of male classic dancers, Bujones, no longer under contract to American Ballet Theatre - his home for the last 13 years - is now at the peak of his phenomenal career, garnering international acclaim wherever he stars. The world of classical ballet is currently Fernando Bujones' oyster. With the unwavering support of fans the world over, the magic of his genius will continue to brighten up our lives."***

What could I say? It was an unexpected but wonderful birthday gift. It made me feel especially good to know that through my dancing I could touch a person in such a way! I immediately called mom and Zeida in Miami and told them to go get the NYT. Then I called Lady Carmen Hall, suspecting that somehow she had something to do with it. I thanked her and asked, *"How in the world did you manage this?"* She answered, *"Never mind...it is a gift, just enjoy it!"*

Lady Carmen Hall and her husband Charles Curkin were determined to make a point. Their point was hardly appreciated by some of ABT's personnel. But in the meantime I took Lady Carmen Hall's advice, minding my own business and enjoying my birthday gift.

Life continued and on June 8, 1986, I had the opportunity to dance once again for President Reagan, when I was invited to perform at the historical Ford Theatre. This was the place where our great President Abraham Lincoln was assassinated! From the stage I could see the balcony box where the President had sat, unoccupied but filled with flowers!

Two days later on June 10, 1986, I went to see ABT perform my favorite ballet "La Bayadere" at the Met. It had been nine months since my parting with them, and I didn't feel comfortable about going to see the performance, but my good friend Toby Leibovitz, urged me to attend, so I went. As Marcia and I walked down the aisle to take our seats a few minutes before the performance, a lady shouted "Bujones!" and began to applaud. As I turned around I noticed that it was Marta Horn, a dear friend and fan, who had spotted me. Within seconds, the entire audience started applauding, and as I acknowledged them the ovation got stronger. On June 12, 1986, **Clive Barnes** in **The New York Post** recorded the incident:

> ***"What a night! And the excitement was not even confined to the stage. When he entered to take his seat just before the ballet started, ABT's Prodigal Son, Fernando Bujones, was given a huge ovation of sympathy from the audience."***

In November, 1986, I traveled for the first time to Copenhagen, Denmark for my debut with The Royal Danish Ballet, dancing the role of James in one of the most loved and important Bournonville ballets, "La Sylphide," with Mette-Ida Kirk as the Sylph. This was very special to me because of my initial training with my teacher Stanley Williams, who schooled me in that technique during my years at the School of American Ballet and taught me to love it.

Now here I was, with this incredible company, in the birthplace of August Bournonville himself. Not far from there was The Royal Danish Opera House, a historical dance treasure. Inside was the original ballet studio where Bournonville personally had rehearsed and created his ballets.

Here Harald Lander created his "Etudes," which I loved to dance, and Toni Lander became a legend and inspiration for a new generation of dancers, including me.

Right from the start, the Danish company and Director Frank Andersen, made me feel at home. My debut performance with the Royal Danish will always hold a special place in my heart. After the show the Danes started singing their traditional songs, and as they lifted their beer mugs, they chanted and cheered for my quick return to Copenhagen. The reviews in the Danish newspapers were to be some of the ones I am most proud of in my entire career.

From **Morgenavisen Jyllands-Posten**, November 2, 1986:

***"Fernando Bujones' guest performance on Saturday evening at the Royal Theatre in Copenhagen enriched the performance of Bournonville's "La Sylphide" with a hint of the big, wide world. This technically, brilliant dancer gave the role of James a totally new dimension which had an inspirational impact on the standard of the entire performance, and he had this effect, although the "Kongelige Ballet" is itself regarded as a specialist in the Bournonville repertoire.***

***Bujones danced the role of James contrary to all standards and traditions, which he certainly did not expect from the Danish dancers either. As a result, the role became much more than simply a demonstration of virtuous high spirits. Not only did Bujones display his technical superiority; he also succeeded in giving wonderful expression to the emotional divide of the shepherd. Even if James is driven to self-destruction because of his dream of sublime love for the supernatural being, despite everything, he also loves his very down-to-earth Effie. Fernando Bujones was the magnetic force on this evening, inspiring all the other performers in "La Sylphide" who, at the premiere of the play, on the whole had given a somewhat weak performance. However, Metta-Ida Kirk is still a captivating Sylphide: the ethereal***

***and gentle counterpart to Bujones' powerful James, whose despair, drama and love which are definitely over at the end, are made so moving by her performance."***

Back home I was surprised and delighted by the news I was to be the recipient of The New York Times / Florida Prize Award for being the most outstanding artist coming out of the State of Florida! The award presentation took place in Sarasota, Florida and Governor Bob Graham was the host presenting it. With it came a wonderful $10,000 check, much appreciated!

Meanwhile in Brazil, a movement had been growing for democratization and change. Marcia received a phone call from Tancredo Neves, the leader for the civilian movement and the first civilian presidential candidate since the military coup of 1964. His party, the PMDB (Partido de Movimento Democratico Brasilero) was trying to get the country away from military dictatorship. He told Marcia the country was changing and that it was time for her to go back, that she had a responsibility to Brasilia, the city her father had founded. At the time, Tancredo was the great hope for change for most Brazilians as well as a close friend of the Kubistchek family. Marcia was now being sought after by this new party, who wanted the daughter of former President Juscelino Kubistchek included on their ticket. The political climate in Brazil was indeed generating opportunities for new people.

For a while Marcia had been toying with the idea of doing something about it. Suddenly, she received the news that Tancredo Neves, right after being elected the first civilian president, and just before his inauguration, had died of a massive heart attack. The entire Kubistchek family as well as the entire country was shocked, stunned and disappointed. Marcia, remembering Tancredo's last words to her, felt motivated to return to Brazil and help in the healing of her country. We decided this would be a good time to move our base to Rio de Janeiro, where the rest of her family lived. Additionally, I had received an invitation from our friend, Dalal Achcar, the Director of the Teatro Municipal in Rio de Janeiro, Brazil to join her as Assistant Artistic Director of the company there.

I still had multiple international commitments and would be travelling frequently. With some trepidation on my part, we sold our apartment in New York City, packed our bags and moved to Rio! This was a major move for me, one that would be taking me away from my environment, from all my friends and colleagues, the city where I grew up, went to school and had called home for all my years.

Once in Rio, we found a huge, beautiful apartment. It had a formidable view of the bay in Ipanema and the Sugar Loaf. The first thing I did as we moved in was to buy a huge satellite dish antenna, so I could continue to watch the Miami Dolphins games on TV! This antenna was to be installed on the roof of the building. When it arrived and the superintendent saw the enormous size of the dish, he refused to put it up. It took all my powers of persuasion to convince him that I would never survive in Brazil if I had to watch the perennial soap operas on Brazilian television! After a week of begging, he finally acquiesced. The monster antenna was hoisted up to the roof and peace once again reigned in the house.

We were finding a new rhythm as a family, and my life kept evolving. Anna Christina had become a young lady, finishing college and was starting a life of her own in Brazil. Julia and Alejandra were enrolled in the American School in Rio, regarded as one of the best in the country.

Marcia was quickly making important political connections, traveling to Brasilia, the capital city. She was well on her way to a new career. I was quickly consumed with restaging my "Raymonda Act III" for the Brasilian company and preparing my next trip to Europe.

CHAPTER 20

# *On My Own*

Thankfully, my now freelance international career continued to bring me new exciting opportunities. Throughout all of the past year without ABT I had been performing many of the major roles I enjoyed with wonderful companies!

In March of 1987 choreographer Maurice Bejart, finally created the ballet for me, which my former company rejected. Titled "Trois Etudes pour Alexandre" the work was based on the legend of Alexander the Great. It was different from anything I had ever done; technically and physically demanding, very rich in details. For me the best part was working with Bejart himself. He was a man whose beliefs were the opposite of Balanchine. He believed that ballet was especially suited for men, and one could see in his works how well he used his male dancers.

I was fortunate to perform "Trois Etudes pour Alexandre" with Bejart's company for its debut in Paris and later on at the magnificent open air theater, Herodus Atticus in Athens, Greece and also in Tokyo, Japan. These performances gave me great pleasure and extended my range as a dancer. I will be forever grateful to Maurice Bejart for his generosity and the time he dedicated to me.

In the summer of 1987, the Australian Ballet asked me to join them for a tour in Japan partnering ballerina Yoko Morishita, in their production of "The Three Musketeers!"

Toward the end of that same year, Jean Luc Leguay director/choreographer of the Torino Opera House in Italy also invited me to perform the leading role in his world-premiere production of "Don Giovanni" which he created for me. I returned to Torino numerous times afterwards and developed a very rewarding artistic relationship with them.

The National Ballet of Canada came through for me magnificently as well, and I danced in many of the company's full-length classics and Galas;

with them I performed the role of "Lensky" for the first time in John Cranko's masterful "Eugene Onegin."

In the following year, I performed with companies I hadn't danced with before, like the Zurich Ballet, Universal Ballet of South Korea, The Ballet of the Teatro Municipal in Lisbon, Portugal; The Ballet of the Teatro Municipal in Lima, Peru; with the Grupo Cisne Negro from Sao Paulo, Brazil at the New York City Center; The Robert Joffrey Ballet at New York's State Theater and at "Le Gala des Etoiles" in Montreal, Canada. The latter was a ballet troupe directed by Victor and Nathalie Melnikoff, who every year brought together some of the best dancers from around the world to perform for a benefit gala. For a couple of years after, I performed with them at their galas, dancing in countries I had not visited yet, like Hungary and Israel.

Much to my surprise, I also received an invitation from Artistic Director Yuri Grigorovich to appear with the Bolshoi Ballet in Moscow. Unfortunately, the invitation could never be finalized, because Russia was going through a political upheaval.

While my career kept taking me around the world, back home in Brazil problems were starting to develop. The ballet company of the Teatro Municipal was in turmoil. There had been new elections, and the new Governor was not in favor of keeping Dalal Achcar as Director of the ballet company. He wanted to replace her with a friend of his. But this friend did not have the track record, contacts, or knowledge necessary to direct a ballet company. And now some dancers were refusing to work under Dalal. There was mutiny at work.

Marcia and I decided to give matters a last try. We met with the new Governor, Moreira Franco, and spoke to him about the importance of preserving the infrastructure of the Ballet company with Dalal as its Director. He listened to us, but we could see he had made up his mind. At one moment during the conversation, he turned to me and asked, "C*ould you not take over and direct the company yourself?... Because for me it would be easier to replace Dalal with you as the new Artistic Director, than to leave Dalal in place."* It became obvious to us Dalal was not part of the new Governor's agenda! *"Governor, I am honored by your invitation, but I cannot accept. I am still performing and traveling constantly; Dalal is the one who brought me here and I would not feel right."* There was silence in the room and that's how it all finished.

We walked out knowing that my days assisting with Rio's ballet company were numbered. A few weeks later Dalal was replaced and soon afterwards I resigned. My work as an Assistant Director with the Ballet of the Teatro Municipal in Rio had come to an end.

Problems were also mounting as Marcia's political activities intensified, and she was hardly ever at home in Rio. She was needed in the political arena of Brasilia, the capital, where everything was happening, while I still had a very busy travel schedule. Christina, Julia and Alejandra were most of the time with their grandmother Sarah in Rio. During one of my return trips, Alejandra came to me and said, *"I miss mommy."* Her words made me see the new reality. I knew then with Marcia's increasing responsibilities and my constant travels, we were becoming a divided family, and things could no longer continue the way they were.

As a family, we still hoped in some way we could work things out, but matters only got worse. In Brazil, when you mentioned the name Kubitschek, doors opened; but for all the support and encouragement Marcia received, she was starting to step into very dangerous waters. The Kubitschek family and I would soon face obstacles that we never expected. Suddenly, political adversaries accused Marcia of not having the legal right to be a politician, because she had lived abroad for so long. This turned into a legal battle, all the way to Brasilia's Supreme Court. After weeks of blood, sweat and tears, Marcia prevailed, and she was voted eligible for a political career. However, the ordeal left scars. She realized times were changing. Brasilia was a far different place from the one she remembered. She couldn't believe the city her father had founded had almost banished her from politics.

Marcia's political campaign began in earnest, and the Kubitschek family and friends went to work. Even I was invited to give one or two speeches. I was hardly a politician, but I decided to put my creative talents to better use. I became the official photographer of Marcia's campaign and recorded every step along the way.

A few months into the campaign Marcia fell ill with hepatitis. The race was a tight one, and she was devastated when doctors told her she was seriously jeopardizing her health. The first thought that ran through everyone's mind was if she could not campaign, she would lose the election. That's when Doña Sarah's fierce spirit was reborn. Marcia's mother was not a young woman, but she suddenly found a new energy. Possessed and driven, she took the reigns, campaigning for Marcia around the clock, as she had done years before for her husband. Every time we saw her, she was in a public plaza giving speeches, or on a television program, or on top of a truck with a microphone rallying the people. She was determined to see Marcia elected.

The night before the election, the phone rang in our bedroom around 3:00 a.m. and Marcia answered. I asked who it was, and she replied, "I don't know. It was an anonymous caller saying I was an illegal candidate and tomorrow all my votes would be annulled." She was going through a nightmare, and I was getting a good taste of what life as a politician's husband was all about.

Right after the anonymous call, Marcia made some calls herself and arranged for security officers to be placed at the most important voting locations and ensure her votes would be properly counted. The tense and hard fought campaign had drained us all, but after a few days when all the votes were counted, we received the great news Marcia had been elected to a congressional seat in The House of Representatives.

I don't know who rejoiced more, Doña Sarah or Marcia, but the fact was Juscelino Kubitschek's daughter had taken the first steps of her political career. We were all proud of Marcia, but we acknowledged the fact Doña Sarah had been the lioness who single-handedly saved the campaign. Marcia would go on to be a busy congressional member, and the first female President of the Foreign Relations Committee in the House of Representatives, responsible for diplomatic treaties and foreign policies. She would also be one of the honorary members of Congress, responsible for writing the country's new Constitution, which prevails today. But Marcia's health had been compromised! She was never very strong physically, and now it was starting to really show.

On the personal side, this new political career was about to bring further changes that would unfortunately start affecting our marriage. I knew her life from now on would be in Brasilia, and our daughters could not be without their mother. And the question finally came to my mind: Could I live in Brasilia? Could I adapt to a whole new world, to a city with no ballet company for me to work for, a limited cultural life, where the only subject for conversation was politics twenty-four hours a day?

I gave it a try, but I just couldn't adapt to Brasilia. The more I traveled abroad to perform, the less I liked it when I came back. And it wasn't only Brasilia; all of a sudden I felt there wasn't much for me to do artistically in Brazil, and life seemed empty. Marcia and I began to lead separate lives, and those personal differences began to take a toll on our marriage.

It was sad to see what was happening to us, but now we were two ships going in different directions and there was nothing we could do. It hurts to think about it, but our marriage seemed to have been destined to last for a certain period, a marvelous chapter in our lives, a chapter now coming to an end.

Late in 1987, Marcia and I were legally separated, and I returned to the United States. Alejandra stayed with her mother and sisters, because with my travel schedule I would be limited in my ability to care for her. Wherever I traveled, Marcia and the girls were still very much in my heart and mind, and I made a point to visit them in Brasilia every year, especially on Alejandra's birthday and during Christmas.

In the meantime, I still missed not being part of ABT. So many difficult changes had taken place in my life in such a short time, I needed something positive to lift me up. Then former ABT principal dancer Bruce Marks, now Boston Ballet's Artistic Director, called. He had seen me perform with the Royal Danish Ballet in Copenhagen, and as soon as he found out I was back living in the United States, he extended an invitation for me to join the Boston Ballet.

In a later filmed interview, Bruce describes the conversation:

**Bruce:** *"I guess I didn't believe this was going to happen... Fernando what would you think about making Boston Ballet your home company?"*

**Fernando:** *"I think that would be wonderful!.."*

**Bruce:** *"I looked around wondering.. was he talking to me? Realizing that his goal was probably to perform in New York, London or Paris, the idea of suggesting that Boston would be his home company seemed to me a real long shot... And his saying "**yes**" changed this company...it changed it, because a dancer of Fernando's accomplishments and prestige raises the level by his presence...he is the mark for which everyone shoots."*

And to Bruce's surprise, I became the company's permanent guest artist. I had found a good home base to work with in America! In my contract with Boston Ballet, I would be required to dance a certain number of performances, but would still have the freedom to continue with my guest engagements around the world. If some doors had closed for me, others were already opening.

My first performance with the Boston Ballet was as Count Albrecht in "Giselle" and I felt great dancing with my new company, like I had been performing with them for years! The following day, October 8, 1987 **Christine Temin**, the dance critic for **The Boston Globe** wrote:

> ***"Last night's "Giselle" was a great performance, not just because of the magnificent dancing of Fernando Bujones, but also because of the energizing effect Bujones seemed to have on the entire Boston Ballet."***

However, I was still hurting inside and not a day passed without the thought of everything that had happened in my life in the last two years. Alejandra was constantly in my thoughts and more than anything I was in need of love and companionship. Boston in the winter was bitterly cold, and after my performances, I walked the few blocks back to the hotel totally alone.

Up to then, I was always surrounded by loving family and friends that had shared my ups and downs. I was living alone for the first time and felt extremely lonely. Those moments were some of the gloomiest and for sure they were the lowest point in my life. The bravos of the audiences were encouraging, but they were only a band-aid to a much deeper wound that only I knew. All my life I had been interpreting roles such as Prince Siegfried in "Swan Lake" and Prince Florimund in "The Sleeping Beauty," story ballets of a prince in search of love. Now my life was no longer a fantasy, and I wondered if I would ever again find the magic of true love.

CHAPTER 21

# *A Girl Named Maria*

Divorced! Just the thought of it was disheartening. Two years had passed since I had legally separated from Marcia and I was still down, feeling lonely, confused, at times angry, tearful and in need of someone to share my life and my feelings. I was vulnerable and fell into a romantic relationship that went nowhere, an emotional roller coaster that plunged me even deeper into depression.

Thankfully, I had some good friends who were very supportive during this difficult period in my life. Larry and Clara Yust and Shelly Birnbaum from Los Angeles; Tobias Leibovitz in New York; Noeli Soares, my agent from Brazil who preserved my performing relationship with that beautiful country; and my longtime family friend, Joseph Rogosik, who at times was like an older brother to me. All of them, very special, warmed my heart with their care and loyal friendship.

My closest family members were also rallying around me. My mother with her words of wisdom, reiterated that each one of us had the right to live our lives in the happiest possible way. When I mentioned to her my concerns for my young daughter Alejandra, she replied: *"You will be a better father if you are happy yourself. You must think of your life now, and if she feels your happiness and your love and care for her, your new life will not change her love for you. Besides, one day she will be a grown-up woman, and she too will be entitled to live her own life."*

Mom's words were right on target and every day that passed I tried to regain my strength and confidence to build a new life. What I didn't know then is as much as we try to help ourselves, life has always something else in store for us and when we least expect it, the surprise is right in front of our eyes.

On September 26, 1988 a sentimental, but happy reunion took place when my former ABT partner Cynthia Gregory and I teamed up for a "Gregory and Bujones Together" program presented for an entire week at the City Center in New York City. Every performance was practically sold out, and we later heard we had broken the record for single ticket sales in a week. Because of the success of that week, Cynthia and I had a heart-to-heart talk in her dressing room. She suggested I consider coming back to ABT. *"Just do it for yourself... forget anybody else and what happened in the past and just think of yourself..."* she said. But that was the problem. I couldn't think only of myself. Too much had already happened in my life with my family, changes I could not overlook. Cynthia was thinking of me and of our partnership, and I understood that, but I simply could not go back to something that, when I left, wasn't working.

Misha was more and more involved in his modern and contemporary works, and less and less in the classics, and kept pushing the company in that direction. A return to ABT was pointless, for as long as Baryshnikov was artistic director, there was no place for me.

In September, 1989, as I prepared for my next "Sleeping Beauty" with the Stuttgart Ballet, my heart and mind were hardly into making another trip all the way to Europe. After all, what was so interesting or exciting about this next trip? My body was tired of traveling and I could dance in my sleep the full-length "Beauty." But I had a contract, so I took that plane to Stuttgart and concentrated on my work.

I was rehearsing in the studio, with Marcia Haydee and her partner Richard Cragun, who were watching my solo from the third act, trying to catch my breath, when I heard a big commotion outside the door. Suddenly I heard some voices. As I turned around I spotted a group of young excited dancers, peeking in, among them a gorgeous young lady with black hair and beautiful eyes, wearing a band around her forehead. My eyes focused on her, and the world around me stood still.

I forgot I was out of breath! In fact, I was breathing better than ever! Suddenly, I began to smile and joke around, and I felt a spontaneous rush of emotions bubbling inside of me. I think no one noticed, but that night the scent of romance fluttered around my soul again.

The next morning after the class, I asked Marcia Haydee about the young lady by the door and if by any chance, as I suspected, was she Latin? There was an exotic and very feminine look about her. Marcia took me by the hand, walked me to her office and showed me a poster with all the company dancers. Then she pointed at one and said: *"Is that her?" "Yes!..."* I answered. Marcia smiled and said: *"Look at her name."* It read Maria Arnillas. Suddenly I remembered... some years before, when I had first come to perform with the Stuttgart Ballet, she had been the young lady from the Cranko ballet school, whose boyfriend introduced her to me at the Opernball. I had just re-discovered the girl who had wanted to meet and dance with me, the girl named Maria! I found out she was from Lima, Peru.

On my third day in Stuttgart, after the dress rehearsal, I approached Maria and introduced myself. I told her I had heard she was from South America. As I continued talking, I felt like a young kid again, slightly nervous and highly curious, and I don't know why I popped a question I never ask, but I did: *"What sign are you?"* She looked at me slightly surprised and said, *"Pisces, March 18." "Really!"* I continued, *"I am Pisces too, and you were born the day after my daughter Alejandra, who is also Pisces, born on March 17."* Maria then asked me if I would take a picture with her, so she could send it to her father. *"Of course, with pleasure!"* I replied. After she took my picture and started to walk away, I asked her one last question, *"Will you have lunch with me?"* There was a moment of silence as she thought, a moment that to me seemed like an eternity. Then she smiled and agreed, *"Ok... tomorrow after the class."*

Next day at lunch in an outside Café, we started getting acquainted with each other. I learned that Maria had started dancing in Peru, but through a three-month cultural exchange program, she came to Stuttgart. Once there she auditioned with the famous John Cranko ballet school, was accepted, and what was supposed to be a visit of three months became a stay of many years. She loved Germany. From the John Cranko School, she went on to perform with various professional ballet companies in the country; and in 1983, she saw her dream come true, when she joined the Stuttgart Ballet, and performed with them all around Europe, South America and Asia.

Before lunch finished, I became more specific with my questions knowing there was a big Atlantic Ocean separating us, and in two days I was going home. If there was any chance for us to keep in touch, I wanted to know more about her personal life. *"Do you have a boyfriend?" "Yes, he is a German fellow studying Chemistry in the university." "I see...*

*and do you love him?"* I asked. I expected Maria to answer that's none of your business, but instead she respectfully replied, "*Well...I have an admiration for him.*" Her answer relaxed me, for I knew that admiration didn't necessarily translate into being in love and perhaps there was a chance for me. Then I asked Maria if she could live away from Germany, if she met a man she really loved. Her answer lit a small spark in my heart. Without any hesitation she replied, *"I think love is the strongest and most beautiful emotion a human being can feel and when one finds it, there are no barriers; one travels wherever they need to find that love and happiness."* I knew then this was a girl I could share my life with.

By the end of lunch, Maria and I felt comfortable with each other. That evening was the opening night performance of "The Sleeping Beauty" and I was inspired, feeling like a prince who was about to meet his princess! And to think I had not wanted to travel to Stuttgart! Before leaving Germany, I visited Maria at her apartment; we talked, listened to music and as I kissed her good bye, I promised her this would not be the last time she would hear from me.

Back in America with the Boston Ballet, news traveled quickly, and I learned ABT's leadership had gone through another major shake up. Baryshnikov had resigned and his assistant Charles France had been fired! The Executive Director, Charles Dillingham was long gone, and Jane Hermann, who was an Executive Director with the Metropolitan Opera House, had been appointed as the new interim Artistic Director.

Then I called Maria in Germany and told her what we had shared really meant something to me. I was traveling to Canada for my debut with The Royal Winnipeg Ballet, and would be at my Florida home for a few days. The day I returned to Florida, Maria called to let me know that she too cared. Weeks went by, and we kept in touch by phone. Not long afterward, I made a trip to Stuttgart just to see her again and confirm my feelings for her were indeed what I thought they were. We developed a romantic relationship and before we knew it, we were involved in a beautiful love affair.

Things were happening quickly and Maria understood if our relationship was going to move forward, one of us would have to make a move. She understood I had just reestablished myself in America. I had a good position with the Boston Ballet and wasn't ready to move again. What's more, I did not speak a word of German and my future was not in Germany. On the other hand, Maria spoke some English. If she liked America, and if after living more than ten years in Germany she would consider making a move, then our chances to be together would improve enormously.

The first step was to get her to like my country. In December, 1989, she visited me at my South Florida apartment and loved it. She adored the tropical climate, the palm trees and the beaches in Florida. However, my work was in the North, so the next step was to see how Boston would fare. Marcia Haydee, Stuttgart Ballet's director, understanding our situation, gave Maria a short leave of absence, so she could travel to Boston and see what would develop.

But before Boston, there was one very special event! I had just received a "welcome back" invitation to perform with ABT! On January 14, 1990, American Ballet Theatre was celebrating its 50$^{th}$ Anniversary and without Baryshnikov as the company's Artistic Director, Jane Hermann immediately invited me to perform with ABT again. Jane and I had always maintained a good relationship, and the moment she took charge, things changed at ABT. Jane made it a point to invite back many of the people who had contributed so much to the legacy of the company, and she extended the invitation for me to dance with Cynthia Gregory in the coda of the Black Swan Pas de Deux.

When the curtain went up at the Met to the orchestra's first beats of the "Black Swan" coda, even before Cynthia and I appeared on stage, we could hear from the wings the roar of the audience in anticipation. By the end, the huge ovation Cynthia and I received from an audience I had so dearly missed, who clearly missed us too, moved us to tears.

On Tuesday, January 16, 1990 dance critic **Anna Kisselgoff** reviewed the evening in **The New York Times**:

> ***"American Ballet Theater celebrated its 50$^{th}$ birthday on Sunday Night at the Metropolitan Opera House with a gala performance that was a grand affair - .... The most noticeably absent figure was Mikhail Baryshnikov, who was artistic director from 1980 until last September, when he resigned prematurely in a dispute with Ballet Theater's board and management. Invited to perform or attend the benefit which he had originally planned, he chose to stay in Paris... The family atmosphere, once typical of Ballet Theater, but absent during the Baryshnikov decade, seemed gingerly restored."***

~

A new era at ABT was starting and I would return to dance with them again, but I was still under contract with Boston Ballet. In February of 1990, Maria joined me in Boston. She had been scheduled to audition for the Boston Ballet and was looking forward to hopefully joining the company. One of the things she liked about the city was its European look. As most Europeans, she was used to walking everywhere; she knew this was the way she could know and enjoy the city better.

The day of the audition was a big day for Maria. She would audition by taking the company class, and Bruce Marks, the artistic director, would evaluate her. I was more nervous than she was, but she came through with flying colors. After the class Bruce ran into me and said *"She is lovely and she dances so beautifully with her upper torso and arms. You can see she comes from Europe, because here in America we don't see enough of that upper body dancing."* A few minutes later Bruce called her to his office singing, "Maria, Maria" from West Side Story... His first words to her were "*Welcome to Boston Ballet.*" She was offered a contract starting the following season, and that was Maria's first job in America. She then went back to Germany to finish her season with Stuttgart Ballet, pack her bags and return to Boston with me.

In the meantime, I was scheduled to perform the role of the Matador in Franco Zeffirelli's "La Traviata" as a guest with the Metropolitan Opera Company in New York City. Suddenly I received a call from Maria's father, saying Maria had been hospitalized. She had suffered a colitis attack, so I found a few days between my Traviata performances to travel to Stuttgart, be by her side, and also attend her sister's wedding. The trip gave me the chance to meet Maria's family as well. Regretfully, her mother had passed away, but I met her father, Luis Arnillas and her three beautiful sisters, Magali, Maribel and Rocio. While in Stuttgart, we all toasted to Maribel's beautiful wedding and to my Maria's quick recovery. She had been released from the hospital just in time for the wedding and was by my side, still a bit frail, but happy.

In the summer of 1990, Maria joined me in Torino, Italy for one of my performances and from there together we made the big move to America.

At first, living in Boston was wonderful and everything seemed under control. Then Maria had a crisis that had been brewing for a bit. She was feeling homesick and missed her past lifestyle. I sympathized with her, but there was nothing I could do. I told her if she needed to, she should return to Germany and give herself the time to decide what she really wanted out of life. Fortunately, the crisis didn't last long, and by 1991 things changed for the better. Without Maria knowing, I called her father in Peru and asked him for her hand, explaining I wanted to marry her. There was a second of silence; then with a warm tone he replied, *"You have my permission."* Next, I went to pick up the ring I had especially made for the occasion.

When Maria came home from her rehearsal, I invited her for a lobster dinner and for an after dinner drink. Maria thought the after dinner drink was very peculiar, but she gladly went along with it. I took her to the top of the Prudential building, which has the most magnificent view of downtown Boston, and told her: *"Just a few hours ago I called your father and spoke to him." "What about?"* Maria was totally surprised. *"Oh, I told him how much I like you, love you, and then I told him that I was calling to ask for his daughter's hand as my future bride and about my plans for a future wedding...that's all I said."* Maria's hands were now around her face, and she was in total disbelief. I then pulled out the small jewel box, gave it to her and waited. *"Well, what do you think?"* She didn't know what to do or what to say. She just sat there looking at the ring, tried it on, kept looking at it, until I finally said: *"Well, do I get an answer? Otherwise I keep the ring."* She smiled, seemed touched, happy and finally replied, *"Yes!"*

That day we looked like the happiest couple in the world, because we were! It wasn't long before a special occasion brought our families together. Maria's father and some of her family members, along with my mother and Zeida, joined us in Boston because on May 4, 1991 Boston Ballet honored me with a 20th Anniversary Gala performance that celebrated two decades of my performing career!

The wonderful event was a sold-out performance, but what it really turned out to be was a one man show. I danced non-stop for two hours, one segment of a ballet after another! Among the many ballets I performed that night were excerpts from "Giselle," "Miss Julie," "Don Quixote," "Romeo and Juliet," Bejart's "Greek Dances," "Etudes," "Raymonda," and others.

I was on fire, running in and out of my dressing room to change from one costume to another. It was my adrenalin and the excitement of the evening that kept me going. At the end of the performance, the standing ovation was the sweetest reward of all and as I stood on stage with the entire Boston Ballet company and my fiancée Maria by my side, our director Bruce Marks came out and handed me a bouquet of flowers and balloons rained down onto the Wang Center stage.

I was honored with two Proclamations from the Mayor of Boston and the Governor of Massachusetts making May 4, 1991, Fernando Bujones' Day. Two days later **The Boston Globe's** dance critic, **Christine Temin** wrote:

> ***"The word on Bujones: Bravissimo" and she finished her review by saying, "Then at the very end, he stood all alone under the chandeliers, playing the role that has seemed to come so naturally to him for the last two decades: the Prince."***

On the early morning of November 1, 1991, Maria and I were officially proclaimed husband and wife, and on the 3rd of November we had our religious wedding at a gorgeous Spanish Monastery in Miami, Florida, where many family members and closest friends from the United States, Peru and Germany attended. The next day Maria and I were on our way to Paradise Island in the Bahamas for our much awaited honeymoon!

It wasn't until after we were married that Maria admitted she had a story to tell me. The first time she saw me dance, she was fifteen years old, in Lima, Peru with her father, mother and sisters watching a video of me in the Don Quixote Pas de Deux! Maria was so impressed, she spontaneously said, *"I could marry this man!"* To which her sisters replied, "*Go ahead, dream on*!"

"*I guess dreams can come true*!" Maria told me with a wink. I was getting the feeling that our relationship seemed to have the word "destiny" written all over it. She continued*: "When I was still in Germany, I called my father in Peru to tell him: "Guess who has just invited me for lunch? Fernando Bujones!"... my father* said: "*Dear, this is an expensive long distance call, so please don't spend time joking around."* It did not take much longer for Maria's father to realize the call had been no joke, I was truly interested in his daughter and that interest became a reality that led to our marriage, a marriage that once more brought a glowing smile to my face and new happiness to my life.

## CHAPTER 22

# *Completing the Circle*

Maria couldn't have come into my life at a better time. She was my salvation, and the more I got to know her the more I knew I was right. Like Marcia, she understood my profession, which made me realize how very fortunate I was. I had an extraordinary first wife; and my second couldn't have been a more perfect match. Now I needed Alejandra, my priceless jewel, to meet Maria. I made it a point to be in Brasilia with my daughter during Christmas and for her birthdays and called her every Sunday no matter where in the world I happened to be. We would talk about her progress at school, about her friends, the movies I had seen and she had seen. Our Sunday phone calls became a ritual and Alejandra grew to know even if I was not with her, she could count on me. She was also thriving at the American School, getting excellent grades and making good progress in her English language.

Soon the students at the American school would have their summer vacation, and I thought it would be the right time to bring Alejandra to the States so she could meet Maria, and the three of us would share some quality time. Alejandra, now eight years old, arrived with her nanny, and I booked a grand suite for all of us in Orlando's Disney World. During the weekend my mother joined us. Alejandra found many ways to make fun of her Cuban grandmother, which of course, mom loved. After that, I made it a point to bring Alejandra to America every summer during her school vacations, and this helped us grow as a family. I was also glad to hear Marcia had married again.

Alejandra was traveling by herself to the States at every opportunity and the three of us enjoyed some beautiful trips by car, so she could get to know the country she was born in. Since she was living with her mother in Brazil and Marcia was still totally involved in politics, Alejandra was becoming very familiar and well versed in the national and international political issues that were constantly the subject of Marcia's life. She was also becoming a very smart, elegant and articulate young lady, usually besting me with her knowledge of world history. She told me after her graduation she would love to come to the United States and go to college here, and for that she had Marcia's blessing, which made me very happy.

We traveled all over the United States. We visited historical St. Augustine in Florida, Savannah and Atlanta in Georgia, Charleston and Fort Sumter as well as two beautiful plantations in South Carolina. We went to Williamsburg and Jamestown, so she could see and feel for herself part of this country's history. The following year we visited Gettysburg. From there, we continued to Washington D.C. and took a tour of The White House. I showed Alejandra exactly where I had performed for President Reagan. I wanted Alejandra to have as much knowledge as possible about our country, so her yearly visits and travels with us became an important part of our lives.

Maria and I were still under contract with the Boston Ballet, and I still had plenty of guest engagements. Then Jane Herman, by now the interim artistic director of American Ballet Theatre called to set up a meeting at my Boston apartment and said: *"So, what is it going to take to bring you back full time with ABT?"* I was a bit startled and happy at her invitation, but replied, *"Jane, I love ABT and New York, but my life has changed and right now I have a good position with the Boston Ballet as the company's permanent guest artist. I can perform with them and still continue to guest around the world. My wife Maria is also a member of the Boston Ballet and very happy here. But I would love to guest with ABT in New York or any other major city where the company may want me."* Jane understood my life had indeed changed, however, she agreed to invite me to guest with the company.

*Jane Herman Remembers:*

*"... couldn't blame Fernando for not coming back full time. ABT had been losing their kind of artistic identity, they lost their point of view. All that started with Baryshnikov, for the ideology and the policy of the company changed considerably when Misha took over. Fernando was*

*one of the first big casualties of that policy. He was forced out of ABT at a period when he was at the height of his power, at the peak of his career. I tried my best to bring the company out of the hole Misha put it in, but by then the finances were no longer there...*

*"Whether you like the New York City Ballet or not, they have a point of view, there is a commitment to an aesthetic. Every single ballet is created for their dancers. Their dancers come by and large from their school. At ABT now you don't know where the dancers come from, you don't know where they're going. They just buy a dancer and they buy a ballet. They bring in the best dancer they can afford, put them on in the best performance they know how to do, and they do their tricks, but there is no specific artistic point of view."*

In the years that followed I returned to ABT for performances, both in New York and Chicago, as a dancer and guest choreographer, and again in Mexico City, dancing the lead of my own production of "Raymonda."

While in Mexico with ABT, a familiar face walked into my dressing room. It was Joaquin Banegas, my first ballet teacher from Cuba, who had not seen me since the days from Varna. He was teaching in Mexico and had come to Bellas Artes to see me dance and see my work as a choreographer.

I felt I was truly experiencing the circle of life. Here was Joaquin, my very first ballet teacher, who during my two early years of dance took care of me and inspired me. To see him act and speak freely this time around, unlike in Varna, reminded me freedom is priceless and whatever sacrifices my mom and I made to leave Cuba when we did, they were worth everything.

Because of my dancing, Maria and I have been able to travel around the world. From the holy city of Jerusalem, to Istanbul, to the mystical Machu Picchu, the magical fjords of Norway and so much more, I have really experienced the world.

*Maria Remembers:*

*"Traveling with Fernando was an incredible experience... He was always so excited about discovering new places. For example, if we went to Norway, he instantly became a "Viking." By then he would have researched the history and traditions of that country and was totally knowledgeable about all he wanted us to see. In the taxi, from the airport, he would say to me:*

*"Don't even think of unpacking now! I have 3 hours before the first rehearsal, so we're going straight to the downtown museum..." and off we went! He loved making very detailed itineraries and every minute was pre-planned, so we never wasted time. He knew exactly the best places to visit in each country, so we always accomplished a lot in very little time. For me, it was like having the best personal tour guide because by then he knew so much about the country.*

*"He was like an explorer, eager to experience everything about the place.. He was unstoppable! He also had natural talent to imitate others. When in France, we would be in a restaurant and he would order food assuming the gestures and mannerisms of the French; when in Japan, he would become all formality and politeness... I had to stop myself from cracking up in the public places while he carried on pretending to behave and speak like one of the natives... he was a lot of fun!"*

By 1993, I was becoming more aware of my desire to choreograph and was teaching wherever I could. I accepted the artistic direction of Ballet Mississippi, and it was there where I really started to direct, produce, choreograph, coach and teach, all of which I grew to love. I invited Peter Stark, a young dancer with the Boston Ballet to join Maria and me at Ballet Mississippi. He accepted, and the three of us were soon confronted with the challenge of our lives, trying to get a dance company going with no budget, no infrastructure, no community support -- only a group of wonderful dancers willing to dance their hearts out.

As a company, Ballet Mississippi attained some outstanding artistic achievements, and I was very proud of my dancers, but ultimately, the city of Jackson could not come up with the necessary funding to support a professional ballet company. The three of us knew it was time to go. By then, we knew we wanted to do more of the same together, if only we could find the right place and circumstances. When we parted, Peter went in one direction and Maria and I went in another. As we said good-bye, I told him I hoped we would be working together again under better conditions. Peter enrolled in a management/business course and learned a great deal about management.

By 1994, I was teaching and choreographing wherever I was invited and traveled several times to Spain, and together with Angela Santos, a popular flamenco and classical ballet teacher, we founded Ballet Clasico Mediterraneo, a company of young talented dancers which shortly thereafter started making an impact in the Spanish dance scene.

In 1995, I became Artistic Director of Ballet de Monterrey in Mexico, an association which lasted three years. At the same time, I began my longtime association with Texas Christian University's Dance Department. Dean Robert Garwell, Chair Ellen Shelton and Professor Stephanie Woods Rand invited me to be Choreographer in Residence of TCU's dance department, and I jumped at it! During what turned out to be a wonderful ten-year relationship, with the special and devoted assistance of the irreplaceable Nancy Carter, my tenure at TCU gave me many, many hours of pleasure and joy.

More and more I wanted to choreograph. I was artistically busy, but it was a grueling schedule for Maria and I. We traveled from Spain to Mexico and back to the States constantly, directing two ballet companies, choreographing and teaching master classes at the Norwegian Opera Ballet, and the Paris Opera Ballet, and still occasionally performing!

Looking back, I don't know how I survived, but I was getting an incredible education!

*Maria Remembers:*

*"Despite the grueling work schedule that we kept at the time, we did manage to find some time for ourselves in between. Fernando loved to take photos, and the first thing he packed, was his camera. So everywhere we went, he took pictures, actually, slides. But Fernando is the only person I know that wanted to take those pictures without people in them! Try doing that in Disney World! He loved the architecture, the landscapes, and nature by itself -- the colors, the sunsets, but no people in the frame! So it was up to me to stop the people, asking them kindly to wait a few seconds while my husband took a picture of the site! I was the traffic cop, running everywhere, stopping people left and right and laughing myself to death!*

*"Once back home, he would gather the old fashioned screen with the tripod, the Carousel projector, the box of slides and start inviting the family for the anticipated travel picture show!"*

All this work was taking a toll on my body, and I could feel my abilities as a dancer starting to fade. Maria and I knew the day would come when I would hang up my shoes and we spoke about it. We both felt I should "quit while I was ahead" and I started to think about having an official retirement before my dancing got to the point of no return.

I spoke to Kevin McKenzie, who had replaced Jane Hermann as the new Artistic Director with ABT, and we agreed my official farewell performance should take place with ABT at the Met. I would dance with my ABT friend and partner ballerina Marianna Tcherkassky in the full-length classic "Giselle." Invitations went out to family and friends to join us for the occasion.

*Alejandra Remembers:*

*"I was twelve years old when my dad had his farewell performance at the Met. I remember receiving the printed invitation at my mom's home in Brasilia and speaking to my father about it. He was so excited*

*about the performance, and he wanted me there to see it! My mother had already arranged with my school to miss a few days so I could go to New York. I had never seen my father dance at the Met, only taped performances, and I couldn't be more excited. I loved watching my father dance -- I was so proud!"*

*"My mom told my father she was going to send me to see the performance, but my father insisted that she had to come as well. My mother wasn't sure if it was proper for her to attend. I really wanted her to go and so did daddy because she had been such an important part of his career! Maria, dad's new wife, called mom and told her that the evening would not be complete without her. Mom had been with dad during most of his career, and it was only fitting that she should be there. She finally agreed.*

*"My mom, dad and I all wished he could have performed "La Bayadere" as his final performance, as it was his favorite role. However, after negotiations with ABT, it was decided "Giselle" would be the ballet for that evening. Looking back, it was a good choice for the farewell performance because it provided one more opportunity for the audience to see how good he was in that role! All of us who attended that evening could not help but leave the theater with tears in our eyes. I knew that the performance I had witnessed marked the end of an era in my father's life.*

*"The day of the performance my mother met with artistic director, Kevin McKenzie, and a small surprise for my dad was arranged between them. I would come on stage and deliver flowers to my father. When the performance was over, I went backstage. I was so nervous when I peeked at the huge audience! They were giving my father a standing ovation and throwing roses on stage. I was really scared to appear in front of so many people so I quickly gave him the flowers and ran off the stage.*

*"I was overwhelmed with emotions that night. I cried because I admired my father so much. I cried because I knew I wasn't going to see him on stage anymore. I was thrilled that I was there to share that moment with him and thankful my mother was there too! My mother's emotions that night are harder to describe; she could not stop crying. She felt that evening was the closing of a chapter, not only in my father's life*

*but in her own! We never talked about that performance again, but I felt how touching and important that evening was for her as well."*

A few days before the performance, I received a letter from President Bill Clinton, dated May 25, 1995 which read:

**Dear Fernando;**

**I am delighted to join your friends and admirers in congratulating you on a lifetime of artistic excellence. Your exceptional contributions to the world of dance have advanced the art form and inspired lovers of ballet everywhere.**

**As you grace the stage of the Metropolitan Opera House for your farewell performance with American Ballet Theatre, you can take great pride in knowing that your vision and talent have touched countless lives. Your career has been a gift to American culture, and I am pleased to commend you for your many wonderful accomplishments.**

**Best wishes for every future happiness.**

**Sincerely,**

**Bill Clinton**

Among the many other letters I received was one from a fan who had followed my career from the very beginning; someone I had never met. The day before the farewell performance, while talking with my mother in her hotel room, I pulled out the envelope and showed her the incredibly touching letter by a lady called Jeanne Bezerra, sent to me at ABT. It read:

*"Dear Fernando,*

*Forgive my familiarity. But I have been watching you dance all over the world since your debut with ABT at City Center when you and I were both still teenagers. My mother and I cheered you on then, as we will on June 2, which I understand is your farewell New York performance.*

*When you first thrilled me with a performance that seemed to defy the laws of physics by which the rest of us are bound, I was still an avid ballet student and balletomane. I frequently fantasized dancing "the Pink Girl" in "Les Patineurs" to your "Green Boy"... Alas, a knee injury ended my dancing days, but not my keen admiration of the art and your gift in particular.*

*While on vacation in England about ten years ago, I treated myself to an evening with the Royal Ballet at Covent Garden As I sat in the orchestra before the performance, I couldn't help noticing the electricity running through the house, which I found quite odd for a British audience, usually so reserved. I asked the gentleman to my right what all the fuss was about, and he replied, "Didn't you know, love, Fernando Bujones will be dancing this evening..." Was I delighted! And I was thrilled that the Brits understood and appreciated your greatness.*

*A couple of years later, after I was living in Sao Paulo with my Brazilian husband's family, I had promised my mother before I left the States I wouldn't travel anywhere with my husband on his motorcycle. One Sunday afternoon as I was passing through the sala (living room) on my way to the cozinha (kitchen), I heard a televised announcement of the final performance that evening of a Brazilian dance company – featuring guest artist Fernando Bujones! I couldn't believe my ears. When I begged my husband to drive me to the box office straight away, he said we'd never get there in time to buy tickets unless we went by motorcycle, thinking he'd be off the hook. Without thinking I said, " For Bujones I shall risk life and limb." I donned a helmet and off we sped. After we bought our tickets (in the very last row) the ticket agent closed the window and turned everyone else away. We had gotten the very last seats! I enjoyed Don Quixote that evening more than I ever have in my lifetime. It was my husband's first time at the ballet, and he was equally thrilled! He kept asking me how you could dance the way you do, to which I replied "Only God and Bujones know."*

*On another occasion, you entered the stage as Prince Siegfried, and half the audience came to their feet to greet you with thunderous applause. Your mere presence on stage electrified the house. It was a grand tribute to your charisma and energy. Which is why, Fernando, you must recognize that you are more than a great talent. You are a phenomenon, a giant among men. I shall miss your star.*

*Most sincerely,*

*Jeanne Bezerra*

As I read the letter to my mother, my voice cracked a few times, and I could not contain my emotions. When I finished reading it, I closed the letter slowly and all my feelings came pouring out. Mom hugged me tight and consoled me, but we both knew this was the end of my performing career — a career that turned out to be so much more than what I could have ever imagined.

On June 2, 1995, I danced my last "Giselle" in a farewell performance with ABT at the Met. As the final curtain closed, Marianna Tcherkassky and I received an incredible and amazing standing ovation. There was a sweet moment when my daughter Alejandra came on stage with a bouquet of flowers for me. I picked her up in my arms and took her forward with the whole company. She was very nervous and eager to get off the stage, and the moment I put her down, she took a quick glance at the audience and dashed off. She later confessed she got scared by the amount of people in the audience.

As I headed back to my dressing room, fans who had come from as far away as Japan were lining up outside the door. For the next half hour, the line extended through the backstage corridor all the way back out into the parking lot! The performance finished at 10:30 in the evening but by 1:00 a.m. I was still signing autographs! On Monday June 5, **Clive Barnes** with **The New York Post** wrote:

> ***"A 15-minute ovation and an ongoing storm of flowers greeted Fernando Bujones and Marianna Tcherkassky at the Metropolitan Opera House on Friday night where they received a reception of Fonteyn/Nureyev proportions. ...Bujones still looking disconcertingly young, but more mature, even more defined than before, acted with superb passion, and danced with style and grace, a powerful closing series of impeccable entrechats demonstrated how little, if at all, his technique has eroded. At one time that technique virtually ran roughshod over his always developing artistry. His career started as an adolescent prodigy with the Eglevsky Ballet, and after he became the first male American to win a Gold Medal in the International Ballet Competitions (Varna, 1974) people more and more tended to regard him primarily as a virtuoso. ....He was always much more than that, and now when curtain feats of male virtuosity – once only the preserve of the likes of a Nureyev, a Baryshnikov or a Bujones – have become common currency, his real artistic virtues of musicality, line, placement and dramatic imagery can perhaps be seen in clever focus. – Bujones has left for his legion of admirers the steel-etched memory of this unforgettable Albrecht."***

By the time I danced my last performance with ABT I had performed in 34 countries, with more than 60 ballet companies around the world, in the most renowned Opera Houses, with the most exquisite ballerinas of the 20th century. I felt I had achieved so much more than what I had ever dreamed.

However, the one thing that made me the proudest of my career was my long association with American Ballet Theater, the company I always considered my own. I joined them as a seventeen-year-old, fresh out of ballet school, jumping in the footsteps of the great dancers that had inspired me as a youth. I grew up with them, forming part of what became, without a doubt, Lucia Chase's "golden age" of classical ballet in America as we know it, of its tradition, dancing its fantastic repertoire, sharing the spotlight with the magnificent dancers, choreographers, musicians and the incredible woman whose vision and determination made that company a legend.

ABT gave me and my family the happiest moments of my life, the most exciting days and nights and the most traumatic times, but American Ballet Theater and Lucia Chase helped make me who I am today. The innumerable friends, colleagues, ballet masters, choreographers and teachers I found there became a true extension of my family and I can only hope my name will forever be a part of ABT's history.

I also feel a special debt of gratitude to the dance critics and reviewers from all over the world who with their knowledgeable commentaries kept track of my career, during the good and the bad times. I hope by sharing their comments and reviews here, it will allow the reader to be part of the moment.

But now, more than ever, I had the urge to continue passing on to the younger generations the knowledge and experiences I had garnered. I would continue directing, choreographing and teaching as much as possible, and remain totally involved in the art form which is my life.

In 1996, I received a second invitation to perform in Russia. Unbelievable, I thought. I was forty-one years old and after twenty-five years of an international career and practically retired from stage, I was being invited to perform in a country whose ballet legacy had such an importance! I felt badly because I would have liked to perform in Russia at a younger age, but it wasn't meant to be. Russia would be missing from my artistic resume.

However, in life, one should never say never. Just when I was ready to finally hang up my ballet shoes, I was presented with an offer I couldn't refuse. So I put those shoes on again, turned on the gorgeous Theodorakis music and on April 12, 1996, danced the solos of Bejarts' "Greek Dances" at the grand theater of the Kremlin in Moscow.

The last performance of my career was created for me by Cuban choreographer Alberto Mendez. I danced the role of "The Phantom" for Puerto Rico's Ballet Concierto in their full-length production of "Phantom of the Opera," and in March, 1997, I went on stage as a dancer for the very last time.

If there was to be a last role for me to dance, "The Phantom of the Opera" was the one, and I really enjoyed myself! As the curtain closed, a most wonderful part of my life came to an end, but a new beginning was waiting in the wings as a full-time teacher, director and choreographer!

Whether I am directing, choreographing or teaching I still feel the need to give the fullest of myself. My goal is to be fair, to respect, encourage and motivate. This approach has allowed me to achieve a special rapport with the many dancers I have worked with.

In many of the dance lectures I have given across the country, I am always asked, "Where did I find my motivation?" "Who helped you in your career?" "What were your biggest influences?" I hope this book can answer some of these questions; but the most popular question was, "What does it take to be a good dancer?" My answer was always the same; "If you want to be a good dancer, you really have to want it! There is no other way to excel in dance except to really want it!"

After I saw the film "Miracle," the story of Herb Brooks, who coached the 1980 U.S. Olympic hockey team to a Gold Medal, I called Zeida and one more time I whole-heartedly told her "thank you!" The film brought back memories of our own work. Like team U.S.A., I knew even against big odds the word "impossible" did not exist for her or for me.

From the beginning, it was obvious to me I had a passion for dance. I still do! And because of it, I was always my own motivator. Many events, people and circumstances can influence you, in a positive way or in a negative way, but in the end, you, yourself are responsible for who you become. When I think back as to how it was I ended up as a dancer, there was never an easy way. How many times while still a student at SAB, I sat watching memorable performances, dreaming of the day when I could do the same. I always wanted to dance. Through hard work and determination, those dreams came true!

Life showed me that talent, combined with passion and perseverance can produce extraordinary things -- an inner joy and happiness, and the most wonderful way to experience the art of living.

CHAPTER 23

# *Orlando Ballet*

By early 1999, I was no longer performing. For the last few years I had still been traveling all over Europe and at home, teaching and choreographing, but Maria and I were looking forward to less travels and settling down in my beautiful condominium in Hallandale, Florida, overlooking the Intercoastal Waterways, closer to the rest of my family.

A couple of Florida ballet companies were searching for new directors at the time and I had applied for those positions. Tampa and Sarasota became possibilities that in the end did not work out. Through my friend Tobi Leibovitz, I received a phone call from the Artistic Director of Southern Ballet Theater in Orlando, Vasile Petrutiu, who asked me to choreograph a number for their upcoming Spring Gala, which I accepted. However, at that time the company was going through a rough transition. So in February I came to Orlando. Working very fast because of other commitments, I put together a ballet which I called "Jazz Swing" as part of the program. It turned out to be a huge success! Tricia Earl, President of the Board of Southern Ballet Theater, and the rest of the organization, were happy with the results.

*Tricia Earl Remembers:*

*"...the ballet was such a hit, he was asked to return as a guest teacher and choreograph another work for the school summer program. During that time, the company was going through an artistic transition. I asked Fernando if he could please help us finish the season while advising us."*

I did. I returned to Orlando as Artistic Advisor and Choreographer for a couple of months to stage another work for them and see how things developed. Now I would have a full three weeks with them. I knew I was being considered as a potential director for the company, and my work felt to me more like an audition for the job. But I was on an adrenaline high. Maria and I pushed on, preparing the end of the season program for May.

A healthy relationship started developing between myself and Southern Ballet Theater. The Board was getting interested in a more permanent participation with the company. The evolution of events had begun. A drastic reorganization of the company commenced with the departure of the current Artistic Director. In a majority vote, the board made the decision to change course and offered me the position of Artistic Advisor and Choreographer in Residence of Southern Ballet Theater.

With its famous attractions providing the highest quality of family entertainment, millions of people were always coming to the city. Yet, their ballet company was a very regional and unknown entity. There was an opportunity here to build an arts organization that could make a difference in the cultural life of Orlando.

In January, 2000, the Millennium kicked in and I officially accepted my affiliation with the company as Artistic Advisor and Resident Choreographer. The opportunity to work with a company in my own state was very heartwarming.

The day I was first introduced to the dancers by Tricia Earl, I found a highly talented troupe, but lacking self-assurance. The dancers were insecure, almost frightened. There was a lot of bickering among them. There were some young Russian, Rumanian and Ukranian dancers, some Cubans, and other Americans from different parts of the country. There were a total of twenty-three dancers and three apprentices. But I was encouraged to see the level of strength and technique of many of them, especially the male dancers!

If there was anything I had learned throughout my career it was artistic leadership was not something you read about in books and then put into practice. Dancers are human beings, artists that need motivation. They must be allowed to grow and express themselves. Having worked with so many different artistic directors through my career, I saw what worked and what didn't and I promised myself I would be open to the idea there would always be a way to find a solution to whatever situation could arise. By then I knew the best way to direct was to guide others by example, by conviction and principles.

I started my very first speech with the intention to ease their worries and build up their confidence.

> *"Let's forget the past, and concentrate on the present, so we can hopefully build a better future. We need to look ahead, work with positive attitudes and put all our efforts into building a company where everyone works with each other and not against each other. I want to create a company full of energy with a team spirit that is interested in reaching greater artistic heights together. Let's give each other a fair chance, and if you see things are not working, I will be the first to step down, but if it works, we will all walk down victory lane with a great deal of satisfaction."*

Maria and I went to work. We set up a schedule for classes and rehearsals and outlined our first program for the Spring Gala in April. It would consist of my restaging of "Paquita," "Gopak Dances," "Grand Pas Classique," "La Vivandiere," closing the program with my own choreography of "Jazz Swing." We were at the studio with the dancers at all times.

*Maria Remembers:*

*"That first year was very difficult for us. We barely slept five hours each night. It was really Fernando's one-man-show. He selected the ballets to be performed, he staged and rehearsed them or choreographed them, designed the programs, the costumes, the sets, the lighting, set up the rehearsals and class schedules, the company's publicity, the ads, simply everything! He listened to and dealt with the dancers' problems, professional and personal. But he only knew one way to do things... 110%. He was committed to excellence.*

*"Fernando had the ability to motivate his dancers, and bring out the best in them; an exceptional gift to inspire them, to make them go beyond themselves... So many times parents and other ballet teachers who came*

*to see the performances told us... "I have been watching my daughter working in class and performances for years and now I see her doing things she never did before..."*

*"Fernando ran a tight rehearsal schedule and really disliked wasting time. He was really a hard task master, incredibly focused, but he also was a lot of fun, incredibly comical and amusing. What an amazing sense of humor he had. The minute Fernando came into a room, he brought with him such a positive and uplifting attitude, it was contagious!"*

Thank God I work very quickly and in five days I already had two thirds of the program done. At that time I also had commitments with other companies, so I could only stay in Orlando for a week and a half, but the ballet mistress would continue taking the rehearsals. I decided for the time being there would be no different categories of corps de ballet, soloists or principal dancers.

With only twenty some dancers, I needed to use them all, everywhere. I spread out the different roles in different casts, so almost everyone had the opportunity to be a principal, knowing by the next performance they would be either soloists or corps de ballet. They understood and accepted it!

The Spring Gala was very successful! Mom, Zeida and Dr. Kathie Sigler, a dear family friend, came from Miami to see it. Afterwards we all went to a fabulous dinner with all the dancers, invited by Tricia and Robert Earl. A week later the Board received a beautiful letter from the dancers:

DR. PHILLIPS CENTER FOR PERFORMING ARTS
1111 N. ORANGE AVENUE, SUITE 4 • ORLANDO, FLORIDA 32804 • TEL: (407) 426-1733 • FAX: (407) 426-1734

To the Board of Southern Ballet Theatre,

As we get closer to the end of our season, we wanted to share with you our thoughts and feelings.

As we all know, the beginning of the year brought with it a lot of uncertainty and for a lot of us much sorrow. By losing our leader we were all unsure of what the future held for us at Southern Ballet Theatre. However, after working with Fernando Bujones and performing at the Spring Gala, we all would like to thank you for bringing this wonderful person to be our teacher, leader and above all our very own Artistic Director.

We are all in agreement when we say how fortunate we are to have this man to lead us through the new millennium and to be with us for many successful years to come

Again, we the dancers of Southern Ballet Theatre thank you all!

The company had previously reserved theater dates for a follow-up engagement in May, right after our Spring Gala. It was a huge challenge to create another completely different program in such a short time, but working under such pressure sometimes produces good results. Thus, a repertory evening was born which I called "The Great Classics," and it successfully closed the end of Southern Ballet Theater's 26th season.

*Maria Remembers:*

*"In the studio, Fernando would never stop while choreographing. Even when the dancers were on a break, he would continue non-stop, moving and choreographing until the day was over; he demonstrated the steps, with such clean execution, that of course, the dancers had this tremendous role model to follow. That's how he motivated and inspired them, because he had the intensity, the ability, the technique to do the steps. He energized them; and the dancers responded in an incredible way.*

*"And then he would say to me "Wow! I just realized I've been on my flat feet all day long, and now not only my feet are burning, but also my brain!..." But you know, I could see it in his face, he had such pleasure while creating his choreography, many times to suit each particular dancer, and when the dancer executed it successfully, his face would glow... he was as happy as he ever was while he was on stage... Many times I asked him: "Do you miss dancing, being on stage?" and he responded "Maria, I had my incredible career. Now I get excited knowing that I am using my brain to create something new, something fresh... it keeps me very alive!"*

On July 1, 2000, I signed my first three-year contract as Artistic Director of Southern Ballet Theater and my wife Maria became Assistant to the Director. With our signed contracts in hand, I located and called Peter Stark and asked him how he felt about coming to work with us again. Luckily he accepted and was soon hired to be the new Director for the Orlando Ballet School, which was part of the organization. Things started looking up real quick.

The company's budget was terribly underfunded, with a very limited budget for an artistic staff. I called Abel Matus in Mexico, the talented former Stage Manager of Ballet Monterrey, and offered him a job. He was wonderfully creative and could come up with incredible alternatives for costumes, sets and lighting effects. He became our Stage Manager, Lighting Designer and even Wardrobe Manager. With him on board, another very important part of my team was put in place. Now I had Maria, Peter and

Abel, all proven professionals with talent and experience, totally committed to the success of our small company.

Tricia Earl started looking for an Executive Director who could spearhead the administrative part; up to that moment, she had a small staff of mostly volunteers who helped with publicity, marketing, ticket sales, etc., and it was mainly her own personal desire, involvement and love for the dance that kept things moving. Born in England, she grew up taking ballet lessons, had friends at Sadler Wells, The Royal Ballet, and elsewhere in the dance world. I was delighted to find in my new Board President someone with the background and knowledge to provide leadership, vision and the motivation to help me build what we both wanted, a world-class ballet company in Orlando.

**Tricia Earl:** *"In my wildest dreams I never imagined that he would be the solution to our problems, or solve them as swiftly as he did"*...

I would call Zeida and Kathie in Miami and keep them aware of everything that was happening; they were helping us set up organizational charts, budgets and everything that up to then had not existed. I started sending a barrage of memos to the Board of Directors. Fortunately, I had one hundred percent support from Tricia and her husband Robert Earl, both confirmed ballet lovers, totally committed to the company. Gradually, their fundraising efforts and our success at the box office started getting attention from the community and pretty soon, Tricia was pulling in new Board members and the cooperation of other area businesses.

She and I visited different local corporations with our new Corporate Membership Program looking for sponsors. A lot of volunteer services started coming in, and even though we could not have afforded it, soon we had volunteer doctors taking care of any injured dancer.

Our new Millennium Season, starting in September would be called "Dances of Distant Lands" featuring "The Kingdom of the Shades" from La Bayadere, Robert North's exuberant "Troy Games," "Le Corsair" pas de deux and my own version of "The Polovetzian Dances from Prince Igor." The season continued in December with my all-new version of "The Nutcracker," followed in March, 2001, by my staging of the full-length "Coppelia" and the season would end in April, 2001, with a program I named "Spanish Sizzle," with the dancers performing to the music of the Gypsy Kings, and Ravel's "Bolero." Everyone was really thrilled and motivated.

*Maria Remembers:*

*"Fernando had an incredible memory! He would remember costumes, set designs and lighting effects of the different productions he had danced in around the world, plus he had impeccable good taste. And all of that served him so well now. With ballet combinations especially, his mind was like a computer; they instantly embeded in his memory never to be forgotten. During one particular class he gave the dancers a gorgeous combination in the center which impressed the dancers so much, that the minute he finished demonstrating, everyone applauded. Fernando looked at me briefly, then looked up and without anyone else noticing, he mouthed: "Thank you Stanley..." This was one of the precious typical center combinations from Stanley Williams' classes at School of American Ballet, which he adored and had never forgotten, since his teenage years.*

*"Fernando had a clinical eye when it came to casting dancers for each role. And then he would create a choreography that would make that particular dancer shine. That's why in all his productions, they said the dancers appeared to "be made just for that role"... well, in fact, it was Fernando creating the sequences and steps that suited each dancer. So it was a win-win situation. The dancer would shine and so would the company! He also insisted in having several casts for each ballet, in order to give as much opportunity to as many dancers! He could have made our life easier by having only one or two principal casts for each production, but he insisted in giving everyone a fair chance, so we would end up with three or four casts for each, which meant three or four additional rehearsals, extra costumes, extra problems... But for this, the dancers loved him. He never took the easy way out.*

*"Sometimes I would say to him: Fernando we don't have the time, nor the budget, nor the number of dancers we need to do this ballet," to which he would reply: "Maria, it will be done!" Many times I thought he was crazy, there is no way we can do everything he has planned! He would say to me: "Maria, trust me, I know what I'm doing" and somehow,*

*people would come together! Staff, volunteers and dancers, and another incredible program was born. And he never forgot the power of praising them, at the right time, of praising the people who were also forming part of the success story that became Orlando Ballet."*

After our initial success, word spread quickly throughout the dance world, and we started getting letters from dancers from all over the world who wanted to come and join our company; we just did not have the budget to hire them all!

Suddenly, the Sarasota Ballet company called and invited us to appear in October as part of their cultural series at their prestigious Aesolo Theater! Now we would also be touring!

Then, in August, 2000, I received a most disturbing phone call from my daughter in Brazil. "Mommy is in the hospital. She is not doing well at all and it seems there may be major complications with her liver. The doctors fear it is too far gone and this may be close to the end..."

Immediately I remembered Marcia's old bouts with hepatitis and told Alejandra that Maria and I would be on a plane to Brasilia immediately. When we arrived at the hospital, Marcia was already in a coma. Anna Christina, Julia and Alejandra were there, too, as was Marcia's current husband. Also there was Be Barbará, Marcia's first husband; Maria Estella, Marcia's adopted sister and Rodrigo, her husband. The attending doctor confirmed to me she was beyond help and nothing more could be done. Alejandra brought me into the room, so I could say good-bye. They say even when a person is in a coma, they still hear your words, and I truly hope Marcia heard mine. As soon as we left the room, we all stood outside the door, in total disbelief. I embraced my daughter and at that moment, we all heard the beeps in the heart monitor go flat. Marcia had just died. And with her went such a beautiful chapter of my wonderful life. We all embraced each other crying. What a sad, sad moment that was.

Alejandra remained in Brasilia to finish high school and moved in with her older sister Christina. She graduated at the top of her class. Throughout all her school years, she had been an exceptional student and was thinking of pursuing a career in International Relations. During her senior year she came to the States and together we traveled to numerous universities, so she could decide what college she wanted to go to. For a while, Alejandra stayed with us but soon was admitted to Northeastern University in Boston and off she went!

Maria became an American citizen and learned to love the history and the culture of America as much as I did. She also became a rabid football fan like me, and no matter where I was dancing, if the Miami Dolphins were playing, there was a good chance Maria, Alejandra and I would be there.

*Maria Remembers:*

*"We were also able to start taking a week's vacation here and there, usually after our seasons were finished, for a much needed rest, however brief. I could see how much good these moments did for Fernando, who also had the ability to disconnect totally from ballet at a minute's notice. Once we took a short cruise to the Greek isles, in the Mediterranean, one of Fernando's favorite places. While visiting the island of Santorini, we rented a small boat with a guide so he could take us out for the day, just the three of us.*

*"As we sailed around those beautiful and peaceful waters, Fernando said: "you see, Maria, finally here we have only the breeze, the sun, this gorgeous water all around us. Here we can get away from it all, you can find peace and quiet..." Suddenly we hear a scream! "BUJONES! Neither he nor I could believe it, but out of the blue, another small tour boat full of Brazilian tourists came close to ours, one of them recognized Fernando, had actually seen him dance at the Met and wanted to get his autograph! Our lives were very busy with work, but also filled with such moments of crazy fun and love!"*

Life moved forward, and I had to admire the strength of character of my daughter. She focused on the positive side of life, despite her huge loss. Her mother had been her inspiration and Alejandra was determined to fulfill

Dance Magazine

Accepting the Dance Magazine Award from Lucia Chase as Dancer of the Year.

Leslie E. Spatt

Leslie E. Spatt

Mom and I.

Jim Houghton

Solor in "La Bayadere"

Martha Swope

Martha Swope

" Bayadere", with Marianna Tcherkassky.

Z.Cecilia-Méndez

Z.Cecilia-Méndez

Romeo, in John Cranko's "Romeo & Juliet" with Marcia Haydee and the Stuttgart Ballet.

Helga Kraus

Rodolphe Torette

Talking with Maurice Bejart about the role he was finally creating for me, "Trois Etudes pour Alexander."

Rodolphe Torette

White House Photographer

With President and Mrs. Ronald Reagan after my performance at the White House Gala.

White House Photographer

Z.Cecilia-Méndez

With Rudolph
Nureyev
In Paris.

Evening Standard

With Princess Diana after my debut with the Royal Ballet at the Covent Garden Opera House.

Maria and I at our wedding.

Exploring Santorini on a donkey.

With my new bride at Machu Picchu.

David Sickl

With Maria at the Boston Ballet.

A quiet moment…
waiting in the wings.

Buddy Myers

Carolyn Huoy

Att the Met, the final curtain of my career, after a most unforgettable performance of "Giselle."

Proud father, at Alejandra's graduation from Northeastern University in Boston, 2004.

Alejandra with her sisters, Anna Christina and Julia, all grown up!,

With my beautiful daughter, cheering our favorite football team!

Just signed my first contract as the new Artistic Director of Southern Ballet Theater. Maria and Dr. Kathie Sigler next to me, Zeida and members of the Board of Directors.

Tanja Schmidt

Teaching company class for the newly renamed Orlando Ballet.

Tanja Schmidt

Tanja Schmidt

Choreographing a new work with the company men...

Tanja Schmidt

With Israel Rodriguez as "Spartacus."

Celebrating backstage with the President of the Orlando Ballet Board, Tricia Earl, the success of the company.

With Robert Earl and Sylvester Stallone, at a fundraising Gala dinner.

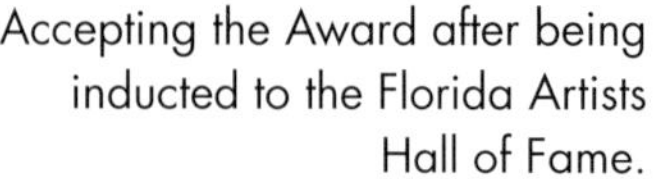

Accepting the Award after being inducted to the Florida Artists Hall of Fame.

Chris Ellis

her mother's wishes for her. I could also see in her some of my own inner strength and determination, and I thought to myself "she will be all right."

Maria and I settled down in Orlando, focused on the new challenges ahead. The new season would be taking up all of our time, but we were loving it. As we embarked on this new chapter of our lives, I was no longer a dancer, but Artistic Director of a dance company. My aim now was to build and preserve a healthy teamwork spirit. It was essential.

By March, 2002, I had already been the company director for two years. I wanted to give the company a better sense of identity and fought very hard to change its name. At first, the Board was hesitant, but I prevailed and we changed the company's name to Orlando Ballet. We were now an important part of the cultural landscape of the city, together with the Orlando Philarmonic and the Orlando Opera.

That same month I was honored to be inducted into the Florida Artists Hall of Fame by Secretary of State Katherine Harris. She handed me the trophy and proclaimed "Welcome to the Florida Artists Hall of Fame. Your name will now be forever inscribed in the walls of our State Capitol in Tallahassee, Florida." I was overjoyed to know I was joining the ranks of such legendary Floridian personalities as Ernest Hemingway, Ray Charles, Jimmy Buffett, Marjorie Stoneman-Douglas, Tennessee Williams, Burt Reynolds and so many other special people.

This award symbolizes for me the incredible journey of my life. Beginning in Florida, where I was born, it took me all over the world, with so many gifts and experiences received at each and every stop. I am so happy to share these gifts with the people of Florida.

# Epilogue

The story does not end here. Fernando continued his extremely successful work as Director of the Orlando Ballet and the exciting ballet seasons followed one after another with critical and financial success up to the year 2005. In May of that year, his contract was renewed for three more years. He also continued his tenure as Choreographer in Residence at TCU. Unexpectedly he was taken ill on September 20, 2005.

Fernando Bujones passed away on November 10, 2005 from Metastatic Malignant Melanoma. He was 50 years old.

During his brief illness he received hundreds of get well messages, cards, and mementos from fellow dancers, fans and friends from all over the world wishing him a fast recovery, wishing him the best and giving him hope. Fernando spread lots of love among everyone who got to know him, and they loved him back. He fought a gallant fight till the end, with the courage, determination, loving nature and humor that had marked his entire life.

He began writing the memoirs of his career and our lives over the last few years. He would send me the chapters as he finished them, and I would then revise, add or edit them as needed. He sent me his latest chapters one month before his illness, but he never expected they would be his final ones.

Most days we find ourselves reliving the wonderful life we shared with Fernando. And the memories are fabulous. He had such a fantastic life, such a marvelous career, packed into 50 short years. Of course, there were ups and downs, but he was, truly, a very happy fellow who brought happiness to his family, to so many of us who loved him.

As a young boy he used to say he wanted to be like a comet, speeding through the skies, shining with the most intense and brilliant light, however brief. Well, he has left behind a spectacular trail of radiant beauty that will shine in our universe forever. His art and his dancing brought so much joy to so many around the world. Throughout his brilliant career he met his challenges and accomplished his goals with unmatched grace, beauty, honesty and love, disciplined determination and courage, but above all, passion. Passion for life, for love, for dance.

He inspired and motivated so many others, and in the end, he became a leader who led by his example. If you close your eyes and listen closely, you can always hear the haunting opening chords of the Kingdom of the Shades from La Bayadere and know he is right there, in the wings, savoring the music and waiting for the moment for his variation to begin. He will come out and explode as Solor the warrior, in his most favorite role of all, thrilling the audiences and all of us who ever saw him dance, one more time, as he takes his leap into eternity.

The story could not end where he left it, for he had accomplished so much more that he never got to say. Many other voices will fill the void to finish this story, the story of a young boy with a tremendous will to excel, and a precious God given talent, who grew up to become one of the finest classical dancers of our generation.

– Zeida Cecilia-Mendez

# Remembering Fernando…

**Olivia Gale, Freelance Writer**

If the dream of a ballet company's Board of Directors is to find Artistic Leadership with the passion and vision to guide their company to heights never before imagined, then Orlando Ballet certainly drew the winning lottery ticket when they hired international Ballet star Fernando Bujones to guide their organization.

In the five-plus years Bujones directed the organization, a lot happened. At his recommendation, the company was officially renamed Orlando Ballet and Bujones' strategy to recruit other outstanding dancers and enrich the company's repertory came into full effect. To that end he brought in exciting new works as well as his own versions of the great full-length classics. To implement his plan, he concentrated on raising the technical level of the company through his personal teaching and coaching.

Little did I know that I'd have the dream come true job, of writing about him, not once, but multiple times. Never in a million years could I have imagined that I'd also have the honor of calling him friend. It is difficult to translate into mere words, how electric was the excitement in his voice and in his eyes when he spoke of his passion for dance and dancers.

If it was one thing Fernando knew well, it was what made a dancer happy. And that was the opportunity to dance. His insistence on multiple lead casts for every ballet consistently expanded the depth of talent and allowed his dancers to grow in leaps and bounds artistically. Morale was at an all time high.

He strove to help them find energy within them that would make the difference between being an ordinary dancer and an extraordinary one.

**Diane Burns, Orlando Sentinel's** dance critic wrote of Bujones first year at the helm of Southern Ballet Theatre:

> ***"In the theater there is an expression 'the fourth wall'. It means the invisible barrier between the stage and the audience. In the season just ended, Southern Ballet Theatre's first under artistic director Fernando Bujones, the company***

***dancers melted the fourth wall with the beat and energy of high voltage dance...***

And to finish her review:

***"The results are even greater than the sum of the parts -good dancing, good choreography, audience development- and for that Bujones is to credit. He has worked the special alchemy that only a charismatic leader can. In Orlando he became one of the hardest working Artistic Directors around: a talented choreographer whose adaptations of the classics were respectful without being stolid: a coach who could teach his dancers not only the grand idea, but also the myriad details that make it genuine. Like all great coaches, Bujones has been able to get his dancers to reach for the rung above the one they thought was possible."***

He was all about the dancer and the dance; about saying "yes" you can, when the rest of the world said "no" you can't. He was about understanding and encouraging the teamwork it takes to reach above and beyond. He was about leaping to the stars and taking everyone with him on the journey. He was about joy. In reality it all comes back to his humanity. Everyone was important to him and he made everyone feel that way in a thousand little ways.

Fernando's passion and energy were contagious. He inspired all those around him to be better than they ever imagined they could be, to reach beyond self imposed limitations. His warmth and generosity of spirit endeared him to everyone who knew him. This is a man who got it right. He understood by treating those in his world with respect and acknowledging the value of each person's unique gifts, the whole would become greater than the sum of its parts. He understood by contributing to and applauding each person's success, our own success is not diminished, but magnified a hundred fold.

**Peter Stark, Director, Orlando Ballet School**

"There are several words one might use to describe Fernando Bujones. These include great dancer, fantastic coach, artistic director, a man who was confident and sure of himself, defiant when he needed to be, smart... But the word that resonates with me the most is generous. Fernando had a great life heralded by a stellar career in dance, and there he leaves a great legacy. Yet I believe some of his greatest contributions were the personal ones. He gave freely and willingly of his knowledge and his time. For those of us who worked with Fernando, he held the highest standards at all times.

When working with dancers he would sometimes get a questioning look in his brow, jump up from his chair and say "try this, it's better for you." He always wanted to make a dancer do and look their best. Countless times I would ask him about a step or a variation and he would give me immediate answers... the right ones... often dancing the variation in the hallways.

When I would show Fernando new choreography, he would watch a whole ballet without saying a word. Then at the end, he would say: "May I?" He would go back to the first step and begin offering suggestions of line, epaulement and structure from beginning to end. It was as if he'd just recite back from a video playing in his head. He had a photographic memory.

But he also had a passion for life. He thrilled in others' successes. The word Fernando used more than any other about dancing was "energy." When he got sick I told him that all energy was kinetic. This means it doesn't end, it just changes. The incredible energy he put out in the studio for us was now living in each of his artists. This is true for us all. Whatever we do with our lives from this time forward, we carry a bit of Fernando Bujones in us to make us better, to push, to improve, to question, to learn, to laugh, to love and to dance."

**Elizabeth Gillaspy, Associate Professor of Ballet, School for Classical & Contemporary Dance at TCU**

Fernando Bujones' legacy in the ballet world is clear: brilliant dancer, consummate artist, generous performer, celebrated and lauded. Yet, it is the part of his life extended past his days as a performer that are less well known, but where he made an equally significant impact. Fernando made the transition from world-famous ballet superstar to teacher, coach, and choreographer with the same ease and grace he employed en l'air. The students, faculty and staff at Texas Christian University's Department of Ballet and Modern Dance, who had the great good fortune to work with him and know him, were changed by his presence.

Just several weeks shy of his farewell performance with ABT, Fernando Bujones came to TCU and taught, shared, laughed and genuinely charmed us all. It is well known a stellar performer may not make a stellar teacher, but that was not the case with Fernando. He was a tremendous teacher. His ballet classes had electricity in them and Fernando was the generator. He responded to passion and heart, and anyone who displayed those qualities received his full attention. He taught without airs or harsh judgment. He shared anecdotes, offered images and crafted delightfully musical enchaînements. At the end of his brief visit, we all knew we wanted him to come back.

With support and vision from Robert Garwell, Dean of the College of Fine Arts at that time, and Department Chair, Ellen Page Shelton, a new position was created for Fernando. He was invited to become TCU's first-ever Choreographer-in Residence and returned to TCU each semester to teach classes and create or restage a ballet for that semester's concert. He always saved room for his TCU commitment. No matter how many international companies or schools wanted his time, no matter how many guest teaching or coaching opportunities he was offered, he remained fully invested in his TCU connection.

Two weeks before Fernando's scheduled fall visit in 2005, I received a phone call from Maria that he was suddenly ill. I couldn't have imagined then we would never see him again. We held a memorial for Fernando in our large studio theater, a space in which he had rehearsed numerous times, on December 10, 2005. In attendance were over 130 friends and admirers, from throughout the Dallas-Fort Worth area, who wished to pay their respects and celebrate his life.

The memorial celebration, which had included video excerpts and live performances, concluded with a slideshow of photographs from all facets of Fernando's life, as a dancer, as a teacher, as a choreographer, and as a friend. His presence resonated in the theater and in our hearts. All of us who spent time with him, knew him and loved him, miss him very much, yet continue to celebrate his passion for dance and for life.

**Heather Lescaille, Ballet Faculty**

"...To me, Fernando was as close to textbook perfect as a classical ballet dancer could get. Even as a female, I would study how he executed the steps watching how clean he was and the beautiful lines he made. When my husband, Alfredo, became a professional dancer and I started teaching dance, Fernando became a staple for dinner conversation whenever ballet came up. I would have my students look at videos of him for comparison and an example and Alfredo would watch him for inspiration. Needless to say, when Alfredo got the job dancing with the Orlando Ballet, it was very exciting, to say the least. I remember when Alfredo first introduced me to Mr. Bujones, I was very nervous and shaking, and as we entered into his and his wife Maria's office, I couldn't believe how nice they were and so down to earth. At the chapel during the funeral, as they carried out his casket, someone said out loud: "Bravo Bujones! I couldn't have said it better..."

**Cynthia Gregory, Principal Dancer, American Ballet Theater**

My wonderful partner Fernando was a legendary dancer, but I want to say what he was as a person; he was amazing, amazing, and to me he was always above all, a gentleman; an elegant, lovely, sweet, warm, generous, giving person who had a great sense of humor; he was down to earth, he liked football, he was somebody who wasn't only interested in dance, he loved life! And to me, that was so unbelievably special.

There are so many dancers that all they do is talk about themselves and their dance, but although he really and deeply loved dance, he was a complete, full person, a family man, a wonderful son, a loving father; he couldn't have been a more lovely person. I am still in shock as I sit here writing this. What a terrible loss! He gave so much to me as a dancer and partner, as a person, as a friend... there are so many beautiful and happy memories of all of us – traveling together, enjoying new places, new audiences, new experiences, I will cherish those for as long as I live."

**Eleanor D'Antuono, Principal Dancer, American Ballet Theater**

"He was among the best of the best. Such a complete dancer. He provided some of the most unforgettable and electrifying moments of my career. I was his partner in his very first "Giselle," his first "Swan Lake," in his first "Theme & Variations," and his first "Coppelia" and will never forget what a pleasure it was working with him as he learned those roles and then exceled in them…"

**Natasha Makarova, Principal Dancer, American Ballet Theater**

"Fernando had a perfect body for ballet, beautiful line and impeccable technique. He was a strong, considerate partner. He made me seem weightless even though I was four months pregnant when we danced at the Edinburgh Festival.

Fernando was my partner for my last performance before I gave birth and my first partner after my son was born, which was at the Metropolitan Opera House, both momentous occasions in my life and Fernando was most supportive.

It is so sad that Fernando's life was cut short. He was devoted to his profession and had so much more to give. My deepest heartfelt condolences to Fernando's beloved family."

**Katie Slattery, Orlando Ballet Dancer**

As a dancer with the Orlando Ballet I was privileged to have worked for five years with the most wonderful person in the world… our Artistic Director, Fernando Bujones. He made us all feel important; we all felt special, he was such a leader, such a motivator, so involved in the overall success of the company. From the first moment he made it clear to us that he cared a lot for us as dancers.

And he knew his dancers very well. If he gave you a role, he knew you could do it, he expected you to do it. If he believed in you how could we not believe in ourselves? He was the greatest coach and made sure that whenever we stepped on stage we would be showing the audiences our best. When he was choreographing or staging a work for us he would say: "Company watch!" And without warming up or changing into dance clothes, he would demonstrate the steps as the incredible dancer he himself was and we would all be fascinated watching him. He could do everything!

Fernando was unique. When have you seen an Artistic Director who is also the company's master class teacher, the principal choreographer, the main coach, he got involved with marketing and publicity, even with selling tickets. He was very involved with the dancers' costumes. Before each performance he had a "costumes parade" and made sure that each dancer looked his or her best. He took care of every single detail, with the sets, the lighting, there was no aspect of the performance he was not personally involved in. The entire company adored him. I will never forget during the performances, and intermissions, he reached for the backstage microphone and we would hear: "Company, this is your director…" and he would go on to encourage us or to tell us "dancers, you've got to keep the energy now" or "you were great, now keep it up, you've got the audience with you.." He let us know what he was thinking, he was very honest and upfront with us, but always positive. He was always there rooting for us, everywhere.

**Martha and Walter Horn, Longtime Ballet Fans**

"My admiration for Fernando followed him everywhere. His artistic creativity became apparent very early in his life, dazzling us with his impeccable technique, stage presence and beautiful and sensitive artistry. His commitment to ballet was total, whatever performing, teaching or choreographing, as was his commitment to his fans. Fernando always had time for us. He gave us his personal attention and was fun to be with, essentially, he was not only such a great dancer, but he was also a great human being. My husband and I were honored with his friendship and will always treasure the happy memories we have of "our dear Fernando" on and off stage…"

**Maria de Varona, ex-dancer and family friend**

I always believed that he was immortal, that he would live forever. I still cannot understand how someone with such talent, such gift of grace can be confined to the laws that govern the rest of us.

Bujones, America's "danseur noble" achieved greatness by determination, hard work and pure talent. The beauty of the art, and not the politics of the artistic elites, was what drove him. His bravura was not a music hall number, but pure perfection; his precision of execution and virtuosity on stage, always within the cannons and traditions of the "dance classique." His musical intuition can be regarded as a six sense.

He was able to surmount all kinds of obstacles, through performances that were spellbinding and mesmerizing. His technique was a unified system and his body the vessel of expression of artistic emotion. He was *"capable of evoking a mood just by dancing,"* the true principles of classical dance (A. Vaganova). Captivating audiences all over the world, his willingness to make friends, to help other dancers, to share, to teach and demonstrate was unparallel, never selfish, never narcissistic. A true giant of this art, he sleeps today among the immortals.

**Veronica Tennant, Principal Dancer, National Ballet of Canada**

"When a shining light in the dance world is extinguished as suddenly and as prematurely as Fernando Bujones, the pain of the loss is palpable. For the National Ballet of Canada, there was a special kinship with this luminous premier danseur. I still remember with clarity the charge of dancing with Bujones for the first time. He exploded into our company as a replacement for Mikhail Baryshnikov, who was unable to dance his scheduled "La Sylphide" in our February 1976 season. Within scant minutes of our introductory rehearsal, at the point when I, as the mischievous Sylph, planted a kiss on his forehead, and he, as James, looked at me startled with such ingenuousness – there were no more thoughts of "instead of" – only discoveries and fun!

We had all heard about this dazzling young dancer's spectacular win at the pre-eminent International Ballet Competitions in Varna, Bulgaria two years before. With pride and charming brashness, Bujones savored his hard-won medals as incontestable proof that he need not take a back seat to the Russian dancers – Nureyev, Panov and Baryshnikov – who, with the help of the media, were dominating the international ballet scene. His smile was contagious. Bujones dazzled audiences with his infectious élan and formidable technique. The word that leaps to mind in describing him is "zest." His exuberance and vivacious personality suffused his dancing. He was a virtuoso and – most important – an unselfconscious one.

Bujones devoured space with panache. His command of the classical technique and his relish in exploring it were inexhaustible. He was very musical, so that the surges in his dancing had arcs of exhilaration and tenderness. As a partner, he was kind and always generous. A stellar dancer, Bujones never took his gift for granted. He committed to the art of classical ballet with unbridled passion. He investigated his own physical and artistic possibilities, then, without pause, served scores of talented young dancers, as he translated his expertise into the roles of coach, teacher, artistic director and choreographer."

**Maria Bujones**
**My Husband and Artistic Director**

"I was 16 years old the first time I saw Fernando dancing. My family and I were at home in Peru watching a video of him performing the Don Quixote pas de deux. I was so impressed that I said out loud "I could marry this man!" My family kindly laughed me off. But guess what, years later I proved to all that dreams do come true!

I was so lucky and had the fortune to share my life and my love with Fernando, to experience his warmth and generosity of spirit, which endeared him to everyone who knew him. A day doesn't go by I don't think how unbelievably beautiful it was to spend fifteen years of my life by his side as his wife and assistant. He showed me the real meaning of life: to live it to the fullest.

He was a happy man, grateful for his life and for the joy he found in it. He found joy in almost anything because joy was within him! He had been blessed with an incomparable talent that took him around the world and made him famous, performing with the top ballet companies and major ballerinas of our times. He was an extraordinary dancer, inspiring teacher, a motivating director, a creative choreographer. I believe everyone that met Fernando carries part of his legacy in their hearts and in their memories, and we have the power to make his art and his spirit be eternal."

# *Roles*

"Abdallah" - Abdallah

"A la Francaix" - Male Lead

"Allegro Brilliante" - Male Lead

"Soldier's Tale" - Soldier

"Apollo Musagetta" - Apollo

"Bach Partita"

"Billy the Kid" - Billy

"Brahms Quintet"

"Carmen" - Don Jose

"Escenas Brasileiras"

"Clair de Lune Pas de Deux"

"Com Amor"

"Concertino"

"Coppelia" Full length- Franz

"Diana and Acteon Pas de Deux"

"Doodles"

"Don Giovanni" - Title Role

"Donizetti Variations"

"Don Quixote" - Basilio

"Esmeralda Pas de Deux"

"Etudes" - Turning Boy

"Eugene Onegin" - Lensky

"Fancy Free" - Rhumba

"Flames of Paris Pas de Deux"

"Flower Festival Pas de Deux"

"Gemini" - Male Lead

"Giselle" Full length - Prince Albrecht

"Glinka Pas de Trois"

"Gopak" Solo

"Graduation Ball" - Drummer Boy

"Grand Pas Classique"

"Grand Pas Espagnol"

"Grand Pas Romantique"

"Hans Christian Andersen"

"Helen of Troy" - Warrior

"Interludes"

"Jardin Aux Lilas" - The Lover

"Jazz Calendar" - Friday's Child

"Konservatoriet" - Male Lead

"La Bayadere" Full length - Solor

"La Fille Mal Gardee" Full length - Colas

"La Sylphide" Full length - James

(A. Bournonville) " (Pierre Lacotte)

"La Traviata" - El Matador

"La Ventana Pas de Deux"

"Le Corsaire Pas de Deux"

"Les Rendezvous" - Male Lead

"Le Spectre de la Rose"

"Les Patineurs" - Green Skater

"Les Sylphides" - The Poet

"Memories"

"Mendelssohn Symphony"

"Miss Julie" - The Butler

"Napoli Divertissements" - Male Lead

"Narcissus" - Narcissus

"Nosso Tempo"

"Paquita" - Male Lead

"Pas de Dix" - Male Lead

# *Roles*

"Peter and the Wolf" - Peter

"Petrouchka" - Title Role

"Phantom of the Opera" - The Phantom

"Pulcinella Variations" - Male Lead

"Raymonda" Full length - Male Lead

"Les Rendezvous"

"Rodeo" - Cow Roper

"Romeo & Juliet" Full length - Romeo

(A. Tudor) (John Cranko) (F. McMillan)

"Sea Change"

"Seven Greek Dances" - Solo

"Shadowplay" - Jungle Boy

"Something Special"

"Swan Lake" Full length - Prince Sigfried

"Tales of Hoffman"

"Tchaikovsky Dances" - Male Lead

"Tchaikovsky Pas de Deux"

" Themes and Variations" - Male Lead

"The Nutcracker" Full length - The Prince

"The River"

"The Sleeping Beauty" - Prince Florimund

"The 3 Musketeers" - Musketeer

"Trois Etudes pour Alexandre" - Alexander

"Undertow" - The Transgressor

"Variations for Four" - Third Variation

"Vendetta" - Male Lead

"Who Cares?"

# Ballet Partners

Lucette Aldous
Anneli Alhanko
Nina Ananiashivili
Ana Botafogo
Susana Benavides
Karena Brock
Ana Maria Castañon
Fiona Chadwick
Florence Clerc
Lesley Collier
Joyce Cuoco
Gisela Cech
Eleanor D'Antuono
Marysse Egasse
Kristine Elliott
Nora Esteves
Carla Fracci
Dame Margot Fonteyn
Jennifer Gelfand
Cynthia Gregory
Kimberly Glasco
Martine Van Hamel
Cynthia Harvey
Vanessa Harwood
Marcia Haydee
Susan Jaffe
Yoko Ichino
Birgit Keil
Cecilia Kerche
Dominique Khalfouni
Gelsey Kirkland
Kim Lightheart
Monique Loudieres
Natalia Makarova
Jolinda Menendez
Julia Moon
Yoko Morishita
Marie Christine Mouis
Kyra Nichols
Galina Panova
Merle Park
Jennifer Penney
Wilfride Piollet
Denise Pons
Noella Pontois
Nadia Potts
Anna Razzi
Maritere del Real
Lisa de Ribere
Zhandra Rodriguez
Galina Samsova
Christine Sarry
Karen Scalzitti
Ludmila Semenyaka
Trinidad Sevillano
Lynn Seymour
Antoinette Sibley
Carla Stallings
Adriana Suarez
Marianna Tcherkassky
Veronica Tennant
Laura Young
Christine Walsh

# *Honors & Awards*

**Gold Medal Winner** &
**Highest Technical Achievement Award**
1974 International Ballet Competitions
Varna, Bulgaria

**Outstanding Young Men of America Award**
Library of Congress, USA 1982

**Dance Magazine Award**
New York City, NY. 1982

**The New York Times / Florida Prize Award**
Sarasota, Florida 1986

**Hispanic Heritage Award**
Washington, D.C. 1989

**Casita Maria Award**
New York, NY 1990

**Proclamation – The Commonwealth of Massachusetts**
**By The Governor of Massachusetts**
**for the "Bravo Bujones – 20th Anniversary Gala"**
Boston, Massachusetts 1991

**The Elliott Norton Theater Award**
Boston, Massachusetts, 1993

**Don Quixote Award**
**Hispanic Heritage Council**
Miami, Florida 1994

**Artistic Achievement Award**
Chicago National Association of Dance Masters, Chicago, Illinois 1998

**Inducted to the Florida Artists Hall of Fame**
Tallahassee, Florida 2002

# *Videos & DVDs*

IRGproductions
**www.fernandobujonesmovie.com**

"The Extraordinary Journey of
Fernando Bujones"
60 minute DVD

Kulture Videos
**www.kultur.com**

"Giselle"
Live Performance
D1289

"Coppelia"
Live Performance
D1120

"The Sleeping Beauty"
Live Performance
D1122

"ABT in San Francisco"
Black Swan Pas de Deux
Bujones/Gregory
Live Performance
D2849

"ABT at the Met: Mixed Bill"
Live Performance
D2024

"Fernando Bujones:
Portrait of a Dance Legend"
Bujones in Class
In His Image
Winning at Varna
D4349